Emerging and Young Adulthood

Advancing Responsible Adolescent Development

Series Editor:

Roger J.R. Levesque, Indiana University, Bloomington, USA

EMERGING AND YOUNG ADULTHOOD
Multiple Perspectives, Diverse Narratives
by Varda Konstam

A continuation Order Plan is available for this series. A continuation order will bring delivery of each new volume immediately upon publication. Volumes are billed only upon actual shipment. For further information please contact the publisher.

Emerging and Young Adulthood

Multiple Perspectives, Diverse Narratives

Varda Konstam

 Springer

Varda Konstam
Department of Counseling and School Psychology
University of Massachusetts Boston
Boston, MA 01778
USA
vkonstam@aol.com

Library of Congress Control Number: 2007926111

ISBN-13: 978-0-387-71032-7   e-ISBN-13: 978-0-387-71033-4

Printed on acid-free paper.

9 8 7 6 5 4 3 2 1

springer.com

To Marvin, Amanda and Jeremy
— my inspirations

Acknowledgements

A special thank you to Amali De Zoysa for providing invaluable support, persistence and steadfastness throughout the process of writing this book. I would also like to thank Phyllis Laffer for her continued support.

Prologue

Having two children, one in the thick of navigating emerging adulthood, the other about to enter it, I found myself struggling between being understanding in terms of how difficult it is to negotiate a seemingly more complex and uncertain environment, and expecting that my children pick up the pace and live their lives using developmental markers that I had internalized. I viewed myself as overly indulgent and involved in the lives of my children. How could I be helpful in my role as parent, friend, and confidante?

It was easy to be judgmental. I was married at 21, had a career that exceeded my expectations by age 27, and my first child at the age of 29. I listened to my internal voice saying, "You don't really get what it's like out there, these are different times that require different approaches, different ways of being and coping." I decided to use my analytic and clinical skills, instead of my well-honed judgmental skills, and convinced myself to be more open to alternative perspectives and ways of thinking about this developmental period. I was going to grapple with the issues, and communicate my newfound understanding to students and potential practitioners in the field, as well as the major stakeholders, individuals negotiating and/or interfacing with emerging and young adults, parents, and employers. I was determined to use my energies constructively and embark on writing a book that was grounded in the academic literature, provided clarity and reassurance whenever possible, but at the same time did not present an overly optimistic picture that was reassuring for reassurance sake.

What happens to emerging adults as they "emerge" from their 20s? How can we integrate their diverse narratives and perspectives and go beyond what we already know about them? My instincts and clinical skills told me they were not a monolithic group, and that the meanings they attached to this developmental period were diverse and textured, informed in part by the experiences they encountered in their 20s. In the process, I would try to decipher and understand what skill-sets, personal characteristics, and environmental contexts enable emerging and young adults to thrive in a highly challenging work and interpersonal environment.

The diverse voices of the major stakeholders are represented: emerging and young adults, parents, and employers. The Chinese ideograph indicating crisis suggests danger as well as opportunity. Listening to the various stakeholders will provide a unique opportunity to view this developmental juncture from multiple perspectives and in the process expand the existing literature.

Contents

	Acknowledgements	vii
	Prologue	ix
Chapter 1	Introduction	1
Chapter 2	Identity	13
Chapter 3	Cultural Considerations and Emerging and Young Adulthood	29
Chapter 4	Voices of Emerging and Young Adults: In Pursuit of a Career Path	43
Chapter 5	Voices of Emerging and Young Adults: From the Professional to the Personal	59
Chapter 6	The "Tyranny" of Choice: A Re-Examination of the Prevailing Narrative	81
Chapter 7	Parental Voices: "Adjustment Reactions to Children's Adult Life"	97
Chapter 8	Voices of Employers: Overlapping and Disparate Views	111
Chapter 9	Running on Empty, Running on Full: Summary and Synthesis	129
Appendix A	Methods	149
Appendix B	Emerging and Young Adult Questionnaire	159
Appendix C	Parent Questionnaire	163
Appendix D	Employer Questionnaire	167
	Index	169

1
Introduction

Negotiating one's 20s has been described as one of the most complex and challenging developmental life stages (Tanner and Yabiku, 1999). Familiar structures such as school and home are removed, replaced by the unknown and unfamiliar, resulting in what frequently feels like an overwhelming present and uncertain future. Depending on the culture, the developmental period of emerging adulthood may vary in length, and it is no longer clear that "the transition to adulthood ... become[s] consolidated" by the late 20s (Arnett, 1998, p. 313).

Cote (2000, 2006) notes that since movement toward adulthood status continues to occur during one's 20s, emerging adulthood "should be expanded to explicitly include the full age period from 18 to 30, at least when college students are studied" (Cote, 2006, p. 108). Recent literature suggests that many of the developmental markers identified by Arnett are inclusive of many individuals approaching 30. This author made a deliberate decision to interview individuals with "fresh eyes" (Cote, 2006, p. 108), and focus on an age range that expands the existing literature, and perhaps more accurately depicts the transition period to young adulthood.

Researchers and writers have generated various possibilities in terms of providing a name for those negotiating their 20s: emerging adults, young adults, quarter-lifers, twixters, and generation Xers. No one descriptor seems to be sticking, although in academic circles, emerging adulthood for those individuals ranging from 18 to 25, appears to be the most-recognized descriptor to describe the transitional period to adulthood. How can we increase our understanding of individuals in their 20s who have been described as self-absorbed, floundering, aimless, irresponsible, delayed, narcissistic, immature, hedonistic, and the like? How does the environmental and cultural context help us understand apparent shifts in behavior, characterized by a delay in developmental markers typically associated with this developmental period?

There does appear to be consensus regarding what the developmental markers and features of individuals who are negotiating their 20s are. Arnett (2006, p. 8) identifies five main features:

1. It is the age of *identity explorations*, of trying out various possibilities, especially in love and work.
2. It is the age of *instability*.

1

3. It is the most *self-focused* age of life.
4. It is the age of *feeling in-between*, in transition, neither adolescent nor adult.
5. It is the age of *possibilities*, when hopes flourish, when people have an unparalleled opportunity to transform their lives.

Although there is acknowledgment that the 20s is an important time for consolidation of identity formation, there is a dearth of research efforts, with most of the efforts primarily focused on the developmental period of adolescence (Arnett, 2004; Waterman, 1999). There is, however, agreement related to criteria for entry into adulthood. These include: (a) accepting responsibility for oneself, (b) making independent decisions, and (c) becoming financially independent (Nelson, 2003). These criteria, are "gradual, incremental, rather than [occurring] all at once" (Arnett, 2004, p. 15), and are consistent with the perceptions of young Americans and their individualistic view of adulthood. Interestingly, marriage is no longer viewed in America, in contrast to more traditional cultures, as the definitive marker that indicates passage into adulthood (Arnett, 1998; Schlagel & Barry, 1991).

Currently, individuals in their 20s and early 30s are engaged in a process that involves making plans for a future that is uncertain. This period has been described as a "... sandbox, a chance to build castles and knock them down, experiment with different careers ...," in the context of a world with "overwhelming choice" (e.g., "40 kinds of coffee beans at Whole Foods Market ..., 295 channels on DirecTV, 15 million personal ads on Match.com and 800,000 jobs on Monster.com" (Grossman, 2005, p. 46)). Given that entry to adulthood is occurring in the context of a fluid unpredictable environment that makes long-term planning difficult at best, how does one plan for the future? Understanding the contextual landscape, as well as listening to the voices of individuals who have emerged from this period of their life enriches the discussion.

A Contextual Perspective

Since the 1980s, motivated in part by corporate downsizing and restructuring, post-baby boomers are assuming new attitudes and behaviors regarding the world of work. Social and cultural changes, emanating from the social movements of the 1960s and 1970s, have led to debates related to lifestyle choices and the questioning of institutional commitments. In response to changing employment situations, emerging adults entering the workforce are advised to assume an open flexible stance, and simultaneously to let go of security-oriented notions such as long-term employment.

Individuals in their 20s and 30s sense uncertainty around them. The rules that have previously enabled them to function and thrive in familiar environments (i.e., school settings) no longer apply. There is a "serious disjuncture" between the period of adolescence and the developmental tasks associated with that stage of development and emerging and young adulthood (Cote, 2000, p. 29). Postponement of the structuring of careers as well as other facets of one's life may be a natural sequel given the overwhelming, complex, on-demand, and unpredictable environment emerging adults encounter.

Flach (1988, pp. 70–71) states:

Perhaps in the absence of sheer necessity, direction is hard to find. Or perhaps these emerging adults feel the need to extend the chaos and take longer than one would expect of them to grow up sensing that the future is indeed quite unpredictable, recognizing the dramatic acceleration of events that has occurred, and following the dictates of nature that suggested that the young, unformed, pliable creature has a better chance of evolutionary survival than the one that matures too quickly and becomes frozen, unable to adapt to a drastically alien environmental condition, the … twenty-first century.

Who are these emerging and young adults, and what meanings do they assign to this time in their life? Sixty-four individuals ranging in age from 25 to 35 were interviewed to capture the experiences of individuals negotiating this developmental juncture. Thirty-one individuals who grew up in affluent suburbs in the northeast, and thirty-three individuals, alumni of a commuter public university that primarily services a diverse body of first-generation college graduates, served as participants. In addition, thirty parents of individuals 25–35 years of age, and thirty employers of this age group were interviewed for the purpose of generating a more nuanced textured narrative of this developmental period. All of the individuals interviewed were volunteers (please refer to Appendix A for a more detailed description of the participants).

Although our understanding of this developmental period is incomplete in general, it is important to note that much of what we do know is limited to individuals in their 20s belonging to the American majority culture (Cote, 2000; Wainryb, 2004). The existing literature on emerging and young adulthood is biased toward representing the views of the middle and upper classes. Given that a significant subset of individuals has been neglected in the literature (e.g., individuals who are poor or working class, immigrants, individuals from minority cultures), generalizations cannot be made from the findings reported in the literature to date. The author attempts here to represent the relatively "silent" population of individuals as discussed in the existing literature. However, it is important to note that the voices represented are college graduates, all of whom are volunteers, located in a specific context, an urban northeastern city and its surrounding communities, and cannot be generalized to other contexts in the United States.

Adam, Laura, and Maria

Adam, Laura, and Maria are three examples of individuals emerging from their 20s with varying experiences and worldviews. Although they do not represent the full spectrum of individuals interviewed and the issues encountered, they do represent a lens to the potential diversity of experiences and possible negotiations.

Adam

Adam is a single, 34-year-old, self-employed consultant in financial services, who is in the midst of launching a second company. At age 27, Adam started his first company with a partner and grew it to a company with 15 employees. He sold the company at age 30 with a considerable profit, and as he describes it, just before an economic downturn, which would have left him in significant debt. Both of his entrepreneurial endeavors called upon his expertise in computers; his latest company is designed to address the need for niche search engines. Since his graduation 12 years ago from a large urban northeastern university, Adam has held four jobs related to financial services. To supplement his existing income from profits made from selling his first company, he currently engages in financial services consulting work.

In my attempt to schedule an interview with Adam, as an outsider looking in, I immediately felt immersed in his world. In establishing parameters related to the interview, Adam responded by expressing no time preference, indicating availability to speak with me anytime during the weekend. Although I attempted to stifle my clinical training, I wondered whether Adam had difficulties with setting boundaries for himself and others. I also wondered whether this young man had a life outside work. In describing himself vis-à-vis his work life, Adam states:

I'm a risk taker, but I am not one of these guys where the business needs to revolve around me. [I] would rather share and have complementary skills. My previous partner and I, we were never on the same page, but it was good. We brought different skills to the table. I do not think I am smart enough. You got to test everything; if you have an idea you have to test it with your partner. You should fight for your ideas, untested ideas. If you cannot convince your business partner, who has the same long-term goals, how are you going to convince anyone else? That is why you need to be open-minded, rather than listening to the ideas that you already know and not feel stress.

At age 30, Adam realized what he needed from his work environment, specifically the work-related conditions that would enable him to thrive. His newfound understanding co-occurred with the selling of his company. He was not happy in the four jobs he assumed post-college in his 20s.

I tried a lot of jobs; was not happy in any of them. The common thread was I could not deal with a boss. I would love a mentor. I like building stuff, and I have a high tolerance for risk. My idea of a good job is working 24 hours six months and then taking a break, opposite to what the average person wants. They have a life and want it. It doesn't work for me. I have been in start ups and they have been extremely exciting.

When asked about the current economic climate and the context in which he works, Adam responded philosophically, stating that the meaning and significance of work, as well as actual practices, are evolving:

It [work] is a continuing part of a total transformation of work and society. Just one example, if you are reasonably willing to hustle, you can survive perfectly well, doing your work remotely on the Internet, maybe visit your clients once a month, and live anywhere in the world. Compare that to 20 years ago. What is happening in India is happening. Fast Internet connections change the nature of work. It is sad for me to think that people don't think there is opportunity out there. The world economy is so diverse. Anyone who is willing to hustle and work hard can find something that they can be happy doing. Not only just surviving ... or staying in jobs that they are not happy with. I was lucky that I did not have to.

Adam provided an historical perspective on the current work environment:

For some people it takes so much longer to figure out what is their place .... In the old days you did not question it as much. You would stay with an unhappy job. People want more from life. People's expectations are higher .... What I am trying to say, is that the idea got out, that there is a big world out there, a lot of fun things to do, interesting things to see. Goes against the idea of being satisfied with a great life but a limited life. People know there is more out there, and they want to experience it.

People are being perfectly rational about it. If you are a woman, are you going to be so quick as soon as you get out there, are your expectations so low, to be married and have kids? That used to be normal. Society does not put that expectation before you any more. Men got away with a lot more. In a more conservative culture, who wants to be an outsider? If you are in a city, in New York or Boston, for example, to be single and 35 is not questioned. It is not strange. Society has become less oppressive. People are delaying putting down roots.

Adam suffers from occasional panic attacks, which he attributes to his entrepreneurial and risk-taking spirit:

Sometimes I have slight panic attacks but nothing bad; the more you do it the better you get at it. I am easily bored. I need excitement. There are socially accepted ways of doing it. We are a spoiled crowd that wants more. I measure myself against people who are interesting and move society forward. I need to build something of value that someone is willing to pay for. If you want individual validation that you are doing something worthwhile, if someone is willing to pay for it that is a good indication. And then you will do well for your employees, and the market is served doing something that someone wants, and hopefully you will make a few bucks.

His reference to delaying putting down roots led to a discussion about relationships. Adam is not currently in a relationship, and has had limited success sustaining a long-term relationship. He views his work life, "Like a roller coaster ... with dizzying highs and lows, and occasionally there is a calm stretch." In contrast, he views his romantic life as "neglected, it's been neglected." With respect to his personal life, Adam states:

I am single, unfortunately; eventually yes, I would like to be married. I wouldn't say tomorrow; when you have had employees sometimes, it does not work out. Made me very careful entering into agreements with people. You don't want to jump into anything that is difficult to undo; you have to do your homework; you have to be careful; there are a lot of steps. You are being foolish if you don't do the steps, the downside is so bad. ... Have to minimize your risk because the downside is so bad. You have to have the patience to follow the right steps.

You got to find the right person; you got to have the right priorities. It will not happen by chance. [It is] painful to fire someone. You have to have your eyes wide open; it's foolish if you don't. And it's risky; it's so much more risk than you want.

I was struck by how Adam spoke of his potential significant relationship. It felt as though he were describing a business transaction, a dispassionate account of his accumulated experiences, using a business model to inform his decisions about choosing a romantic partner and making a long-term commitment to her. Although Adam alludes to boundaries, he seems to have difficulties applying his knowledge to his life.

When you are in the middle of one of these startup experiences it consumes every minute if you let it. Always racing against the clock because there is an infinite amount of things that you need to do. Personally, you have to have boundaries.

There appear to be no boundaries between Adam's work life and personal life. For example, during the time when Adam owned a company with 15 employees, his employees provided him with his primary source of social interaction. Interestingly, Adam uses his current business partner, as well as his previous business partners, as major sources of support in his life. His relationships with his partners seem to provide him with emotional sustenance and emotional balance as evidenced by the following statement Adam made, "When there are problems you really internalize; that is why you need a business partner because they will be feeling up when you are feeling down."

Adam understands the need for balance, the need for complementarity in his life. I personally wondered if and how Adam was going to make it happen in his personal life. He had found a rhythm, albeit a nontraditional one, and a sense of fulfillment in his work life. He did express a sense of unease about his personal life, but at the same time communicated that this area of "neglect" would receive attention at some point in the future.

Whereas Adam in describing his work life conveyed a sense of mastery and confidence, never questioning the notion that he is the navigator of his ship, Laura, a 33-year-old single female, spoke of her work life in contrasting terms. Unlike Adam, the course of her ship had been redirected by unfavorable and uncontrollable work conditions, leaving her somewhat frustrated and anxious about her ability to stay the course and reach her destination point.

Laura

Laura did exceptionally well in high school, attended an urban northeastern university, and assumed a job in the publishing industry after graduating from college. Her second job left her in a highly responsible position, taking a new publication, and trying to bring it to the marketplace. She immersed herself in her job, serving as an empowered devoted employee. Laura was granted an unusual degree of autonomy and latitude in terms of decision making, particularly given her level of training and previous work experience. Laura thrived, but the publication did not. Two years later, following a series of mishaps, in large part caused by the rules governing startup companies, Laura found herself laid off despite outstanding evaluations and a tremendous sense of gratification. She subsequently assumed several positions in small start-up companies that resulted in lay-offs as well:

I feel like I am in constant danger of being laid off. I used to be really paranoid about it. I will have been at this job for three years; maybe it is complacency. There are no guarantees anymore. Employers don't have loyalty. I have blind faith that I am here for a while but that could change. There are risks in my job right now. In a bad market, I am out of a job if retrenchment takes place.

In my current position, [there are] no hierarchies, no way for me to go. My goal is not to get fired or laid off, to leave myself with a portfolio of work that will leave me bulletproof. It is hard to have long-term goals when you don't know what the situation is going to be. That may be overly pessimistic of me.

Laura did not have a sense that her story and experiences related to work were unique. In fact, she viewed her work experiences as fairly "typical:"

If you got involved in the story of the Internet startup companies, I am typical. Seventy percent have stories like mine. I would log on to a site (fuckedinternet.com) and my story, especially compared to those from Silicon Valley, would be rated G …. Among my friends, I've had worse luck. I don't know if it is circumstance or because the companies I worked for were small, more entrepreneurial; that is part of what I am trying to figure out.

In describing some of her work environments, Laura uses metaphors suggesting a war zone. Her stated short-term goal includes constructing a portfolio of work that would leave her "bulletproof." Although that represents one view of the work environment and her place in it, she also sees other possibilities. She is currently enrolled in a creative writing program and hopes to gain skills that will enable her to further pursue writing professionally:

I don't have long-term corporate goals and strategies. Maybe move on to a bigger company, being head of creative services, but my personal goals are more important …. Would love to quit my job and do freelance journalist writing. The outlets for freelance writing are not as good. I have bills. I have a pragmatic streak. I do not have a bad job, but it is not me being authentic to the world.

In my 20s I wanted to be head of a company; now it seems okay to be in a fairly low-level job in my niche, and do what I have to do. My personal goals are to get my degree, put together good novels, short stories, and just start writing books. Turn my back on the nine-to-five thing. I would not necessarily be John Grisham, but if I needed to go to Europe for three months and live off my savings, I could do that.

In keeping with Laura's guarded outlook, she views her work world with a "good measure of cynicism," which she perceives as adaptive to the current work context:

I have observed at least two ways of coping: a conformist nonquestioning do not rock the boat path. The other is a healthy dose of cynicism, or humor to get through it. Or be in a position where work is not the end-all or be-all of your life. Work is only 40 hours a week. Be sure to have loved ones in your life, hobbies, something waiting for you at home on Friday. Your career is not who you are. Do not get caught up in trappings or excitement of saying you are a doctor or vice president of a company …. Have a healthy personal life or satisfying one. The work, in the form you know it today, is not always going to be there. It is an artificial benchmark.

Laura's worldview is in part informed by what may be seen as a healthy dose of cynicism as well as a sense of humor (albeit an edgy one). Her experiences have taught her that despite outstanding job performance evaluations, the work world is unstable at best, unpredictable, and that although she has been praised for the wonderful work that she was doing, it can all go awry without notice or warning. Work for Laura has evolved into something she "does" rather than a part of what she "is." She is disillusioned with the world of work, "the dream of fulfilling... [herself] as a person at work had tarnished" (Josselson, 1996, p. 192).

Laura expressed disillusionment in her romantic life as well. She sustained a relationship for nine years, which has recently ended. Laura's boyfriend worked 80 hours a week on the average, and seemed "spent" when with her. Differences in work values created a rift that could not be reconciled for Laura. Her boyfriend's success moving up the corporate ladder created a permanent schism in the relationship. Laura aspired to a committed, nurturing, and mutually supportive relationship, one that allowed for the co-existence of a satisfying work life and home life for each of the partners. She terminated the relationship, given her assessment that it was not possible to "be" in a relationship with her boyfriend, given his emotional and physical unavailability.

Maria, in contrast to Laura and Adam, chose a career prematurely, and regrets not having sufficiently experimented with alternative choices. She has come to terms with her career choice and derives satisfaction from the process of teaching. She hopes to open doors to adolescents who like herself may not have the support or know-how to actualize their dreams.

Maria

Whereas Adam and Laura are single, without children, Maria is a 30-year-old single parent, trying to navigate a career, raise her two children, and maintain a vibrant network of friends. She immigrated to this country from Spain at the age of eight. Her father passed away when she was five, an event that mobilized her mother to pursue a better life for her two children, as "there was very little opportunity for education." Maria did exceptionally well in school, and has been teaching for the past eight years. She is currently seeking a second Masters degree so that she can function as a high school guidance counselor, in part to help others, like herself, take advantage of the educational and career opportunities of which they may otherwise not avail themselves. She discusses her goals and hopes, "I hope to be a guidance counselor. I really value education and I see it as an equalizer, and I hope to inspire students from that high school [referring to high school she attended] to go to college."

Maria reflects on her career choice with some regret. Although she enjoys the process of teaching, she regrets not having sufficiently explored and experimented with alternative careers post-college. Maria selected a career prematurely, without considering the myriad options available to her:

I would have never studied business .... I think I should have majored in something like cultural anthropology. I really liked learning about cultures, their histories .... I never before found a major that incorporates all the things I wanted.

She attributes her inability to find a suitable major as foreclosing opportunities. Maria has been able to satisfy her need for exploration and experimentation via travel. She enjoys immersing herself in other cultures and learning from those experiences. During her college years, as well as her early 20s, Maria traveled a fair amount, supporting her travels via part-time work.

After teaching for eight years, Maria chose to pursue a career in guidance counseling, building on her strengths and experiences as a teacher. She is currently in the throes of completing her second Masters degree in counseling, and appears to have come to terms with her career choice.

In speaking about her personal life, Maria assumes a more questioning and confused stance. Although she is able to have satisfying long-term relationships with female friends, her intimate relationships with men have left her disappointed and frustrated. She dated during college, but did not wish to be in a long-term intimate relationship.

When I was in college, I never wanted to be in a relationship, never saw myself married. I dated a lot. I wanted to do well in school. Not in my plans. I knew I wanted to be married eventually. I did not want any part of it in college. I wanted to study, date, and travel. A lot of my friends wanted a relationship. I did not see men as that great. My mother told me you have to be perfect, to be clean, to be a virgin, to be the perfect girl, so that a man will want me.

Maria, in describing her relationships with men post-college, describes scenarios whereby she is in relationships with controlling and/or duplicitous men that are primarily motivated by physical attraction, or in relationships that are devoid of physical attraction, that ultimately lead to disappointment and sadness.

Maria's first serious long-term relationship was tempestuous, one in which physical abuse occurred. She immediately ended the relationship, after seeing "a side of him [she] did not see before, an indication of what [her] life was going to become." However, she was pregnant and did not consider abortion an option, in large part due to her religious beliefs. Maria continued to assume a social life, juggling her multiple roles: mother, working woman, daughter, sister, and friend. With respect to dating, she tried a different tack, making deliberate choices to date men who were not physically attractive to her:

I went on dates, no one I was physically attracted to. A lot of successful men [I was] not physically attracted to them. Let me try a guy I am not attracted to. Maybe an attraction will come. Before, I was dating guys that there was a physical attraction, and those ended pretty terribly.

Her second serious long-term relationship was guided primarily by a desire to make a relationship work that was not exclusively organized by physical attraction. Maria became pregnant, and although she and her male partner tried to make the relationship work, lack of passion on her part served as a significant barrier. Maria is currently resolved to living her life without a male partner, raising two children, with both fathers assuming some responsibility for the emotional and financial well-being of each child. Although Maria yearns to find her soulmate, she assumes a fatalistic stance:

I have given up on the idea of finding a husband. I leave it up to God. If it is meant for me to be married, I will. If not, I accept that. Maybe God put me on this earth to do other things and being married would interfere with that.

She reflects on her previous relationships, stating that although she would prefer to be married, she is not willing to be in a relationship where she has to "give up herself."

I want to be married. I can't be a stay-at-home mom and that's it. He [the father of her second child] wants someone like his mom, who never worked. She did not work until he was 18. He needs someone like that.... I was trying to do my best, to be there for him, but I was not going to give up my self. He said there is something missing from the relationship. We don't have the same goals. If you are going to be married, that person needs to be perfect. If he needs someone to make him the center of her world, then I guess I am not that person. He should have who he wants. He should not have to make sacrifices like that. I want to be right for that person. He wants to feels that he is my everything too.

Maria expresses sadness in terms of her personal life. She wishes that her life would have unfolded differently. However, she also takes pride in being an educated woman who was able to travel and see a larger world.

I don't think I would have established a strong relationship in college. If I had gotten in a serious relationship, I would not have traveled, seen so much, learned so much. I do regret getting pregnant out of wedlock. I should have been responsible with sex and wasn't. I do love my children.

Her attitudes toward men and marital relationships are strikingly different from those of her Spanish mother. Maria seems to have incorporated an alternative model, one that strives toward autonomy and differentiation. She is struggling with the need to come to terms with disparate, seemingly incompatible models for being a woman in her current cultural context.

Summary

Adam, Laura, and Maria present a window to the diversity of voices of individuals who describe their attempts to transition to young adulthood in a context in which legal, social, and economic authority, in comparison to previous generations, occurs in a delayed fashion. The following chapters explore current understanding of identity development and cultural considerations, followed by an analysis and discussion of the results of the interviews conducted with emerging and young adults, parents, and employers. Their rich and diverse narratives attempt to illustrate and capture the complexity as well as nuance of this developmental period.

References

Arnett, J. (1998). Learning to stand alone: The contemporary American transition to adulthood in cultural and historical context. *Human Development, 41*, 295–315.

Arnett, J. (2000). Emerging adulthood. A theory of development from the late teens through the twenties. *American Psychologist, 55*, 469–480.

Arnett, J. (2006). Emerging adulthood: Understanding the new way of coming of age. In J. Arnett & J. Tanner (Eds.), *Emerging adults in America: Coming of age in the 21st century* (pp. 1–3). Washington, DC: American Psychological Association.

Cote, J. (2000). *Arrested adulthood: The changing nature of maturity and identity—What does it mean to grow up?* New York: New York University Press.

Cote, J. (2006). Emerging adulthood as an institutionalized moratorium: Risks and benefits to identity formation. In J. Arnett & J. Tanner (Eds.), *Emerging adults in America: Coming of age in the 21st century* (pp. 85–116). Washington, DC: American Psychological Association.

Flach, F. (1998) *Resilience: How to bounce back when the going gets tough!* Long Island City, NY: Hatherleigh Press.

Grossman, L. (2005, January 16). Grow up? Not so fast. *Time*, 42–53.

Josselson, R. (1996). *Revising herself: The story of women's identity from college to midlife.* New York: Oxford University Press.

Nelson, L. (2003). Rites of passage in emerging adulthood: Perspectives of young Mormons. *New Directions for Child and Adolescent Development: Cultural Conceptions of the Transition to Adulthood, 100*, 33–49.

Schlegel, A. & Barry, H., III. (1991). *Adolescence: An anthropological inquiry.* New York: Free Press.

Tanner, J. & Yabiku, S. (1999). Conclusion: The economics of young adulthood—One future or two? In A. Booth, A. Crouter, & M. Shanahan (Eds.), *Transitions to adulthood in a changing economy: No work, no family, no future?* (pp. 254–268). Westport, CT: Praeger.

Wainryb, C. (2004). The study of diversity in human development: Culture, urgencies, and perils. *Human Development, 47*, 131–137.

Waterman, A. S. (1999). Identity, the identity statuses, and identity status development: A contemporary statement. *Developmental Review, 19*, 591–621.

2
Identity

The tasks associated with entering and negotiating adulthood, including identity development, are daunting. Emerging and young adults in an industrialized society such as the United States face a global environment that is fast-paced, increasingly complex, demanding, and ever-changing. The future is uncertain, and for some, replete with choices and possibilities. Rules are less clear and more contextual, and there is less institutional guidance pointing to clear developmental pathways. Hence, there is a need for greater individual maneuvering that requires a strategic approach in planning a life course (Cote, 2000; Moses, 1998).

Emerging and young adults often feel that they are living in a different environmental context in comparison to past generations. Adults, positioned in the past to provide them with tangible and emotional support, may no longer be able to provide assistance. Given lack of institutional supports, and parental inexperience and/or expertise in providing know-how regarding how to best navigate these new environmental contingencies, a key question, ". . . Who am I, and where am I going," is experienced by many emerging and young adults as overwhelming, particularly given an environment that leaves it up to the individual to figure it all out (Cote, 2006, p. 127).

Identity development is informed in part by historical and cultural context. For example, whereas symptoms associated with neurosis were most prevalent in Victorian times under conditions of emotional repression, identity issues appear to be paramount in these times of limitless possibility, and no single vision. Although the diagnosis of borderline personality disorder is highly controversial and sex-role linked, it is currently one of the most popular diagnoses in psychiatry, an umbrella term that covers a multitude of symptoms that all seem to point to those individuals who are needy, scattered, and present an uncertain self (Cote, 2000). The diagnosis appears to be symptomatic of our fluid, ever-changing context, a context that challenges the abilities of the individual to internalize a coherent self (Sue, Pharam, & Santiago, 1998).

Cote (2006) takes the position that given the current environmental context, specifically with respect to lack of adequate structure and support, "People tend to be confused or lose their sense of place in society" (p. 136). He argues that the abundance of choice is "problematic" and that emerging adults struggle individually (Cote, 2006):

In late modern society, we seem to have a population that tends to be confused about "who they are." Lacking a secure psychological foundation, people have a difficult time making the transition to "adulthood." In turn, an increasing number of people seem to become "adults" (in terms of age) who are "immature" in comparison to adults of earlier periods. This all seems "normal" now. (p. 136)

There is a rich literature on identity development that primarily addresses the period of adolescence. Some developmental psychologists discuss identity in binary terms, as either immutable and stable, in contrast to others who tend to view identity development as primarily dependent on external contingencies and prone to change (Lipford & Bradely, 2005; Zunker, 2006), introducing an artificial polarity to the discussion of identity. It is the perspective of the author that identity is a multidimensional construct, characterized by shifts in one's sense of self that are informed by environmental contexts. Identity may vary over time and across settings (McCarn & Fassinger, 1996; Tanner, 2006). Moreover, changes in identity do not necessarily represent a switching of loyalties, but are responses to expectations and constraints of particular environments (Hays, 2002).

Identity in emerging adulthood is an "initial formulation" that is reconstructed and reformulated throughout the lifecycle (Marcia, Waterman, Matteson, Archer, & Orlofsky, 1993, p. 21). It evolves over time and does not end in our 20s (Bauer & McAdams, 2004). It is tested, recalibrated, and/or redesigned to "fit with new experiences" (Phinney, 2006, p. 120). Belsky (not dated, p. 110) states that we are "works in progress throughout our entire lives," and that revisiting and revising our identities is consistent with the human condition. Our lives are "prone to being disrupted," requiring periods of reassessment and revision (Belsky, not dated, pp. 110–111).

Josselson (1996, p. 30) provides a cogent discussion of identity, and reinforces the notion that we are responsive to our environment, capable of assuming a self that is nuanced, organized, and informed by environmental expectations and contingencies:

We are not the same in all regions of our lives, and how we make meaning may change across situations or over time. Identity is what integrates our own diversity, gives meaning to the disparate parts of ourselves, and relates them to one another. Identity is how we interpret parts of ourselves, and relate them to one another. Identity is how we interpret our own existence and understand who we are in our world.

Marcia (1966) identified four identity groups based on the theoretical underpinnings of Erickson (1959): *Guardians, Pathmakers, Searchers,* and *Drifters. Guardians* tend to execute a life plan that they mapped out in their childhoods, or was mapped out by their parents. They are the carriers of culture revealing the highest level of obedience to authority, respect for rules, and the lowest levels of anxiety, when compared to the other three groups (Josselson, 1996). They hold on to tradition as they navigate their 20s and their lived experience reflects the belief: "This is how I am because it's how I was raised, or how I've always been" (Josselson, 1996, p. 35).

Pathmakers are action-oriented and are not inclined to be very introspective. They engage in a process of exploration, reach resolution, and "make identity commitments on their own terms" (p. 35). They struggle with options, and then make their choices, although they decide with less conviction than *Guardians*. Their lived experience reflects the belief, "I've tried out some things, and this is what makes most sense for me" (p. 35).

Searchers engage in exploration, but are in a period of struggle, unclear about how to execute perceived available choices. Their lived experience reflects, "I'm not sure about who I am or want to be, but I'm trying to figure it out" (p. 35). Most *Searchers* choose only after an extended period of self-examination and experimentation and remain aware of their internal conflict and struggle.

Drifters are most delayed in structuring their identity. They are "without commitments . . ., either feeling lost or following impulses of the moment" (p. 36). *Drifters* have difficulties discerning their desires and dreams, and these desires and dreams are ever shifting. They struggle to "find themselves within their own volatility, but are vulnerable to being appropriated by someone else's design" (p. 241). Their lived experience reflects the belief, "I don't know what I will do or believe, but it doesn't matter too much right now" (p. 36). Their struggle is most often an individual effort, characterized by a paucity of support from others. The high percentage of *Searchers* and *Drifters*, according to Cote (2000, pp. 134–135), can be understood in the context of a society "in which choice-making is both possible and problematic."

It is important to note that the identified four identity groups are not fixed, and may shift over time. The categories are not etched in stone. Given the complexity and nuance of individuals' lived experience, many individuals can be seen as fitting in more than one category, and significant overlap may exist. The categories as presented are meant to be viewed on a continuum, with no fixed boundaries. Although some individuals may stay stuck in one group, others may enter and exit the identified categories over time (Waterman, 1999). Critics such as Belsky have pointed to the reality that individuals may identify with one group in one area of their life (e.g., interpersonal relationships), but in another domain may identify with another group (e.g., career choice, religiosity). In other words, it may not be helpful to categorize individuals in one group, especially given the negative value judgments associated with the categories of *Drifter* and *Guardian* (Goosens, 2001; Kroger, 2000).

It is also important to recognize the instability that is characteristic of this developmental period (Montgomery, 2005; Shulman, Feldman, Blatt, Cohen, & Malhler, 2005). A longitudinal study conducted by Cohen, Kasen, Chen, Hartmark, and Gordon (2003) reports that only slightly more than half of the participants at age 25 are fully independent of their family of origin. In addition, extensive variability exists with respect to individual trajectories. Participants ranging in age from 17 to 27 fluctuated considerably between increasing and decreasing dependency.

Identity and Group Membership

Group identity informs the process of identity formation (Phinney, 2006). Although meaningful discussion of identity needs to recognize the influences of race, gender, social class, ethnicity, religious orientation, sexual orientation, and disability, the literature is sparse (Schwartz, Cote, & Arnett, 2005). bell hooks (as cited by Phan, Torres Rivera, & Roberts-Wilbur, 2005, p. 310) discusses models of identity development and notes that they have not sufficiently incorporated cultural influences and have understated the effects of "discrimination, oppression, prejudice, sexism, racism and White supremacists' ideas" on identity development.

In homogenous contexts, group identity exploration may not express itself as a primary concern (Phinney, 2006). In more heterogeneous and global contexts, individuals are increasingly likely to explore issues related to group identity and the negotiation of self in relation to other groups, particularly if they have encountered "discriminatory attitudes and evidence of their lower status and power in society" (p. 130). Temperamental style, personality characteristics, level of education, phenotype, and degree of group discrimination experienced are variables identified by Phinney as important in determining likelihood and extent of group exploration. In addition, some individuals are more sensitive to perceived discrimination (e.g., depressed individuals).

With regard to ethnic identity, some people feel a strong need to belong to a group; they may seek out people who share their ethnic background and obtain information about their ethnic heritage as a way of developing a place to belong. Others feel less need to belong or else fulfill the need within a different context, such as family or friends . . . . Experiences of being treated stereotypically or discriminated against, or being asked to label oneself ethnically, can be strong motivators of exploration, regardless of the larger context. (Phinney, 2006, p. 130)

Harrison (1995) provides further clarity with respect to understanding the relationship between identity development and cultural group memberships. All individuals seek an identity, "A specific individuated personhood" (p. 379). Identity includes that "idiosyncratic constellation of qualities in each of us that persists over time," and is context-dependent, and "multifaceted" (p. 379). Among individuals belonging to marginalized communities (e.g., homosexual men), having been exposed to stigmatization, prejudice, guilt, and shame is likely to lead to the incorporation, integration, and expression of these experiences. The incorporation of these experiences provides opportunities to express a need for "self-assertion against prejudice" and inform identity development (p. 379). In addition, it is important to recognize the intersection and interrelationships of cultural group memberships such as race, ethnicity, gender, and social class, particularly among individuals with "multiple oppressive identities" (Constantine, 2002, p. 211).

Although it is critical to acknowledge the significance of cultural influences and the isms associated with these influences (e.g., racism, sexism), it is also important not to overgeneralize, stereotype, and confine one group of individuals to a specific limiting narrative. For example, bell hooks (1996), states that in order "to understand the complexity of African American girlhood we need more work that documents that reality in all its variations and diversity . . . . There is no one story of African American girlhood" (p. 13). Above all, we need to see and incorporate the other as he or she is located in idiosyncratic cultural contexts, and incorporate the dynamic meaning systems constructed by individuals informed by membership in a variety of cultural groups. In response to projections by others, a Black female emerging adult states the following, ". . . [E]veryone sees what they want to see. But no one seems to want to see me" (Williams, 2005, p. 279). Encountering the other includes seeing and experiencing the other, embracing all complexities, contradictions, and nuance.

Agency and Identity

Schwartz, Cote, and Arnett (2005) investigated the relationship between agency and identity across three American ethnic groups (non-Hispanic Whites, non-Hispanic Blacks, and Hispanics). They evaluated differences in identity indices between clusters of participants organized according to patterns of agentic personality scores. Results revealed few ethnic mean differences in the indices of agency and identity. "Agency is positively related to exploration, flexible commitment, and deliberate choice making, unrelated to closure and conformity and negatively related to avoidance and aimlessness" (p. 222). The authors conclude:

These results support the cross-ethnic generalizability of Erikson's (1968) theory of identity as well as that of neo-Eriksonian identity theories proposed by Berzonsky (1989), Cote and Levine (2002) and Marcia (1966). More specifically, this finding supports Cote's (2000; Cote & Levine, 2002) contention that agentic functioning is an important component of individualized identity development and, hence of effective adaptation to postindustrial societies, in emerging adulthood (p. 222) . . . . What appears to be key is [one's] ability to capitalize on the relatively unstructured and unguided task of forming an identity in contemporary American society. (Schwartz, Cote, & Arnett, 2005, p. 222)

Across all three groups, for those emerging adults who evidenced commitment to a set of goals, values, and beliefs, the commitments appeared to provide resources for them to "counteract the anomie and lack of collective support associated with identity formation and the transition to adulthood in the United States, and perhaps in other postindustrial societies" (Schwartz, Cote, & Arnett, 2005, p. 223). It is important to note that the conclusions are based on a sample of private high school students. Therefore, results are context-specific and cannot be generalized to other high school settings such as public schools, nor can they be generalized to older emerging and young adults.

Schwartz, Cote, and Arnett (2005) state that although the range of alternatives available to emerging adults (e.g., career paths, romantic attachments, and world-views) has expanded, "The collective support for identity formation has decreased" (Cote & Levine, 2002). Accordingly, if emerging and young adults are to make enduring life commitments (e.g., romantic commitments, career choices), they must first undertake the psychological tasks of individually forming a stable and viable identity that can guide and sustain these commitments, particularly given the replacement of community-oriented policies and production-based lifestyles by market-oriented policies and consumption-based lifestyles (Furong & Cartmel, 1997, p. 202). Emerging and young adults actively negotiating the formation of identity in a "proactive and agentic manner," are more likely to situate themselves such that they are more able to negotiate for social resources and position (Schwartz et al., 2005, p. 203).

In summary, individuals have many discrete "selves" and the search for a solitary purpose or unidimensional identity is foolhardy. However, there appear to be idiosyncratic qualities in each of us that persist over time. Thus, there are many "stories" that represent who we are, and growth is a process of "rewriting, revising, and interweaving these narratives" (Josselson, 1996, p. 256). "A sense of identity is never gained nor maintained once and for all . . . . It is constantly lost and regained" (Erickson, 1959, p. 118). Thus, identity is:

The backbone of a life story, provides unity to a life as lived by choosing versions of one's history that "fit" often editing out what is incongruent. The past is reconfigured to make our present identity seem inevitable—or if not inevitable, at least meaningful . . . . In retelling our lives, the past also absorbs aspects of the larger culture's narratives (so that we all feel like products of our times) . . . . Some individuals live a single story; others live many . . . . these stories intermingle and influence one another. The "plot" tends not to be linear. Identity encompasses all these selves, forming a narrative that weaves them together. (Josselson, 1996, pp. 256–257)

A Diversity of Paths: Emily, Ryan, Tracey, and Sergio

Emerging and young adults navigate their lives in myriad ways, in part reflecting their perceived freedom and existing lack of clearly demarcated social norms (Arnett & Tanner, 2006; Tanner, 2006). Absence of strict codes of behavior create a context in which emerging and young adults feel freer to explore and expand their search for identity:

Social control and social norms set boundaries for what is acceptable and punish behavior that is outside the boundaries. When the boundaries are broad, as they are in emerging adulthood, a wider range of individual differences is allowed expression, on the basis of a wide range of individual tendencies and preferences (see Arnett, 1995, in press). Thus, for example, adolescents are "supposed to be" not yet in a committed long-term romantic relationship and young adults past age 30 are "supposed to be" in one, but it is acceptable for emerging adults to be in a committed relationship, or not to be in one, or to be semi-committed, or any of a wide range of gradations along this continuum. Because of their freedom from social control and the lack of social norms for the 20s, emerging adulthood is the most volitional period of life, the time when people are most likely to be free to follow their own interests and desires, and those interests and desires lead them in an exceptionally wide range of directions. (Arnett, 2006, p. 15)

The context described by Arnett creates a rich environment for exploration of possibilities. Emily, Ryan, Tracey, and Sergio illustrate the multifaceted, nuanced, and diverse ways emerging and young adults are negotiating the ongoing dynamic process of developing an identity. Sergio provides a context for understanding the immigration process and how it intersects with identity development.

Emily

Emily is a 31-year-old, single female, with a degree in environmental science. Her 20s have been characterized by a series of adventures: she has sailed around the world twice, working on ships that allow her to utilize her training and expertise as a research scientist. She has pursued time-limited "projects," typically on boats that have taken her to a range of work sites including the Galapagos Islands, Hawaii, and Alaska. Emily's sense of self is informed by a lifelong commitment to learning and exploration. She has spent two years working as a lecturer on a recreational boat, as well as two years teaching English in a more formal context to students in Japan.

Emily speaks to the importance of friendships and family and how she creates family given her peripatetic existence.

My sister and I are exact opposites. She and I are the ying and yang of the family. My sister sees family as not being important to me. [That is not the case]. I am able to create family where I go. I consider the friendships I make, family members, whereas for my sister, immediate family is her focus. She does not have friends outside of family. Friendship is much more important to me. My friends' families embraced me as a kid. [Once I started working] I never come home for Thanksgiving. I have kept that tradition of spending time with other people's families, depending on where my friends are, and where I am in the world. What I have had for the past years are incredible experiences, but I need money to survive. I don't need a lot.

Emily thrives on work opportunities that provide for growth, adventure, and freedom. Satisfying her intellect, immersing herself in scenarios where she is forced to adapt, learn, and grow is consistent with her view of herself:

I have so much freedom. My work life is what I make it. The positions I hold have vague outlines for my responsibilities. So for example, on the boat, I was required to teach four 45-minute classes a day. But the atmosphere encourages you to do whatever you want based on your interests. So I was giving environmental lectures. I did a series. I coached a basketball team, taught kickboxing, letter writing workshops. I worked 12 hours a day, [and I was] only required to teach for four hours.

Personal freedom is a value that Emily cherishes. Her parents married in their early 20s, raised a family soon thereafter, and although currently satisfied, they have expressed a sense of regret to Emily for not having had the time and money to travel and pursue their respective interests. Emily's mother was incapacitated with a back injury during most of her adolescence, positioning Emily as the major caretaker of her family. Perhaps Emily's need to explore and interact with a global world, embrace difference and diversity, is related to her adolescence, where she may have felt confined by her premature role of caretaker for a family of five. Personal freedom is key to Emily's view of herself, "Knowing that I can do anything, having the freedom, knowing that I can do anything anywhere, and to do it alone as well, is important."

Emily thrives in the current environment she has chosen for herself. She is emotionally and intellectually drawn to challenging and potentially growth-enhancing experiences. Adversity is framed by Emily as a learning opportunity, and overcoming adversity is core to Emily's sense of self:

If I am not happy, I immediately come up with a list to figure out what it is that I need to do to make me happier. For example, the work I did in Galapagos, I was working with all Spanish speakers. That was quite hard on me to camp on a desert island with people I could not communicate with very well. But it was really up to me. I really studied and made an effort to communicate, and at the end, I had made lifelong friendships. At the end, I was able to understand, understand Spanish I should say. The fact that there is a challenge, where I have to do something, that I can learn as a person and grow, that draws me.

Family and friendships are key to Emily's view of herself, but she negotiates these important domains in a nontraditional way. When asked how she would rate herself in terms of overall personal satisfaction (on a scale from one to ten, ten indicating maximal satisfaction), she rates herself as close to ten:

The downside, I make these really close friends for a short period of time, for three to four months, and then we go our own separate ways. I keep in touch with people I meet through e-mail and visit them again and again. However it would be nice to stay long enough to keep those friendships for more than a few months.

When asked about friendships and how she negotiates them in the long-term, Emily states:

Some dwindle, some don't. There will be 10–20 people [on a project that I will connect with]. We will get along and feel really close. When we part, we all write to each other. After a year, four or five friends stay in the circle, and after five years, I might keep in touch with one or two of the most important people. My group of friends is the one or two of the groups that I have had. [However] if I knocked at the door [referring to the original circle of friends], I am sure they would let me in, but I don't keep in touch with them on a regular basis. My connections are sporadic. I might write for a week every day and then not for three weeks. My closest friends would hear from me once a month at least.

When asked how she would rewrite the story of her personal life, Emily states:

There are a couple of guys I would not have dated (laughs). Other than that, I wish I had more time. I wish that I spent more time just hanging out with friends. At times, I get very focused on my projects and I should socialize more and work less.

Emily does not have a clear sense of what her future holds. When asked how she envisions her life ten years from now, she states:

I'm not so good at envisioning the future. I could be doing the same thing I am doing now, or I could be inspired and go back to school and get a PhD and be in a profession. It could go anywhere. I don't think I would have guessed what would have happened from graduation to now. I never guess the future. I will still be in connection with many of my friends and make new ones.

With respect to intimate relationships, Emily does not have a clear vision. Rather, she thinks there is a good possibility that she will give birth and raise a child as a single parent. She has observed that her intimate relationships have changed based on revised expectations:

I think I exhibit a lot of the same behaviors time after time. The biggest change, in my earlier 20s, I knew I could date people and neither one of us would be serious. And then as I get older, I still may not be serious; it seems like relationships seem to have more purpose. I don't like going into a relationship knowing that someone is looking for a wife. It puts unnecessary pressure on it. So I think my behavior is more cautious now, whereas before I would say sure for a date or two [when asked to go out], now I would not bother so much unless I was really interested.

Emily has chosen a less traditional path, one that is informed by her need for exploration, growth experiences, and a connection to a larger global world. Ryan, in contrast, has chosen a more traditional path, laying a foundation that includes consistency in his multiple roles.

Ryan

Ryan is a 26-year-old married scientist, who has a clear sense of where he is and where he wants to be professionally and personally. His love of tinkering with computers as a child, as well as his respect for the creative process, has blossomed into a career as a research scientist. He has channeled this love of inventing to his current job, whereby he is involved with other researchers in executing and testing new inventions for the marketplace. Ryan has been married for two years. His wife, an accountant, has a clearly articulated life plan, a plan that Ryan jokingly states, "was conceived in the womb."

Currently, Ryan is relatively happy in his career as well as his home life. He continues to grow professionally, and is entertaining the possibility of eventually starting his own business. Economic concerns are in the forefront for Ryan. He has accrued significant debt from his undergraduate and graduate degrees. Although he and his wife generate a combined income that is substantial, he is not able to envision owning his own home before having children, a goal that both he and his wife hold. His future includes assuming most of the financial responsibility for his wife and his family. He hopes to have two children by age 35. Ryan also mentions the possibility of having to help support his two parents when they retire.

Ryan is relatively satisfied in his professional and personal life (on a scale of one to 10, Ryan rates his overall satisfaction professionally and personally an 8.5). His life is comparatively regimented and routinized, and he wishes that he had more time for leisure. Given the significant work demands both he and his wife are negotiating, weekends are filled with errands and responsibilities. Ryan laments that he does not have sufficient time to "hang out" with his college friends and misses those associations. Although he plans on reconnecting with them at some time in the future, he has not done so to date. He thinks about the future in a larger context, and is concerned about what he perceives as pressing social issues:

I wonder if we are going to be the generation that will have to grapple with the world's biggest problems—global warming, transportation, social security. There are a lot of issues we will have to grapple with. My generation is self-centered for a reason. We never felt that the institutions were there for us. Long-term jobs and pensions are not there. Social security is going to disappear. You know what? I have to take care of myself. I feel screwed in my 20s. The baby boomers, their gain is my loss.

Ryan states the above in a matter-of-fact way, belying the possibility of anger toward his parents' generation, the baby boomers, for being irresponsible and leaving his generation with escalating problems that should have been addressed. Ryan entertains the likelihood that his generation will most likely be in the position of having to re-examine major assumptions, and struggle with important and complex issues such as global warming and social security. Although Ryan feels burdened, he also has faith in his generation, reaffirming their competence, creativity, and energy.

Tracey

Tracey is a 33-year-old black, married, female, with a one-year old son, and second child on the way. After graduating from an elite college, Tracey took a series of low-paying jobs (secretary, receptionist) that barely paid her bills. Her expectations were "pretty low," and at the time, she was not thinking about "personal or career development."

I really had a hard time in college . . . . I did not have expectations of what my future would be like. I did not have a vision. I could not see a future. And I think it was easy to not think about it. My parents were not saying come home and figure yourself out. There was an attitude of there's time, you are young, and you need to figure things out.

At age 26, triggered by a turning point in a relationship, Tracey, with the help of a therapist, broke the cycle of low-paying jobs that held little personal satisfaction. She confronted a dysfunctional relationship in which she was physically abused. Tracey had been living with a heroin-addicted man, Ben, for two years, who was stealing money from her to maintain his habit. Previous attempts by Tracey to leave him escalated to Ben attempting suicide and promising to change, which in turn left her clinging to possibilities and hope for the relationship. She sent him "back on a plane to his mother," during a violent episode, when she realized that she would not be able to "rescue him and that she needed to rescue herself."

The loss of her therapist to cancer also sparked a crisis for Tracey and mobilized her toward action. She remarks, "I didn't know what to do with myself. I didn't have much direction. You don't know how much time you have to do something and I always had an interest in government."

Tracey returned to her "roots," setting up an apartment with her sister, entered graduate school in the field of government, and took a more responsible job at an insurance company to support herself. She sought therapy with a Black therapist who helped her come to terms with herself as a woman of color. With help from her therapist, she explored feelings of alienation and not belonging while growing up in a relatively privileged neighborhood, feelings that were replicated in her elite college experience. Tracey summarizes her experience in therapy as helping her to understand and accept herself in context. She was able to reflect on her experience of being marginalized and struggled with "the complex interplay of racist, sexist, classist . . . oppression" she had experienced (Williams, 2005, p. 282). It was the first time Tracey began to think about a "career versus a job."

Prior to graduate school, my expectations were pretty low. I would make enough money to support myself, would not be too bored, but I was not thinking about career development, professional development, or personal development.

Tracey completed her degree in government, and decided to enroll in a PhD program in counseling psychology, while working to support herself. She successfully completed her doctorate in counseling psychology as well as a clinical post-doctoral internship. Her clinical experiences suggested that she had not found an optimal fit with respect to her career choice. Tracey worked in a clinical setting that included crisis management, a demanding on-call schedule that left her feeling overwhelmed, overscheduled, and emotionally depleted.

At age 29, Tracey met a very supportive nurturing Black man, whom she married a year later. She describes her husband as kind, stable, and committed to family. She is struggling with her choice to stay at home and mother her soon-to-be-two children:

I am an overeducated woman, with some money, who is staying at home and having children. I got really burnt out doing therapy, doing my post-doc. There are people who can do it. Great, but I am not one of them. After-hour crisis is not what I want to do. I do not want to do on-call work. I hope there are a lot of paths available. I worry about what is the impact of my taking five to six years out of the workforce. [It is] really scary to not have my hands on my wheel. How do you define yourself; how do you keep yourself from just being a mom? Other people have views? People assume that you are not interesting, that you do not need intellectual stimulation. I have a real split between my more analytic side and my clinical side. I loved doing statistics for my dissertation and I also love the feely-touchy piece of clinical work. I could set up a small practice, but it is hard at times to know what to do.

Tracey fluctuates between assuming a reassuring stance, and at more vulnerable moments, assuming an anxious stance that focuses on her identity as a professional woman:

It will work out. I have always worked it out before, and the path will become clear when the time is right; that is my healthy zen side speaking to me. Learning to trust that the world will be okay, that there will be enough for me. [I am] trying to live what I believe. It comes out of years of trying to live an authentic life, figuring out what I value, what I hold dear, and trying to live that . . . . I hope there are a lot of paths available. At my worst, my anxiety gets very high. No one will hire you. You will have to work at McDonalds, although there is nothing wrong with honest labor. I will become this mindless person. [I] will be boring. [I] will be living my life through my children. I fear how I will make this all work, knowing that I am a control freak. I like to plan . . . I worry. What is the professional impact of my taking five to six years out from the workforce? [It is] really scary to not have my hands on my wheel. How do you define yourself? How do you keep yourself from just being a mom and how do you deal with other people's views of who you are? No one will speak to me at cocktail parties when they find out I am a mom. People assume that you are not interesting, that you do not need intellectual stimulation.

Tracey is currently trying to lead an authentic life, one that does not compromise her sense of herself as an adult Black woman, trying to raise children to be responsible mature adults. Her self-esteem appears to be fragile, reinforced by an environmental context that does not appreciate the choices that she has made, most recently to take time out and stay at home and raise her children:

I am coming out of years of trying to live an authentic life, figuring out what I value, what I hold dear and trying to live that. How do I help my son grow up to be who he is, help him explore his gifts, his passions, his interests? How do I help him develop competence and self-esteem as opposed to an inflated self-esteem? There is an I am an okay lovable person, and I am enough, as opposed to a self-esteem that is not grounded in reality. How do I help him connect with himself and other people? How do I help him have authentic connections, to help him know who he is and what he is offering?

Tracey is trying to live her life authentically, making choices in the service of her family that leave her feeling underappreciated, vulnerable, and marginalized. Understanding Tracey's struggles requires an understanding of the importance of cultural context and the complex interplay of racism and sexism (Williams, 2005). The questions she rhetorically asks regarding her son seem to apply not only to her struggles, as they are embedded in a larger cultural context. Tracey continues her search for an identity that includes a nonmarginalized view of herself as an authentic Black professional woman, wife, and mother who is "seen."

Sergio

The immigration process, leaving one country to resettle in another country, presents interesting challenges for the emerging and young adult. The individual immigrant is not only experiencing instability and uncertainty associated with his or her immigrant status, but is also likely to experience "flux" associated with this developmental period (Walsh, Shulman, Feldman, & Maurer, 2005, p. 414). Sergio, a 26-year-old immigrant from Bulgaria, exemplifies the intersection of these two processes.

Sergio arrived from Bulgaria as an adolescent, attended college in the United States, and is currently studying for a degree in business administration. He alludes to a self that was "shaped" in part by a communist regime. Immigrating to this country has afforded Sergio an opportunity to revisit and revise his worldviews. Sergio provides a poignant metaphor that speaks to this process:

The image I get is that of a bird, a canary that has been in captivity, that someone has caught it and kept it in a cage. And now the canary has gotten freedom, and it is now experiencing life as it should have been. I would say the door has always been open, but the bird has always been scared. My own personal self-imposed cage.

The environmental context that Sergio depicts is one of "captivity." However, he interposes an additional layer of complexity, suggesting that he places "self-imposed" limits on his freedom, in addition to the limits of freedom imposed by a communist regime.

Sergio describes his social context in Bulgaria. He alludes to different norms regarding dating expectations within an atmosphere of secrecy. In addition, he speaks of himself as a shy awkward adolescent:

Would have liked to have had some sort of a love interest in high school. And then of course, I would have liked that I was more sociable. I would hang out with people and go to the parties we had. I would have liked to be less shy. I went to high school in my country . . . It was during the time a communist regime was still around. You could not have a love interest; you could not be public with it. It was not something that was expected. People would have other people that they would like, but nobody would know about it.

You would not tell your parents, because the expectation was [that] you would reach a certain age and then you would get married. High school age was not considered the age to be seeing other people. We were closed to the rest of the world. You would not see movies [as] boyfriend girlfriend [out in the open]. Don't ask don't tell. It helped communism by subduing people, not allowing them to do what they liked.

Sergio is informed by the norms of his current cultural context. He hopes to have a career in place by his early 30s. He also hopes to experience "three to four long-term relationships," and to be married by the age of 35. He states that had he not immigrated to the United States, he would be committed to a career in Bulgaria, and most probably be married. Sergio has not had a long-term relationship, in part due to his shyness, and in part due to the freedom he perceives with respect to what he deems as culturally and developmentally appropriate. He recently met a woman on the Internet, a relationship he hopes will continue to develop and thrive.

Sergio is availing himself of choices and opportunities with respect to his career. He has had several jobs, none of which have been an adequate fit. Sergio gets bored easily, and does not appreciate repetitive tasks. He states, "After working someplace for some time, I get bored. Trying different things is what I really really like, and seeing what I like."

In describing himself vis-à-vis work, he depicts an image of himself as a bee:

A bee going from flower to flower and having the nectar from different flowers. I am taking a sample of different flowers, in a sampling mode, trying different things, and that is why I have that image of a bee. I think it has been a really good thing for me. The nectar would be the skills—software skills, people skills where you interact with different kinds of people. Improved my communication and people skills, which would be the money.

He recognizes that there are consequences to experimentation:

You don't get the feeling of being settled till much much later in life. Always feeling you could do something better. There is always more out there to try. That is a feeling of being uneasy, not being happy with your life, one of the consequences. There are more different types of jobs that are available. A lot more opportunity, a lot more choice. And since there is so much choice, people feel they can move if they don't like particular positions.

The book *Rich Dad, Poor Dad* by Kiyosaki and Lechter (1998) has had a profound influence on Sergio and the way he thinks about his career:

I found it [*Rich Dad, Poor Dad*] very inspirational. I wish I read it a bit earlier. It talks about how rich people and poor people think. Basically, before reading that book I had no idea what I wanted to do with my life. I was basically in school getting a degree to get a job. But then after reading the book, I found that it may not be the best path to follow. There are other options out there. Investing, starting a business. Things like that. On top of that, the author talks about even if you work all your life, [you are] not guaranteed anything at the end of it. Like pensions. [With the] information age, people are becoming millionaires really really fast. . . . At least the book gave me hope, gave me a direction, options you never thought about exactly.

I was raised in a family where money was not discussed. Go to school, get a degree, get a job, and you are all set. Almost like I did not know anything else. I could not possibly have known about these other choices, like fish in the water, they don't know there is anything outside of water.

Sergio speaks of premature foreclosure, closing off consideration of options:

When I started college, I made the mistake of deciding what I want to do and focusing on that only. When I finished school, the whole dot com just fell and I could not find a job, and so I had to try different things. Had I been more careful, had a broader view of things, I could have taken different kinds of classes and I think that would have helped me.

Given that Sergio experienced a communist regime as a child and adolescent, choice and experimentation are particularly salient for him:

It comes down to choice. If there was not so much choice, people would go with what they have. I would equal it with someone entering a store, buy whatever, being swamped with everything they can buy. If they had three or four choices they would just get done with it. Because they are looking at all these different things they are spending time looking at all these choices, rather than going in and getting out.

On a personal level, people get the feeling I have tried all these different things in the end I chose what is closest to my own personality. On a broader level [it is] probably affecting our society, with people not deciding early enough on relationships or work, getting philosophical. If they will not marry till late 30s early 40s, they will have fewer kids, will make our society older. [There is] a bit of a down side, they're not getting married till their 30s, not having more than one kid or no kids, won't be as many kids around. The society begins to lose its edge. Kids bring in the new things. A lot of innovation is done for the young people or by [young] people. They see the future. Innovation suffers. Society begins to get older. Loses its edge. The hope is by people trying different things, deciding what they really like, it will make us a lot happier in our life, more adjusted in our society.

In summary, choice and freedom are paramount issues for Sergio, a function in part of his experience of "growing up" in an eastern European country. Sergio provides an intricate narrative, one that is interactive, nuanced, and incomplete. He is continuing to revisit and revise his sense of self, informed by diverse socio-cultural political experiences.

The lives of Emily, Ryan, Tracey, and Sergio exemplify the diversity of experiences related to identity formation, and capture the range of paths taken professionally and personally. Whereas Ryan is following a path more consistent with *Guardians* and *Pathmakers*, as identified by Marcia (1996), Tracey appears to be least differentiated with respect to her career path, yet more directed and differentiated in her personal life. Emily and Sergio have identified their respective interests, and are in the process of connecting those interests with a career path, one more traditional, the other less traditional. Both remain unattached, although Sergio identifies a path he would like to follow with respect to his emotional and social life, whereas Emily remains unsure.

Conclusions

This chapter has focused on the dynamic process of identity formation and the significance of environmental context. Identity development is a daunting task for emerging and young adults. Absence of strict codes of behavior create an environment in which emerging and young adults feel freer to explore and expand their search for identity. There is clearly less institutional guidance available to assist emerging and young adults to maneuver developmental pathways, in a context of seeming limitless possibility.

Identity development is an ongoing process, nuanced and informed by environmental expectations and contingencies. The lives of emerging and young adults are dynamic and fluid, requiring periods of reassessment and revision. Interviews with emerging and young adult participants illustrated the diversity of experiences related to identity formation, and the range of paths taken professionally and personally. The following chapter focuses on culture and class and how it informs the narratives of the participants, followed by chapters four and five which capture the voices of the participants with regard to their work and personal lives.

References

Bauer, J. & McAdams, D. (2004). Personal growth in adults' stories of life transitions. *Journal of Personality*, *72*, 573–602.

Belsky, J. (n.d.). Constructing an adult life. Retrieved August 3, 2005 from http://wwwuncwil.edu/gc/pdf/BELSKY_chapter_11pdf#search='belsky%20emerging%20adult.

Cohen, P., Kasen, S., Chen, H., Hartmark, C., & Gordon, K. (2003). Variations in patterns of developmental transitions in the emerging adulthood period. *Developmental Psychology*, *39*, 657–669.

Constantine, M. G. (2002). The intersection of race, ethnicity, gender and social class in counseling: Examining selves in cultural contexts. *Journal of Multicultural Counseling and Development*, *30*, 210–215.

Cote, J. (2000). *Arrested adulthood: The changing nature of maturity and identity—What does it mean to grow up?* New York: New York University Press.

Harrison, J. (l995). Roles, identities and sexual orientation: Homosexuality, heterosexuality, and bisexuality. In R. F. Levant & W. S. Pollack (Eds.), *A New Psychology of Men* (pp. 359–382). New York: Basic.

Hays, P. (2002) *Addressing cultural complexities in practice: A framework for clinicians and counsellors.* Washington, DC: American Psychological Association.

hooks, b. (1996). *Born African American: Memoirs of childhood.* Boston: South End Press.

Josselson, R. (1996). *Revising herself: The story of women's identity from college to midlife.* New York: Oxford University Press.

Kroeger, J. (2000). *Identity development. Adolescence through adulthood.* Thousand Oaks, CA: Sage.

Lipford, J., & Bradley, C. (2005). Multiple-lens paradigm: Evaluating African American girls and their development. *Journal of Counseling and Development. 83,* 299–304.

Montgomery, M. J. (2005). Psychosocial intimacy and identity: From early adolescence to emerging adulthood. *Journal of Adolescent Research, 20,* 346–374.

Moses, B. (1998). *Career intelligence: The 12 new rules for work and life success.* San Francisco: Berrett-Koehler.

Phan, L. T, Torres Rivera, E., & Roberts-Wilbur, J. (2005). Understanding Vietnamese refugee women's identity development from a sociopolitical and historical perspective. *Journal of Counseling and Development, 83,* 305–312.

Phinney, J. (2006). Ethnic identity exploration in emerging adulthood. In J. Arnett & J. Tanner (Eds.), *Emerging adults in America: Coming of age in the 21st century* (pp. 25–36). Washington, DC: American Psychological Association.

Schwartz, S. J., Cote, J. E., & Arnett, J. J. (2005). Identity and agency in emerging adulthood: Two developmental routes in the individualization process. *Youth and Society, 37*(2), 201–229.

Shulman, S., Feldman, B., Blatt, S. J., Cohen, O., & Mahler, A. (2005). Emerging adulthood: Age-related tasks and underlying self processes. *Journal of Adolescent Research, 20,* 577–603.

Sue, D., Pharam, T., & Santiago, G. (1998). The changing face of work in the United States: Implications for individual, institutional, and societal survival. *Cultural Diversity and Mental Health, 4,* 153–164.

Tanner, J. (2006). Emerging adulthood, a critical period of life span human development. In J. Arnett & J. Tanner (Eds.), *Emerging adults in America: Coming of age in the 21st century* (pp. 1–3). Washington, DC: American Psychological Association.

Waterman, A. (1999). Identity, the identity statuses, and identity status development: A contemporary statement. *Developmental Review, 19,* 591–621.

Williams, C. (2005). Counseling African American women: Multiple identities-Multiple constraints. *Journal of Counseling and Development, 83,* 278–283.

Zunker, H. (2006). *Career counseling: A holistic approach.* Belmont, CA: Thomson.

3
Cultural Considerations and Emerging and Young Adulthood

A notable feature of emerging and young adulthood is the opportunity for extensive identity explorations in the areas of love and work. A consolidation of identity explorations typically occurs, characterized by "pervasive and often simultaneous contextual and social role changes" (Schulenberg, Sameroff, & Cicchetti, 2004, p. 799). The multiple contexts in which an individual resides determines in part the developmental course of that individual (Arnett, 2000; Bronfenbrenner, 1993). Cultural standards and experiences are particularly salient during emerging and young adulthood (Harding, Leong, & Osipow, 2001; Santrock, 2006). A discussion of cultural factors empowers us to adopt a more nuanced and complete understanding of this dynamic period, whereas exclusion of cultural considerations can lead to a flattened and constricted perspective.

Definitions of culture are bountiful (Hays, 2001, p. 10). It cannot be reduced to a singular dimension such as ethnicity, gender, or race. Rather, culture is:

A broad-based concept comprising a host of interrelated dimensions that include, but are not limited to, race, religion, ethnicity, age, gender, or sexual orientation. . . . It is the intricate interaction between and among these dimensions as well as how each informs the others, that ultimately shapes how an individual defines oneself. These dimensions also have a profound impact on the relationship(s) that one person develops with another. (Hardy & Laszloffy, 2002, p. 569)

Culture is not a fixed or static process. Thus, an individual can simultaneously assume roles that are divergent (e.g., a white upper-class homosexual male).

Among the emerging and young adult participants, social class was most consistently identified as a dimension that informed the self during the period of emerging and young adulthood. That is not to say that other significant variables such as gender and race were not relevant to this discussion. Rather, analysis of results revealed that individuals attributed significance to the dimension of social class in informing the direction and navigation of paths taken during this developmental juncture.

This chapter first addresses criteria for adulthood status and how it is informed by cultural context. Two contexts that provide opportunities to gain a greater understanding of cultural influence are discussed—mandated religious and military experiences and filial piety—followed by a discussion of social class and emerging and young adulthood, using case illustrations.

Criteria for Entering Adulthood: A Cultural Lens

Emerging adulthood is informed by a culture's values regarding when and how individuals are expected to take adult responsibilities (Arnett, 2004). There are similarities and differences across cultures. For example, emerging adults in Argentina, Israel, and China rate accepting responsibility for the consequences of one's action as the most important criterion for adulthood. However, it was not rated as necessary for adulthood by American emerging adults (Arnett, 1998). In Israel, the capacity to withstand pressure was rated as required and necessary for achieving adulthood status, a finding that is congruent with political realities (Mayesless & Scharf, 2003). Facio and Micocci (2003, p. 92) report that it is not surprising that in Argentina emerging adults emphasize the capacities of the family to provide stability "in a way the world of work does not," given that Argentina has been beset by economic upheavals. For Chinese emerging adults, having control of one's emotions was viewed as a necessary criterion for entry to adulthood (Nelson, Badger, & Wu, 2004). None of the above criteria was rated as necessary for entering adulthood by American emerging adults (Arnett, 1998).

In general, what defines adulthood for Americans are processes rather than discrete events. These include accepting responsibility for one's self, making independent decisions, and becoming financially independent. Based on the above findings, it can be argued that specific cultural contexts inform beliefs and behaviors related to emerging adulthood including criteria for entry to adulthood.

Arnett (2003) compares three ethnic minority groups in the United States with respect to defining features of emerging adulthood: African Americans, Latinos, and Asian Americans. He found that minority status was associated with a bicultural conception of emerging adulthood. Minority groups, in comparison to Caucasian Americans, endorse both individualistic and collectivistic notions of obligations toward others, incorporating views of the majority culture as well as views of their respective ethnic-minority cultures. For example, although the three minority groups, African Americans, Latinos, and Asian American, endorsed individualistic criteria such as accepting responsibility for one's actions, when compared to Caucasian Americans, they were more likely to endorse views consistent with obligation to others (e.g., become less self-oriented, develop greater consideration for others). These results suggest incorporation of values and beliefs that are textured and inclusive of more than one cultural context. Cheah and Nelson (2004) studied the role of acculturation (the process by which individuals adapt or react to a foreign culture) among a sample of Aboriginal emerging adults in Canada. They found that the more an individual identifies with his or her heritage culture, in contrast to the majority culture, the more the individual is likely to endorse criteria representative of his or her heritage culture's beliefs and values.

Mandated Religious and Military Experience

Mandated experiences during the period of emerging adulthood provide special opportunities to gain greater understanding of the significance of cultural context. Mandated religious obligations and mandated military service provide two opportunities for enriching our understanding of the interface between prescribed mandates associated with a specific cultural environment and the developmental period of emerging adulthood. Filial piety and how it informs belief systems and behaviors of emerging adults is examined as well.

Religion and Mandated Rites of Passage

Religious culture informs human development. Individuals develop their faith through a series of stages (Fowler, 1995). Emerging adulthood is a period in which changes occur, and over the course of one's college years, commitment to religious beliefs tends to decline in the United States (Barry & Nelson, 2005). Beaudoin (1998) proposes that emerging adults in America tend to be more "suspect" of religious institutions and value personal experiences involving religiosity.

Arnett and Jensen (2002) report that emerging adults attach great importance to thinking critically about spiritual issues rather than accepting dogma in its entirety. Hervieu-Leger (1993, p. 141), argues that emerging adults use religions as "symbolic toolboxes" picking and choosing what fits best in accordance with their beliefs and values. Barry and Nelson (2005) state that "emerging adulthood may best be characterized as a time during which young people: (a) question the beliefs in which they were raised, (b) place greater emphasis on individual spiritually than affiliation with a religious institution, and (c) pick and choose the aspects of religion that suit them best" (p. 246).

In Utah, religious rites of passage associated with the Mormon religion provide meaning and purpose, and inform adulthood status. The Mormon religion has an embedded structure that requires codes of behavior (i.e., attending the temple; serving a mission between the ages of 18 and 27; adhering to the Law of Chastity; abstaining from alcohol, tobacco, and illegal drugs; and caring for others including family and church members). The structure provided during one's emerging adulthood "enforces" established beliefs and values. This structured and clearly prescribed context is associated with a shorter timeframe for experiencing the developmental period of emerging adulthood, in comparison to the American majority culture. Although emerging adults in the United States are delaying marriage, the average age of marriage in Utah (70% Mormons) is 23 for men and 21 for women. At a Mormon university, 60% of men and 45% of women are married when they graduate (Jarvik, 2002). Mormons are taught to put family responsibilities first to have as many children as they can afford to care for, and not to postpone having children for selfish reasons (Oaks, 1993).

The research findings of Barry and Nelson (2005) reinforce the findings described above. The authors report that a university context can influence behavior either by reinforcing established cultural standards and beliefs, or create an environment whereby students are more likely to explore their identity including religious beliefs. For example, the authors report that attending a Catholic university was related to greater adherence to some aspects of students' faith. Students did "believe in God, practice[d] their faith, and adhere[d] to norms to a greater extent than public university students" (p. 253). Mormon students attending a

Mormon university voiced movement toward religious beliefs, emphasized emotional control, and supported greater interdependence rather than autonomy. In contrast, individuals attending a public university tended to subscribe to norms that indicated movement toward greater religious liberalism, autonomy, and complexity. Thus, religious culture, particularly when highly structured in institutions such as university settings, can influence development. It is important to note that the samples represented in the studies reported above are urban and middle-class, and do not represent the range of societal sectors (i.e., rural). It may be, as Arnett (2003) suggests, that cultural differences within countries may be as great as or greater than differences between similar groups across countries.

Mandated Military Service

Shulman, Feldman, Blatt, Cohen, and Mahler (2005) conducted a study involving emerging adults in Israel, a country that mandates military service. Israeli society is described as individualistic on the one hand, consistent with other developed industrialized Western countries, but also highly committed to family and communal values (Peres & Katz, 1981). The developmental tasks that are associated with emerging adulthood in Israel speak to the complexity related to understanding the influence of a cultural context, one that provides mixed and competing messages concerning individualism and communalism, independence and dependence.

Emerging adults in Israel navigate a setting that is steeped in mixed societal messages regarding social roles and behavioral responsibilities to self and others such as family and community. Findings by Shulman et al. (2005) revealed that for a substantial number of Israeli emerging adults, like their Western counterparts, the period of emerging adulthood is experienced as a complex time, characterized by periods of confusion and uncertainty. The experience of mandated military service was associated with the promotion of enhanced maturity in areas that include personal responsibility, independent decision making, and impulse control (Lieblich, 1990; Mayesless, 1993). Mandated military service was also associated with behavior patterns that may interfere and postpone experimental behaviors, which may in part be a response to military service, an experience that is typically highly demanding, rigid, and authoritarian (Gal, 1986). The Israeli mandated military experience informed and propelled behaviors associated with maturity, and on the other hand postponed experimental behaviors associated with emerging adulthood in developed industrialized Western countries.

Filial Piety

The teaching of Confucian doctrine affects views of emerging and young adulthood. The Confucian teachings of filial piety support the belief that it is the responsibility of a mature adult to support and take care of one's parents and family. This tradition includes obeying parents and living close to them while they are alive. "As a culture, Chinese value caution, rather than adventure," and tend to value norm compliance with an emphasis on "obedience, conformity, and cooperation"

(Nelson et al., 2004, p. 33). They endorse responses consistent with a collectivistic culture, including learning to have control of one's emotions, becoming less self-oriented, developing greater consideration for others, and demonstrating a commitment to others (e.g., preparing to take care of parents financially, avoiding behaviors that would bring dishonor to one's family). Whereas 89% of the Chinese American sample associated capability of supporting parents financially with adult status, only 16% of White American emerging adults did so. Chinese Americans reported behaviors that indicated commitment to others, and tended to emphasize needs and interests of the family and community.

Interestingly, Chinese emerging adults (in Beijing Normal University) are not inclined to use the developmental period of their 20s to explore to the same extent as in the United States. Nelson et al. (2004) suggest that contextual considerations such as lack of exposure to outside religions, as well as inability to change schools, may explain the relative lack of exploration observed among Chinese emerging adults attending Beijing Normal University.

Economic Context, Social Class

Social and economic forces have changed the meaning of the transition to adulthood. Globalization has certainly informed the dialogue. The complexities inherent in this changing economy have been described by our cohort as overwhelming and difficult to navigate. "Youth are shortchanged in their preparation for adult roles" (Nelson et al., 2004, p. 255). The authors assert:

That either the economy is not prepared for this generation, or this generation is not prepared for the economic terrain they must navigate. A mismatch between available jobs and the qualifications of those who are seeking employment became apparent.... Indeed, poor parenting, inadequate education, and the paucity of settings in which adolescents are able to develop adult skills have serious repercussions during the transition to adulthood. Moreover, minority groups and subpopulations face particularly daunting challenges that impede their advancement toward economic independence and stability. (Nelson et al., 2004, p. 255)

Findings suggest that many of the participants experienced an economic context similar to the one described by Nelson et al. (2004). Emerging and young adults with limited economic resources were particularly challenged.

Social Class

Social class membership is an important lens in understanding the experiences of the participants. Difference in social class emerged as a salient variable in terms of informing the experiences of the two cohorts of emerging and young adults. Emerging and young adults in the less affluent cohort were more likely to encounter dilemmas in large part due to economic considerations. Economic constraints determined decisions and choices, which at times served to narrow opportunities for change, and limit access to range of experimentation. It is important to acknowledge that exclusion of discussion of group memberships such as race, ethnicity, gender, and social class, and their combined synergistic effects constricts the narrative (Constantine, 2002; Ponterotto, Casas, Suzuki, & Alexander, 2001). Nevertheless, the voices of the participants in this study identified social class as an important variable in terms of informing their experiences. For this sample of participants, social class was identified as influential in informing and shaping the navigation process.

For both groups, navigating the terrain was highly challenging. They encountered a set of environmental and economic circumstances captured in the following description by Mortimer and Larson (2002).

What is clear is that, across social strata, rapid social and institutional changes place a premium on youth's initiative, creativity, and ability to navigate a multidimensional labyrinth of choices and demands. For both rich and poor, the future puts greater responsibility onto their plate, requiring them to be volitional and agentic and . . . manage diverse components of fiscal, human, and social capital. (p. 14)

The interface of social class, environmental and economic contexts described above informed the freedom of range emerging and young adults, particularly those with more limited economic resources, could navigate. When faced with a set of circumstances described by Mortimer and Larson (2002) and others (e.g., Shanahan, 2000), those with more limited economic resources navigated paths that were experienced as constricting and confining. The cases of Eric and Jim are representative of the challenges faced.

Both Eric and Jim speak of personal struggles that are informed in part by their class status. Both are attempting to navigate limitations imposed by economic considerations. Eric assumes a philosophical stance, exhibiting an uncanny ability to view life predicaments from multiple perspectives, within a sea of calm. Eric is relatively resolved to redesigning his dream with a vision that is more limited in scope, in comparison to his original dream. He appears to have come to terms with a dream that will not be realized, a dream that included the pursuit of journalism as a career choice, and being fully immersed in what he perceives as the creative process of writing.

Jim, on the other hand, in telling his story, reveals a contained angry stance, a silent volcano that may never erupt. The writer found herself wondering about the emotional, physical, and social costs to Jim in assuming this stance. Jim is trying to stay true to his values, provide for his family, and to the best of his ability uphold the American dream. First, a discussion of Eric, followed by a discussion of Jim.

Eric: "Parallel Ladders"

Eric is a 32-year-old Portuguese male, married for two years to a nurse, with a child on the way. He grew up in a divorced household, with some economic instability. His career path is characterized by an attempt to negotiate a desire to continue the pursuit of creative ambitions, which include writing feature stories for magazines, with the reality of having to support himself and his family as a marketing consultant within a corporate hierarchical organizational structure.

When asked to provide a metaphor that describes his career path, he responds, "parallel ladders." The metaphor refers to his current position as a marketing consultant, and his interest in growing a business as a photographer and writer.

Eric navigated a circuitous path in his successful attempt to graduate college. He supported himself while in college taking a series of service-oriented jobs. He discovered his passion for writing in his fifth year of college, and pursued a degree that enabled him to enter the field of journalism. He graduated in seven years which he attributes to two givens: (1) a need to support himself, and (2) having no clearly formulated future goals. Upon graduating from college, Eric tried to pursue a career in journalism, but assessed that he could not support himself. He found a job in editing, did not like the job, and quit shortly thereafter, without having an alternative job offer. According to Eric, the decision to quit placed him on a trajectory that forced him to take jobs he was not particularly well suited for, one of which included marketing. The marketing job did provide him with security and benefits, which in turn led him to his current job as a marketing consultant. In describing his current job, he states the following.

I don't have the creative outlet I would like. I am not a big fan of corporate life. I don't like the bureaucracy and the politics involved. I am not saying it would not be anywhere. At some point, I would like to start my own business [in photography and writing]. I am currently working on getting there, starting my own business on the side. Photography and magazine writing, the two go hand in hand, and go back to my roots.

When asked if and how he would rewrite the story of his career, Eric replies:

I would have starved more at college and accepted the fact [that in order] to start in a creative field you have to suffer more than in corporate life. [I would] more steadfastly stay on a creative career path rather than a corporate career path. I have no illusion that hindsight is 20/20. Not that I wanted to get rich quick. But basically I did not want to make any changes in my lifestyle. I targeted my job for the lifestyle I wanted, and now it is close to impossible given my domestic situation.

I did what I did, but if I were to rewrite it, I suppose I would have taken lower-paying positions that I was offered, and worked at that for a while so that I could get publishing credibility, build my resume in that field. At the time, to be honest, I just could not afford to live on what they paid me.

Eric expected to be a little bit further "ahead" at this point in his life, owning a house, and having a child. He states:

I did not have a full vision for my personal and social life. I knew that as I approached my 30s. I would want a house and family, but I did not set my own personal goals [for] how to get there.

Eric articulated a sense of regret in not recognizing that he had more "space to make great leaps" than he understood. Given that he is married and going to be a father soon, he feels that he is currently "guided by more conservative choices." Because of his decision to quit a job without alternative economic resources, and take a job that paid the bills, Eric currently assesses that he is limited by the choices he can make. He has more to "lose" in comparison to peers who are not married, do not have children, or have the economic flexibility to experiment and pursue their dreams:

Less to lose can be a good thing or bad thing. I think my friends who are single, they can take big leaps. If they fall, they will be okay. They can pick themselves up. I felt that way before just a few years ago. I could almost say, people in my place, they don't make fewer choices, they make more conservative choices.

In offering advice to other emerging and young adults, he states, "As best you can, know when you have the space to make big leaps and know when you don't. When you are in your early 20s, it is hard to conceptualize."

In summary, while navigating his 20s, Eric feels that in hindsight he had more "space" to pursue his dreams, imposing unnecessary constraints on himself. Currently, he is guided by more "conservative choices," but appears to have come to terms with the decisions he has made. He states that he wanted a minimal standard of living during his 20s, and did not tolerate poverty well. He might have revisited that choice if given the opportunity. He envisions growing a business in photography and writing, while working full time in a job that is less than satisfying. Currently he spends 95% of his time doing his work related to marketing, and 5% growing his business. He hopes to turn that around, where most of his time is spent growing his business, and ultimately spending less than 50% of his time working in marketing. He also envisions owning a small house, with his wife and two children. With respect to the metaphor he provided—"parallel ladders"—he is currently climbing both ladders, but hopes to eventually direct his focus and energies to climbing one ladder, realizing his dream of having a business that fully supports him and his family.

Jim: The System Is Broken

Jim is a 30-year-old architect, married, with two children from a previous relationship. He is entrepreneurial, started his own solo practice as an architect, and could not make a go of it. As he states:

I met a wonderful woman, decided I needed to be a grownup, make more money, and be able to get married and provide for my kids a lot better. I was getting by. I took the opportunity to work for someone else and make more money.

Currently he is working in an architectural firm, and is unhappy at work:

Prior to meeting my wife, I made a lot of poor personal choices and as a result I have baggage from the mistakes I made in the past which provide irritants to my current personal life. I don't regret having two wonderful children. It was a dark time in my life. What made it dark is that I had committed myself to a relationship where we were totally incompatible . . . . because I failed in a previous relationship I did everything I could to make this person happy including sacrificing everything I was. I had become hollow, nothing left to me. I was a huge angry empty shell. The relationship took everything out of me and I did not know how to love any more.

Jim feels that he needs to quit his current position and start his own architectural firm, but cannot afford to do so. He expresses regret regarding losing track of his value system which serves as his anchor. Jim is trying to stay true to his values, but finds it difficult to live in a capitalistic enterprise that has gone "out of control." He states the following:

We are all born with a value system. And whether we know it or not, we have a moral compass that basically lends itself to that value system. That compass directs us . . . to the right place . . . .. a value of mine is to not to let money control my profession. I did not want to do a job because of money . . . .. [However] to get the job I want, [having my own business] would put an unfortunate financial burden on my family. I would not be able to make it right now, and right now is when you need to pay the mortgage and car payments . . . . I have student loans. It is not easy to come out of college with those financial burdens . . . .. We live month to month, and that does not make sense to me. I make twice as much as my parents do. Capitalism is spilling out of control. Young people these days are so driven by [the need] to have more. They never look at themselves as established. They are always looking for something better, they are afraid to look at themselves and say, hey I am happy, why do I need more.

I think video games [are a good example]. Every year there is a new video Game Boy, it renders obsolete a system that everyone is capable of being satisfied with for a very long period of time. Instead, Play Station 2 is no good any more; now it is Game Boy, Game Boy Advanced, Game Boy DS; now it is Game Boy Mini DS. You cannot keep up with it. And, if I don't have the latest Game Boy, there is something wrong with me. It is wrong not to have the best of the best. Therefore, we are never satisfied.

Jim presents as a man who is trying to do right by his wife and his two children, guided by his moral compass. He hopes to be able to negotiate a new position in a firm that is a better cultural fit. He, however, feels constricted and frustrated by his perceived options. He views himself as buying into the American dream, but is unable to actualize it. He is in considerable debt, stressed at home and at work, and is constricted by the choices he can make. He would like to start a business of his own, but his current financial commitments prevent him from taking the risk, despite the fact that he perceives himself to be well educated, hardworking, and committed to trying to make it all work.

Debt, Class and the Emerging and Young Adult

The American dream has been ingrained in our psyche, located in a rich history that is grounded in the belief that freedom and opportunity are key ingredients. Although many emerging and young adults espouse the American dream, external realities and pressures are shaking their belief system in terms of its viability.

Jim poignantly expresses the frustrations of trying to live the American dream. A first-generation college graduate, he feels stuck, unhappy in his current job setting. He feels saddled with financial obligations that are in large part related to debt he has accrued. Jim's dilemma is reflective of a reality facing many emerging and young adults. An article that appeared in the *Village Voice* by Koerner (2004) provides perspective with respect to the issue of debt among individuals in their

20s and early 30s:

The average collegian in the U.S. isn't graduating into a world of boundless opportunity, but rather is $ 20,000-plus in the hole thanks to student loans and credit cards. So begins the snowball effect: The most desirable entry-level jobs often pay wages too low for the indebted, who must fork over a large percentage of their salaries to Sallie Mae or Citibank. Other posts are reserved for those who can afford to work unpaid internships, or whose parents can support them through an extra year or two of graduate studies.

Furthermore,

High levels of debt preclude the young from getting the sweetest mortgage deals, and they often end up in the clutches of sub-prime lenders. On average, people who had to borrow their way to a graduate degree are already behind $ 45,900; median debt for grad students has increased 72 percent since 1997. (Aspiring doctors have it the worst, with average loans of $ 103,855.) Add to those obligations an investment in a humble bungalow, and you're on the hook for a quarter million or more—not counting interest.

The cumulative effect is that merely keeping one's head above water, rather than getting ahead, has become the top priority for Americans between the ages of 18 and 34. Pursuing the relatively modest dream of doing better than the generation before requires serious capital—up front in the form of tuition and loans, and hidden in the form of lost opportunities.... But it's really more of a gamble, as there's no guarantee those tens of thousands of dollars will get you where you want to go.

The next generation is starting their economic race 50 yards behind the starting line,...They've got to pay off the equivalent of one full mortgage before they make it to flat broke, in order to pay for their education. They can never get ahead of the game, because they're constantly trying to play "catch-up."

And once you've got accumulated debt, the debt takes on a life of its own. It demands to be fed, and it takes that first bite out of the paycheck. And it means the opportunity to accumulate a little, to get a little ahead, to maybe put together a down payment—it's just never there.

Jim, despite debt accrued for college tuition, has been able to purchase a "bungalow," but at a tremendous cost. He is unhappy at work (rates his job on a scale from one to ten, a 4.5), but given his debt commitments that "demand to be fed," feels stuck and unable to find an alternative lifestyle that would be compatible with his desire to be a good husband, father, and architect.

Jim bought a relatively modest house as a way of entering the housing market, and from his perspective, enabled him to lay a foundation in which he can live the American dream. However, as Koerner (2004, p. 1) states:

Adding yet another fixed cost to his debt load might seem like an unwise choice, especially since ... [Jim] doesn't have much in the bank for a down payment. But the way house prices are going, it feels like a now-or-never proposition. If housing prices continue to escalate, at least you'll be on the train.... As the train moves, you'll move with it. But it's also a high-risk proposition if it's going to take your income and your spouse's income to make the mortgage payment every month.

Jim states that he has lost sight of an important value of his, that is, to not allow money to control his professional pursuits. As a result of being committed to loans accrued to cover costs associated with his college and graduate degree, he feels stuck:

I do not want to do a job because of money . . .. To get the job I want would put an unfortunate financial burden on my family. I would not be able to make it right now, and right now is when you need to pay the mortgage and car payments . . .. I love being an architect, I just don't like being an architect in this firm. I have to be an architect in a firm because of my commitments, if I'm to continue to be the husband and father I want to be.

According to Jim, the system is broken. He questions the pursuit of things deemed critical for our happiness, and is relatively sophisticated regarding marketing ploys that encourage acquisitive behavior. Jim views himself as having a value system, a "moral compass" that directs his actions. However,

I think we are, simply because the demands society has put upon us, in a position to seek work or stay at jobs with which we are dissatisfied. We cannot survive financially unless we do. Capitalism—I do see it as an evil that is destroying our society. It is like the play *Little Shop of Horrors*, a story of a Venus flytrap who grows from a little beautiful bud to a monster. I don't think we take care of anybody any more . . .. I make twice as much as my parents, we live month to month, and that does not make sense to me. Capitalism is spilling out of control . . .. We are a society that is hyper focused on money and getting ahead . . .. I've got to find a way to completely balance all the things in my value system without one being too compromised, compromising one at the expense of the other.

In summary,

From the vantage point of the Kid and his millions of real-life contemporaries, one big answer is obvious: The system punishes the young who dare strive for something better. For those on the young side of 35, debt and its ripple effects have made upward mobility a fiction more often than not. (Koerner, 2004, p. 1)

So the Kid pays his ambition tax in virtual silence, like that stereotypical sarariman putting in a 16-hour day with nary a complaint. Somewhere on the other side of the world, a Japanese youth preparing for his first trip to the U.S. may read the Kid's woeful tale and marvel, "How tedious, how pointless, how restrictive, how dreadful." He'd be right.

Both Eric and Jim express frustration related to career and personal trajectories imposed by economic constraints. Eric emphasizes the importance of knowing when to make "leaps." He speaks of missed opportunities to "leap" toward a more satisfying career trajectory. Eric feels confined by his need to make more conservative choices, although he seems at peace with the choices he has made to date. Jim also expresses frustration, feeling stuck in a job that keeps him paying the bills that are associated with debt accrued while trying to establish himself professionally. The personal narratives of Eric and Jim poignantly reveal the import of social class and its influence on the developing self.

Conclusions

Consideration of cultural factors empowers us to adopt a more nuanced and complete understanding of this dynamic period. A review of the literature with respect to the importance of cultural context was provided. Mandated religious obligations and military service served as examples for understanding the interface between prescribed mandates associated with a specific cultural environment and the developmental period of emerging adulthood. Filial piety and how it informs belief systems and behaviors of emerging adults was examined as well.

Analysis of results revealed that participants, particularly those in the less affluent cohort, tended to attribute significance to the dimension of social class in informing the direction and navigation of paths taken during this developmental juncture. Economic constraints determined decisions and choices considered, limiting experimental behavior and resulting in more "conservative" choice selections. The following two chapters capture the voices of the participants and their diverse perspectives regarding their professional and interpersonal lives.

References

Arnett, J. (1998). Learning to stand alone: The contemporary American transition to adulthood in cultural and historical context. *Human Development, 41*, 295–315.

Arnett, J. (2000). Emerging adulthood: A theory of development from the late teens through the twenties. *American Psychologist, 55*, 469–480.

Arnett, J. (2003). Conceptions of the transition to adulthood among emerging adults in American ethnic groups. In J. Arnett and N. Galambos (Eds.), *New Directions in Child and Adolescent Development, 100*, 63–75.

Arnett, J. & Jensen, L. (2002). A congregation of one: Individualized religious beliefs among emerging adults. *Journal of Adolescent Research, 17*, 451–467.

Arnett, J. (2004). *Emerging adulthood: The winding road from the late teens through the twenties.* New York: Oxford University Press.

Barry, L. & Nelson, L. (2005). The role of religion in the transition to adulthood for young emerging adults. *Journal of Youth and Adolescence, 34*, 245–255.

Beaudoin, T. (1998). *Virtual faith: The irreverent spiritual quest of generation X.* San Francisco: Jossey-Bass.

Bronfenbrenner, U. (1993). The ecology of cognitive development: Research models and fugitive findings. In R. Wozniak and K. Fischer (Eds.), *Development in context: Acting and thinking in specific environments* (pp. 3–44), Hillsdale, NJ: Erlbaum.

Cheah, C. & Nelson, L. (2004). The role of acculturation in the emerging adulthood of Aboriginal college students. *International Journal of Behavioral Development, 28*, 495–507.

Constantine, M. G. (2002). The intersection of race, ethnicity, gender, and social class in counseling: Examining selves in cultural contexts. *Journal of Counseling and Development, 30*, 210–215.

Facio, A. & Micocci, F. (2003). Emerging adulthood in Argentina. *New Directions for Child and Adolescent Development, 100*, 21–31.

Fowler, J. (1995). *Stages of faith: The psychology of human development and the quest for meaning.* San Francisco: Harper.

Gal, R. (1986). *A portrait of the Israeli soldier.* New York: Greenwood Press.

Harding, E. E., Leong, F. T. L., & Osipow, S. H. (2001). Cultural relativity in the conceptualization of career maturity, *Journal of Vocational Behavior, 58*, 36–52.

Hardy, K., & Laszloffy, T. A. (2002). Couples therapy: Using a multicultural perspective. In A. Gurman & N. Jacobson (Eds.), *Clinical handbook of couple therapy* (pp. 569–593). New York: Guilford.

Hays, P. (2001). *Addressing cultural complexities in practice: A framework for clinicians and counselors*. Washington, DC: American Psychological Association.

Hervieu-Leger, D. (1993). Present day emotional rituals: The end of secularization or the end of religion? In. W. Swatos (Ed.), *A future for religion? New paradigms for social analysis*. Thousand Oaks, CA: Sage.

Jarvis, E. (2002, December 15). Reading, writing, rings at Y. *Deseret News*. Retrieved, July 13, 2006, from http://www.desnews.com.

Koerner, B. (2004, March 17–23). Generation debt. The ambition tax: Why America's young are being crushed by debt—And why no one seems to care. *Village Voice*.

Lieblich, A. (1990). The transition to adulthood during the military service. In K. Binyamini, S. Kugelmas, & R. Butler (Eds.), *Conceptualization and application in psychology* (pp. 84–98), Jerusalem: Magness, Hebrew University.

Mayesless, O. (1993). Attitudes towards military service among Israeli youth. In D. Ashkenazy, *The military in the service of society and democracy: The challenge of the dual-role military* (pp. 32–35), Westport, CT: Greenwood Press.

Mayesless, O. & Scharf, M. (2003). What does it mean to be an adult? The Israeli experience. *New Directions for Child and Adolescent Development, 100*, 5–20.

Mortimer, J., & Larson, R. (2002). Macrostructural trends and the reshaping of adolescence. In J. Mortimer and R. Larson (Eds), *The changing adolescent experience: Societal trends and the transition to adulthood* (pp. 1–17). Cambridge, MA: Cambridge University Press.

Nelson, L., Badger, S., & Wu, B. (2004). The influence of culture in emerging adulthood: Perspectives of Chinese college students. *International Journal of Behavioral Development, 28, 1*, 26–36.

Oaks, D. (2003, November). The great plan of happines. *Ensign, 72*.

Peres, Y. & Katz, R. (1981). Stability and centrality: The nuclear family in modern Israel. *Social Forces, 59*, 687–704.

Ponterotto, J. G., Casas, M. J., Suzuki, L. A., & Alexander, C. M. (Eds.) (2001). *Handbook of multicultural counseling*. Thousand Oaks, CA: Sage Publications.

Santrock, J. (2006). *Life-span development*. New York: McGraw-Hill.

Schulenberg, J. E., Sameroff, A. J., & Cicchetti, D. (2004). The transition to adulthood as a critical juncture in the course of psychopathology and mental health: Editor's introduction. *Development and Psychopathology, 16*, 799–806,

Shanahan, M. J. (2000). Pathways to adulthood in changing societies: Variabilities and mechanisms in life course perspective. *Annual Review of Sociology, 26*, 667–692.

Shulman, S., Feldman, B., Blatt, S., Cohen, O., & Mahler, A. (2005). Emerging adulthood: Age-related tasks and underlying self processes. *Journal of Adolescent Research, 20*, 577–603.

4
Voices of Emerging and Young Adults: In Pursuit of a Career Path

Mom: Are you here to stay now?
Biff: I don't know. I want to look around, see what's doing.
Mom: Biff, you can't look around all your life, can you?
Biff: I just can't take hold mom. I can't take hold of some kind of life.

Death of a Salesman, Arthur Miller, 1949 (As cited
by Schulenberg, Bryant, & O'Malley, 2004, p.1119)

Given the lengthened period of time to reach key milestones in comparison to previous generations (i.e., career, marriage, and children), emerging and young adults are potentially well positioned to make informed career and personal decisions. Increased possibilities and opportunities for exploration co-exist within a work environment that also offers no assurance that hard work will be rewarded, and that the American dream will be realized. This chapter focuses on the experiences of emerging and young adults trying to "take hold of some kind of life" professionally. Their perspectives provide a window to understanding the diversity of meaning and importance of consolidating a professional identity.

Settersten (2005, pp. 534–535) sets the stage for understanding the unstable changing terrain emerging and young adults are encountering. These changes include:

... [An] expansion of secondary and higher education; a decline in the availability of full time jobs; an increase in the proportion of individuals concurrently pursuing higher education and work; an increase in the labor force participation of women; an increase in cohabitation; delays in marriage and childbirth; a decline in fertility; and the expansion and retraction of welfare state policies and programs. Major cultural shifts include weaker normative controls on behavior and greater individualization, both of which have allowed young people more freedom to plan and live in accordance with their interests and wishes, and the emergence of feminism, which has reoriented the priorities of women.... [These changes have] altered the nature of the entire life course.

In addition, a vacuum exists with respect to institutional structures designed to facilitate and support the transition to young adulthood. Schulenberg, Sameroff, and Cichetti (2004) describe the realities emerging adults are encountering:

In comparing the transition into adolescence with the transition into adulthood, it becomes evident that there is far less institutionally and culturally imposed structure on young

43

people.... On the positive side, this relative lack of structure can allow for greater self selection of paths and activities. ... However, for some young people, the relatively sudden drop in institutional structure can be debilitation, creating a mismatch between individual needs and contextual affordances. This discrepancy can result in avoidance of life tasks during this time. (p. 801)

Jeff, a 29-year-old participant, captures the experience of transience of many of the participants:

Everything is temporal; nothing is permanent, compared to prior generations. [It is] easier to move, to get divorced, to live in temporary housing, much easier to pack up and live life as you know it. Put your stuff in the back of a car and move foreword.

In speaking about their work lives, common themes emerged for the participants in the study. Themes applicable to both cohorts of emerging and young adults include: (1) disconnection between school and work: changing the rules, (2) lack of loyalty, (3) pursuit of passion, and (4) expectations revisited. First, a summary of findings with respect to work satisfaction levels.

Satisfaction Levels at Work

Both cohorts were asked to assess the degree to which they were satisfied at work (using a Likert scale, ranging from one to ten, ten indicating the greatest level of satisfaction). Emerging and young adults in the affluent cohort reported less satisfaction. For the less affluent cohort, a mean score of 7.72 (SD = 1.81) was reported for work satisfaction. In contrast, a mean score of 6.94 (SD = 2.09) was reported by the affluent cohort.

When asked to identify what would need to change in a positive direction in order for participants to assess their work lives as optimal (ten on a Likert scale, ranging from one to ten), interesting differences as well as similarities emerged between the two groups. For the less affluent cohort, 30.3% of the participants identified the ability to "make more money," which they associated with increased satisfaction levels. They also identified the following with greater levels of satisfaction; (1) ability to procure more challenging work (12.12%), (2) ability to exercise more independence and choice at work (12.12%), (3) ability to procure more fulfilling work (12.12%), and (4) ability to report to more competent and supportive managers (12.12%).

For the affluent cohort, 16% of the participants identified the need to have more responsibility at work, as well as the need to work fewer hours. They also identified the ability to exercise a greater degree of independence and choice (8%), a greater degree of appreciation of their abilities by their respective employers (8%), "more money" (8%), more security, primarily attributed to outsourcing (8%), and the ability to spend a greater amount of time working directly with colleagues (8%). Common to both cohorts was the desire to make more money, as well as the desire to exercise more independence and choice in their respective work settings. The less affluent cohort focused on the ability to report to more competent and supportive managers, whereas the more affluent cohort focused on the ability to be appreciated by their supervisors. The narrative data support the finding that emerging and young adults are seeking more responsible, challenging work that involves the exercise of independence and choice.

Given that age 30 has been reported as a developmental marker for many emerging and young adults, work satisfaction was analyzed by age (participants, ranging in age from 25–29 were compared with participants ranging in age from 30–35). Analysis of mean scores for work satisfaction reveals a mean score of 7.23 for participants 25–29 years of age (SD = 2.09) and 6.86 (SD = 1.59) for participants 30 and above years of age.

With respect to their professional lives, participants 30 to 35 years of age identified the following with greater levels of satisfaction: (1) ability to generate more money (21.74%), (2) ability to exercise more independence and choice (13.04%), and the ability to have more fulfilling work (13.04%). For those participants 25 to 29 years of age, the following were identified with greater satisfaction: (1) ability to generate "more money" (18.18%), (2) ability to work fewer hours and work and report to more competent and supportive management (12.12% respectively), and (3) ability to have greater opportunities with respect to professional advancement and promotion, as well as the opportunity to engage with more challenging work (9.09% respectively).

Disconnection Between School and Work: Changing the Rules

In both cohorts, participants entered their 20s with expectations regarding how their lives would unfold. Upon graduating from college, many encountered "reality checks" that were difficult to incorporate and integrate. They reported feeling unprepared for the abrupt shift that occurred once they entered the workforce. Individuals in their 20s who were particularly prone to feelings of disconnection were those situated in entry-level jobs that required no specific skillsets other than a college degree. The disconnection was often jarring. Rules mastered during their college years no longer seemed to apply. In speaking about the transition to work, Carol states, "You know what it feels like, like white water rafting and ending up on a huge lake. [College was] very intensive, very pressured, very directed, and now it is open sailing. Trying to figure it all out is hard."

Many of the participants implicitly or explicitly believed that their work life would approximate college life, with some modifications. Their work expectations allowed for the possibility of restructuring job responsibilities to capitalize on their individual strengths. In addition, many held the expectation that they would be valued and respected in the workplace. There was also an expectation that their work-related activities would matter, and that they would be able to have influence in work-related decisions. Representative comments were varied, and ranged from the philosophical to the mundane as Ruth describes:

I felt like my brain was turning into mush, the tedium of it. Yes, in school you are held accountable. At the end of the day, in school, it is still all for you. In a job, no one really cares if you are learning. That is something to get used to. There is much more mundane tedium. And you are not working at the same level as college. You are going backwards intellectually. During my college years, my brain was working more than it is now. Now, it turns into mush. On the other hand, what I do like about work, I learned so much about the way the world goes around, the way the world operates. So many things I still think of. I became worldly, wise.... I grew up a lot.

Raymond summarizes his work experiences as follows, "In school, I was being challenged. At work, I am being underutilized and understimulated." Another participant, Erica, states:

I think that I worked very hard during college. It is hard to adjust to not doing rigorous intellectual work. I had the expectation that there would be a lot of menial work, but that I would still get a chance to get intellectually involved with something. I also thought that I would be well received by supervisors because I am smart [and that did not turn out to be the case].

Alex and Elise echo the frustration expressed by Ruth, Raymond, and Erica, specifically with respect to the lack of growth opportunities they encountered at work.

Alex: I expected it to be more satisfying. I expected when I started, that there would be more growth in what I was doing and there wasn't.

Elise: You come from an educational environment that caters to you and nurtures your strengths, designed for you to do your best. In the workplace, you are not in environments that are designed to bring your best out, and permit you to grow. We don't worry that we are putting people in environments that are not designed for them to excel. There is a huge disconnect between the world of work and education.

There was also an expectation among many emerging and young adults that they would have an impact on their work environment, and that they would have opportunities to make a difference as described by Ruth and Jill below. Ruth spoke about the disillusionment and alienation she experienced in a job she had procured at an architectural firm. After immersing herself in the job, she expected that the results of her labor, specifically the recommendations she was expected to generate, would be seriously considered:

Ruth: Within the firm, there were no private clients, just municipalities, institutions. It was frustrating there.... A number of times I encountered very bad luck, the wrong set of political circumstances, change in staff, and then they would decide they didn't want to do the project. We were hired as consultants to give our opinion.... I was idealistic, and the process left me feeling [that] this is so useless, and what I am doing is so useless.

In addition, there was a sense that there was little respect for the individual's time outside of work, and with the advent of technology, boundaries between work and home were viewed as unclear and blurred.

Jill: With e-commerce, it is more fast-paced, there are no boundaries. E-mails, Black-Berries, cell phones. You're always on.... It does give people flexibility, but the division between work and home interferes with people's lives. The old-fashioned attitude, "I am not at work; you cannot talk to me," is not respected. You are seen as a slacker if you take the view that I don't want to be available at all times; you cannot talk to me at all times.

Jill: I am attached to my BlackBerry. I literally get anxiety when my cell phone rings. I literally turn it off. I was so overwhelmed by my personal and professional life. [I] felt I had to literally leave the country to turn off my BlackBerry and cell phone. [It is a] rat race, 150 e-mails a day, nonstop. I cannot keep up with it hardly, . . . not really improving your quality of life.

Andrea and Mark refer to the work climate they encountered post college.

Andrea: I did not expect to be yelled at ten times a day. Intellectually, work did not meet my expectations. I think I also discovered that client service industries are a drag. People call you to scream to you about something that I have no control over.

Mark: I was unhappy. The actual job was like filling gas, dirty tough work. I sampled water, installed moderating walls. [I] did not need a masters degree to do what I did. Some of the people who did it were high school dropouts. You really did not need much advanced training to do what I did. [I] did not feel respect from supervisors, only in there for themselves. They did not care about you, which is why turnover was so high.

In summary, many individuals in their 20s, in the process of trying to "take hold of some kind of life," found themselves disillusioned. Those entering highly differentiated fields, (i.e., engineering, medicine, law, and investment banking), fields that required specific valued skillsets, were less likely to articulate these concerns. Nadia (a 27-year-old participant) and Maria (a 25-year-old participant), and a blogger, comedian, and writer, Adam Karo (2005), capture the experiences articulated by many of the participants interviewed, particularly those who graduated from college with no specific valued skillsets.

Nadia: We were not prepared for the world of work, underfunctioning, and having our brain turning to mush.

Maria: You go to college, graduate somewhere between 22 and 25, [your] undergraduate degree is worthless without a graduate degree, and you realize it. . . . You think you are spending $120,000; you expect to get a job. That is a hard reality to face. You are treated without respect, lowest on the rung. Once you start working, you really realize that is how it works. Everyone in college tells you [that] you are so smart, people validate you, and you measure yourself against other people. You may develop a sense of entitlement that sort of pushes you into feeling, what am I doing working at entry-level jobs when I just worked so hard to graduate?

Karo: There's nothing worse than realizing that a monkey could do your job. It happens to everyone. You're sitting at your desk doing mindless busywork, and you think to yourself: You know what? Throw some Banana Republic khakis and a blue button-down on a chimp and he could probably do what I do. Once I swear I saw the cubicle next to mine being fitted for a cage. (Karo, 2005)

Loyalty or Lack Thereof

In describing their current work environments, emerging and young adults identified lack of loyalty as an important variable in informing their career-related decisions and behaviors. Mindful of the impact of globalization, ongoing advances in technology, and potential economic downturns, participants tended to view the marketplace as highly fluid. Disposability in work settings was viewed as an ever-present threat, and job elimination and/or replacement of personnel, a reality. The current work climate placed increasing demands for productivity on its workforce, while simultaneously providing fewer benefits and overall a more compromised quality of life. Gone were the days of guaranteed lifetime employment.

Participants, children of the boomer generation, observed their parents (particularly fathers) devastated by job elimination, and feeling betrayed by previous employers, big business, and big government. Some of the participants' parents were unable to recuperate financially and/or emotionally. Durkin (2005) captures the sense of disillusionment the boomer generation, (and through osmosis their children) experienced in response to the economic conditions that prevailed: "No matter how hard they worked, they were vulnerable." She asserts, "If companies were not going to be loyal . . . there was not reason to be loyal to them" (Durkin, 2005, p. 16).

Durkin (2005) proposes that lack of loyalty is in part responsible for decreased job satisfaction and that American companies are being shortsighted with respect to potential profits. Employee loyalty leads to customer loyalty, which drives brand loyalty, which drives profit (p. 199). Loyalty, according to Durkin, can be developed and nurtured, regardless of the nature of the industry or size of the company. It requires leadership that is committed to the success of the company and the individuals responsible for its success. According to Durkin, the economic challenges for business in the future will be best addressed with "[a] strong, loyal workforce, with employees who are empowered to achieve their personal ambitions while creating company growth" (p. 199).

Participants spoke to the issue of lack of loyalty and how it informed their view of work. They changed jobs more frequently in comparison to their parents' generation, and attributed their search for better work environments in part to lack of loyalty. Representative comments by Jennifer, Jeff, Amanda, David, Ashley, and Sharon speak to the issue of lack of loyalty in the workplace. Jennifer, a 29-year-old participant, currently in a technical field experiencing shortage in availability of personnel, states:

I think in the past, our parents' generation, loyalty was extremely important. If you worked for a company for a short period, people would look at you differently, they would think you are an unstable person. Maybe not very focused in terms of setting your career goals. And now, more and more are getting higher education. Most companies are looking for talent. Most of my employment experiences do not exceed over two years. Some managers ask [why two years], but it is never a concern for them.

Jeff: I think they think, my personal experience as an analyst, [that] we are basically resources taken advantage of as much as possible. . . . In corporate America, 20-year-olds are just resources to be exploited.

Amanda: I think people are a lot less loyal. Companies are not loyal to them. My parents worked for their companies for more than 20 years.

David: You can't expect someone to make a commitment to anything long term, if fewer and fewer people make a commitment to them.

Ashley: I think on the lower end of the job scale, people are replaceable. I think that an entrenched workforce is more expensive for companies. Companies like part-time people. Then again maybe you don't have good workers. People are chasing, looking for something better.

Sharon: Employers think . . . you are not fully loyal to them but they are not fully loyal to you. I do think the expectations change from industry to industry. . . . In [some industries] it is the nature of the industry because the clients are not loyal to the industry. It may be worse now, you become a commodity; they trade employees like they trade baseball cards.

Given participants' perceptions regarding lack of loyalty, they actively experimented with a variety of jobs, trying to grow and direct their careers. Most participants perceived few opportunities for "grooming," and in turn felt compelled to look out for themselves, with many moving every one to two years in the service of opportunity. This was particularly true of individuals who graduated college without specific skillsets and/or were unclear in terms of career goals. Given their perspective that the marketplace viewed them as commodities, dispensable at will, many of the participants felt they had to fend for themselves. A Rutgers–University of Connecticut poll indicates that 58% of workers surveyed were of the opinion that most top executives are only interested in looking out for themselves, even if it harms their company (Durkin, 2005).

Their peripatetic search for better jobs was in part informed by a perception that changing positions frequently would allow them to build their skillsets, and overall better position them to thrive in a highly competitive challenging marketplace. The quest for passion and meaning guided their search.

In 1911, Walter Dill Scott, a visionary psychologist wrote the following regarding treatment of employees: "[If you treat them] like machines, look at them merely as cogs in the mechanism . . ., they will function like machines or find other places" (as cited by Durkin, 2005, p. 45).

In Pursuit of Passion: Looking for Personal Fulfillment and Meaning

Follow your passion and the rest will take care of itself.

(Ruth, a 26-year-old participant)

You have to do whatever floats your boat.

(Shandra, a 28-year-old participant)

A striking number of participants subscribed to the belief that following one's passion(s) was key to finding meaningful work. Both cohorts subscribed to the importance of finding meaningful work. When asked to provide advice to individuals about to enter the developmental period of emerging adulthood, 51.85% of the affluent participants and 25% of the less affluent participants most frequently responded by subscribing to the importance of either pursuing one's "passion" and/or pursuing work that they would "love" and "enjoy."

For many, passion served as a marker in guiding their job search. They aspired to find work that would be satisfying, engaging, meaningful, fun, and at times even exhilarating. For many emerging adults, advice given by parents, teachers, and friends reinforced the central role of finding passion in one's work.

Most participants reported working hard during college, and their expectation was that they would be embraced by a job market that would afford them opportunities, enjoyment/fulfillment, and growth. For many, particularly those with college degrees that did not provide them with specific skillsets, disillusionment, alienation, and a feeling of being shortchanged followed. Opportunities did not abound for a majority of the participants in the study. They entered the workforce with an unspoken contract in hand: I worked hard in college, pursued my studies with great diligence, and in return I will be rewarded. Participants entered the contract in good faith, trying to follow their passion(s), and anticipated that they would be rewarded for their efforts. Many participants experienced frustration and disillusionment along the way.

Nick: You're told to pursue your passion.... And then you get out into the world, and pursuing your passion does not get you anywhere necessarily, and you have to figure out a new approach. It is a big adjustment.

Daria: People have this desire to find out what their passion is, and what their true calling is. People don't want to just be a cog on a wheel the way people have been in the past.

A parent of an emerging adult succinctly echoes the sentiment expressed by Nick:

Clara: They've worked so hard and they feel gypped. The world did not deliver a set of goods promised.

Similarly, Drew, a 27-year-old political science major, attempted to heed the advice of his parents: "Do what you love, follow your passion, because you will be better at what you love, and that is important." Drew encountered an unwelcoming job market and many rejections along the way. He had lived up to his end of the bargain, worked hard during college, and found it difficult to fathom how underappreciated and undervalued he felt. Messages imparted by his parents, as well as significant adults in his life, did not resonate with the numerous rejections he received in the pursuit of trying to procure employment. Once employed, Drew felt bored and frustrated in the positions he held. Currently, he is applying to a doctoral program in political science.

Many emerging and young adults noted that their parents worked hard in demanding, all-consuming jobs that provided them with little gratification. Motivated by the desire not to replicate their parents' experiences, they sought jobs that would provide them with fulfillment and meaning. However, for some participants, the pursuit of a fulfilling job proved to be elusive and illusory. In the process, they became anxious and despondent about future prospects. Some appeared to flounder, taking jobs that left them frustrated, unfulfilled, and/or stalled. Others assumed an experimental stance, trying a new job every one to two years, attempting to find their "calling," whereas others immersed themselves in work, pursuing a career path that had been envisioned for them by a parent. Daria, a 31-year-old actuary, expressed frustration related to not taking the time necessary to reflect on her career choice, in part due to the demanding number of hours necessary to succeed in her job, in part due to her experience of being on a treadmill since high school with no time to think about what she wanted for herself:

Work, work, work. You're on a path, without trying to figure out what it is you want to be. You almost don't know what your opinions are, what your thoughts are. Everyone has been thinking for you. You don't have the skillsets [to think for yourself]. You have been doing, doing, doing, without really questioning.

When asked what advice they would offer to other individuals in their 20s and 30s, most of the participants focused on the importance of being happy, finding meaning, having fun, and making sure that they experienced no regret regarding career choices. Marla, Frank, Jim, Robert, Susan, and Thea, when asked what advice they would offer to other emerging and young adults, spoke of the importance of finding passion and meaning in one's work.

Marla: Whatever you choose to do, you should make sure that it is really what you want to do, not what other people want you to do, and that you are happy to do it. At the same time, work is not college, not every aspect of work is fun, but if you find something meaningful in a piece of your work, at the end of the day it is worthwhile; it is worth doing.

Frank: Don't let the pursuit of financial success interfere with that internal compass that tells you I am satisfied, that I am happy.

Jim: Do the best you can. Do something that makes you happy. Too many people get into bad situations. Find out what you like doing and do it. . . . Please don't be miserable and bored. . . . Don't have regrets and say I wish I did this. You owe it to yourself to do cool things you're interested in.

Robert: People want to do something meaningful, whether it is for society or for their company. They want to make a difference.

Susan: I think it is really important to be working in a situation that you believe in what you are doing, and the purpose of what you are doing. I don't like it when people say work is work, I don't like it. I want to be able to say this feels like fun, this does not feel like work, although I realize this takes a lot of discipline.

Thea: I always believe that it is important to like your work, to enjoy what you are doing. There is a sense of integrity that goes with that, and fortunately for me, wherever I have worked, that has been valued. . . . I have always believed it is not just a job that gives you money, but it is something that you are passionate about.

In addition, many participants expressed concern related to their observations of a workforce that was all too often bored, unhappy, and from their perspectives, lacking meaning. They were determined not to replicate what they viewed as lives lacking meaning and passion, as discussed by Clifford, currently a 27-year-old teacher, who began his career after college in real estate. His plans include continuing to teach as well as investing in real estate:

When I was in college during the summers, I started to work summers in my dad's law firm. I could see how unhappy people were. Pushing papers all day. Working in a job they were not invested in. Working there for 20 to 30 years, monotonous, boring, uninteresting. It is kinda sad. I made a decision then if I was going to have a job, it was going to allow me to have flexibility, do what I want to do, work from home if I wanted to, take a couple days off, and it would not make a difference. Make my own life. What I put into it, is what I got out of it. The amount of time and effort I put in was going to be directly related to the amount of money I made.

Hassler's (2005) assertions regarding the role of passion in our work life is illuminating given the emphasis on the pursuit of passion by participants in the study. Most individuals in their 20s, according to Hassler, are not adept at identifying their passions. Although 80% of her sample (women only) reported that passion was lacking in their work, 90% of her sample could not identify their respective passions. Hassler (2005, p. 275) illustrates this theme: "Passion has become a buzzword, although many of us don't even know what it really means. As a generation, we have become obsessed with finding our passions, and a lot of us have found suffering instead."

Following one's passion, according to Hassler, implies, that there is a "fire burning in our bellies," that will drive us toward career fulfillment and a life of happiness (p. 275). If we aren't passionate about work, we are doomed to a life of unhappiness and lack of fulfillment:

Rarely, [are] individuals born with so strong a love for art or work. . . . [A] far more common approach to discovering what we want, is to follow the natural progression of events. Without any experience in the fields of our so-called passions, it is hard to know for sure that we would even want to be able to make careers out of them. (Hassler, 2005, p. 275)

According to Hassler (2005), whereas for some, careers fulfill a need for purpose and passion, for others, the process of finding passion in one's work can be a more elusive process:

We put a tremendous amount of pressure . . . to first realize our purpose (which society brands as "passion") and then to immediately generate careers that serve it. One reason that previous generations did not complain about a twenty-something crisis is that they weren't consumed by their passion-finding trend. People placed more emphasis on working to support lifestyles that made them happy. . . . We make our career decisions with so much urgency and finality that many of us get side-tracked and do not follow the flow of our lives or our purpose [and thus we sense an absence of passion]. (p. 276)

Furthermore, for many emerging and young adults, according to Hassler (2005), work has taken center stage in terms of organizing one's identity. Work can define us as individuals, at the expense of other domains awaiting further development. Investment in one's career is attributed in part to uncertain times, a way to take control of one's life. She suggests that it is critical to separate what one does from who one is. Otherwise: "If we do not separate what we do from who we are, our identity will always be dictated by something external—our jobs—and that can significantly weaken our foundation. . . . No job can fill a void or complete us" (p. 272).

For many emerging and young adults, focusing on one's career appeared to be key to taking hold and control of one's life. Macko and Rubin (2004) describe emerging and young adults and their commitment to career investment. They suggest that investment in the self may be the most reliable strategy in terms of taking hold and control of one's life. In reality, investment in self translates to investment in career, according to Macko and Rubin. Hassler (2005) suggests an alternative potentially freeing strategy for those unable to identify their passion or frustrated in their career search: "We have to look at the dream jobs, determine which of their elements we can attain, and then try our hand at those" (p. 277).

The overemphasis on passion and the pressures we feel to do and have it all propels us into one of two states: either we put ourselves on an accomplishment timeline, or we waver because we don't know what we want. As much as we want to figure out what to do so we can start doing it, not knowing is part of process of ultimately discovering our purpose. (Hassler, 2005, pp. 290–291)

Optimally, career decisions are based on the "intersection of... [one's] skills and passions" (Trunk, 2006, ¶ 10). Although some emerging and young adults may be unable to either identify or pursue their passion(s), they are able to describe a specific dream job, a job that may be outside their realm of possibility. An impediment to finding fulfillment is the pursuit of passion in conjunction with the pursuit of perfectionism. Deidre, a 26-year-old participant reflects this view, "It's not enough to have a good job and nice friends and family.... Older people might think it's enough, but I want more."

For emerging and young adults, particularly for those in the affluent cohort, the quest for passion may co-occur with the quest for the perfect life. For some, the quest for perfection occurs in one domain, most typically the work domain; for others the quest for perfection includes the perfect job, perfect mate, and the perfect life. For those emerging and young adults who strive for both passion and perfectionism in their work and personal lives, confusion and angst frequently follow. Daria expresses a sense of confusion regarding her inability to take hold of a career, particularly given her assessment that there exists a fair amount of economic opportunity available to her:

Maybe people expect more out of a job, and it is hard to find it.... People don't settle for jobs. People are searching, trying to find their passion, their true calling. You go to different positions to try to find it [passion]. You don't settle.... What should be satisfying is that there is so much opportunity and so many things that you can be doing. You don't have to settle on a personal or professional level. At the same time, it is hard to figure it out. It is frustrating to know that you have all these opportunities and options, but not to know what the right one is for you.

Implicit in Daria's assessment, is that there is one "right" job, and that it is her responsibility to "figure it all out." To pursue a job that is not "the right one" suggests that she is settling for less.

The fear of settling for less is a concern that has also been raised by emerging and young adults in other technologically advanced countries such as Japan. Woods (2005) in an article appearing on the front page of the *Wall Street Journal*, focuses on Japanese emerging and young adults who seemingly are electing not to enter the workforce. They are holding out for "dream jobs" in an economic environment that is desperately looking for personnel to replace an aging population (twenty percent of Japan's population will be over the age of 65 by the year 2006, and it is expected to reach 35% by year 2050).

A study conducted by Nomura Research Institute, surveying work attitudes of 1000 Japanese employees, found that three-fourths of individuals in their 20s and 30s reported feeling unmotivated in their existing jobs, half reported that they would quit if given the chance, and that overall they were "tiring of corporate life" (Woods, 2005, ¶ 20). It is estimated that 640,000 young Japanese, ages 15 to 34, although able to enter the job market, have not done so, holding out, ostensibly looking for better jobs. The existence of "slackers," also called *NEETS* (not in education, employment, or training) has mobilized the Japanese government, alarmed by the growing scope of the problem, to spend 8.5 million on programs designed to inspire youths to enter the workforce. These structured programs have been relatively unsuccessful. One interpretation for the current work attitudes among *NEETS* in Japan is:

Many Japanese in their 40s and 50s who sacrificed their lives for stable but grueling corporate jobs don't want their children to do the same. As a result, they're encouraging them to pursue dream jobs—even seemingly unattainable ones—and are willing to support them in the process.... Young people, too, are tiring of corporate life. The parents entered a company and stayed there their entire life and their children are looking for more diversity. (Woods, 2005, ¶ 19–20)

Given abundance of choice, and given that finding a "dream job" is like "finding a needle in a haystack," experts question the wisdom of seeking a job that is designed for an emerging adult's unique strengths and skillsets: "the chance of stumbling upon that one perfect profession is about as likely as winning the lottery" (Woods, 2005, ¶ 26).

The following prescription offered by a career consultant working in Japan, perhaps cynical and limiting, captures the dilemma emerging adults are facing in their search for a dream job: "Dreams are for when you're asleep.... When you're awake, you have to think about reality" (Woods, 2005, ¶ 27).

Expectations Revisited

Many of the participants were still in the throes of resolving dilemmas related to career choice, rethinking basic and nuanced assumptions related to the meaning of work. As participants approached the age of 30, they were more likely to calibrate their work expectations. Erin, 34 years of age, spent seven years as a lawyer and is currently pursuing a second career in public relations. She states:

If you can do it, just be kind to yourself and lower your expectations of yourself. It is the only thing I can think of, which I find difficult to do. I cannot figure out how not to be hard on myself, but that is the goal. To just accept where you are and just sort of have that be okay. To acknowledge there really is no superwoman. And to be kinder and more forgiving of yourself for not living up to your own and or others' expectations of you.... I think that is why you have a lot of people switching jobs. Kids are trying to fulfill expectations, go to college, get that graduate degree, but then after the fact, they realize it was rushed.

Ruth tried to follow her passion and need for perfectionism for ten years. She experienced a series of disappointments related to her jobs, which have led her to conclude:

People need to take practical things into consideration. Will you truly be happy not making money? One has to follow their heart and yet be practical. You have to have a practical bone in your body. Do you really want to pay off school loans till you are 70?

She summarizes the disillusionment she felt regarding the dictum she tried to follow, "Follow your passion, and everything else will fall into place:"

[My parents] have been very supportive. It is kind of good and bad. It is nice to have parental support, but at the same time because I have floundered, I wish their attitude was one where they said, you just gotta figure it out for yourself. With my own children, they have to do what they want to do, but I might learn from my not necessarily good example. I would tell them to choose more wisely. Whereas my husband would say, you have to get a practical degree, something between me and him is about right. So much to be said about a liberal arts degree being a valid pursuit as an end in it of itself. When else are you going to have the opportunity? But on the other hand, you have to pursue a degree that will give you value, where you will be appreciated for your skills.

Marla similarly has calibrated her expectations:

I think I was more idealistic. . . . I wanted to be doing something I loved all the time. I realize that now it is almost impossible . . . especially at entry level. . . . Hopefully, I held out for something I wanted to do. I am unique in that way. If I get what I want, I have lowered my expectations to a point where hopefully I will meet them. I don't know if I lowered my expectations. I have a better grasp on reality in terms of what I should expect. I may have expected something that was not reality.

A period of adjustment and calibration followed for Marla and many emerging and young adults who participated in the study. Many of the participants, including John and Jill, found it difficult to balance their need for meaningful purposeful work with external realities that prevented them from realizing their dream. John, despite graduating with honors, disenchanted and disillusioned concludes:

John: I was not ready for the reality, not the way I was brought up. Things I was told that were not the case.

Jill: You are told you are the future, you are the leaders, you are the ones that will make a difference. In fact you are not leading the world. just bringing in an income, and I would say that was the hardest part. I felt my first job was so meaningless relative to big ideas in college. Things take a lot longer than you think they do. I think I used to be able to turn something around in a day. Lowering expectations of what you can produce and the contributions you can make, I like being reasonable with my expectations so I am not disappointed. I know my job is not that important, and I kind of laugh at it. In the grand scheme of things I am insignificant. I can make this person happy for one day. Setting small bullets for yourself; no one is steering the ship, it is a big ship to steer. If I was working for a small company, sometimes you can make a bigger difference. Managing expectations, don't get too excited about something too good, or too bad, things are never as good or bad as they seem.

Niedzviecki (2004) captures the disappointment and alienation experienced by the participants. Emerging and young adults grew up with the assumption that given hard work and determination, they would be able to realize their dreams, assumptions reinforced by their educational experiences. Instead, they encountered an environment that was highly regulated. Participants were emotionally and intellectually challenged not to internalize the rejections and sense of failure they experienced. A process of correction for many emerging and young adults took place, and as Erin states, "We try to go back and correct what they may perceive as mistakes, what I perceive perhaps [as] incompleteness."

Conclusions

The career paths participants took were varied. Some were "on track" and typically entered professional or graduate schools post-college. Many actively experimented with job possibilities, with most of the participants in pursuit of "passion" and/or "skillsets" to guide their journey. They reported feeling unprepared for the abrupt shift that occurred once they entered the workforce. Many became disillusioned and struggled with jobs that were not synchronous with their intellectual capacities and talents. The primacy of developing a satisfying and meaningful career pervaded their narratives. Most of the participants revisited and reassessed their career expectations and choices to date, some with more deliberate forethought, others more randomly, and by age 30 most of the participants were on a career trajectory that they viewed with more permanence. Most acknowledged that their career paths would shift over time, given current marketplace realities, and maintained a flexible open stance. The following chapter focuses on the interpersonal lives of the participants, specifically the developmental tasks of developing and sustaining intimate relationships and friendships.

References

Durkin, D. (2005). *The loyalty advantage: Essential steps to energize your company, your customers, your brand.* New York: American Management Association.

Hassler, C. (2005). *20 Something, 20 Everything: A quarter life woman's guide to balance and Direction.* Novato, CA: New World Library.

Karo, A. (2005, January 31). Ruminations [Weblog entry]. Retrieved May 3, 2006. *Monkey Business.* (http://www.aaronkaro.com/issue.php?id=36).

Macko, L. & Rubin, K. (2004). *Midlife crisis at 30: How the stakes have changed for a new generation-and what to do about it.* New York: Plume.

Niedzviecki, N. (2004) *Hello, I'm special: How individuality became the new conformity.* Canada: Penguin Canada.

Schulenberg, J. E., Bryant, A. L., & O'Malley, P. M. (2004). Taking hold of some kind of life: How developmental tasks relate to trajectories of well-being during the transition to adulthood. *Development and Psychopathology, 16*(4), 1119–1140.

Schulenberg, J. E., Sameroff, A. J., & Cicchetti, D. (2004). The transition to adulthood as a critical juncture in the course of psychopathology and mental health. *Development and Psychopathology, 16*(4), 799–806.

Settersten, R. Jr. (2005). Social policy and the transition to adulthood. In R. Settersten Jr., F. Furstenberg Jr., & R. Rumbaut (Eds.), *On the frontier of adulthood: Theory, research, and public policy* (pp. 534–560). Chicago: University of Chicago Press.

Trunk, P. (2006, March 5). If you can do more, try a few careers until you're sure. *Boston Sunday Globe,* p. G1.

Woods, G. (2005, December 29). Generation gap: In aging Japan, young slackers stir concerns; Changing attitudes prompt people to quit job search; A demographic time bomb; Mr. Isozaki's lack of urgency. *Wall Street Journal,* p. A 1.

5
Voices of Emerging and Young Adults: From the Professional to the Personal

Analysis of demographic as well as social behaviors suggests important changes with respect to emerging and young adults and the environmental contexts in which they reside. Interpersonal and social codes of behavior have been removed, with no clear rules for engagement in place. A vacuum exists, with many emerging and young adults experimenting in an environmental context characterized by "social chaos" (Straus, 2006, p. 134).

Instability, characteristic of this time period, had a profound impact on the interpersonal and social development of the participants. Participants, in speaking about their personal lives, expressed a diversity of values, attitudes, and expectations. Their narratives were textured and rich, with common threads. For the majority of the participants, intimate and social relationships were informed by a sense of primacy of developing satisfying and meaningful careers. For some, consuming careers challenged notions of clearly defined boundaries between one's work and personal life. Participants tended to value experimentation and diversity in their relationships, and were hesitant to rush into what they viewed as premature marital commitments.

Whereas the previous chapter focused on the professional lives of the participants, this chapter focuses on their interpersonal and social lives. Based on an analysis of the narratives, the following themes emerged: (1) career preceding commitment to a life partner, (2) fluidity in relationships, (3) experimentation associated with minimization of risk, (4) the process of negotiation: let's make a deal, (5) technology and its influence on relationships, (6) friendships, (7) too many expectations, and (8) philanthropy and the need to make the world a better place.

Career Preceding Commitment to a Life Partner

The majority of the participants followed a pathway that included "identity-before-intimacy," that is, having one's career in place, before launching a long-term committed relationship (Dyk & Adams, 1990; Macko & Rubin, 2004). "Investment in oneself" frequently translated to investment in one's career (Macko & Rubin, 2004, p. 22).

Males and females evidenced similar pathways with respect to career commitment and consolidation of identity. Women were as likely as men to postpone marriage, and focused their energies in pursuit of career-related goals. A minority of women in the less affluent cohort followed a path that not only included investment in career, but also simultaneously included investment in their role as single parent.

Career status informed participants' assessment of readiness for marriage. For example, Robert, a 29-year-old MBA student, states the following:

First, you evaluate yourself in your job. If you are evaluating whether you need a new career, it is not the time to jump into a relationship. If you hate your job, it is not the time to commit, or buy a house. Be complete as a person, before you expand in relationships and family, relationships that lead to marriage.

Mike, a 26-year-old male considering a career in urban planning, expresses his hesitance to enter a committed relationship that is likely to lead to marriage. He emphasizes financial resources as a critical variable in determining readiness for marriage:

I feel like I am not ready [for marriage]; I feel like I am too young. I would think by the time I figure out what I want to do in my career, I will think about a wife. So, financial status is a big part of this in terms of my view.

John, a 28-year-old male, speaks to the expanding economic opportunities for women, which in turn results in marital delay, particularly in fast-paced urban contexts. He contrasts his observation with his experience as a graduate student in the Midwest:

People take longer to settle down. [It is] easier for women to get their degrees. A lot more people are focused on their career, which is good. People have less time to focus on their relationships. More of a focus on a career, especially for women. It has become okay. If people focus on careers, it takes them longer to settle down.

In the Midwest, [where I was a graduate student], people are more integrated with their faith and their church, [and there is] less distraction than in the city. People tend to settle down more quickly. Here [Boston], it is completely different.

Overall, participants expressed traditional goals regarding marriage and children, a finding that is consistent with reports in the literature (Twenge, 2006). A preponderance of the participants expected that their spouse or partner would work and assume joint responsibilities for their child(ren). However, there was diversity with respect to the timing of marriage. Although a minority of the participants chose to formally commit to each other via marriage by age 25, the majority of the participants were single during their 20s. With respect to those participants who were married by age 25, one or both of the partners tended to be focused and launched in their career path(s). The age range of 30 to 35 seemed to be an important developmental marker, albeit a flexible one, a yardstick for determining whether participants were launched personally and professionally. For women, the biological clock vis-à-vis the choice to have children influenced their assessments.

Participants were invested in developing themselves before marriage, preferring to have a sense of themselves as "complete," capable of making a commitment to another who is also "complete." They tended to view investment in self as increasing the likelihood of a successful marriage and/or a long-term commitment.

According to Sheehy (1995), as individuals approach the age of 30, a "dramatic shift" occurs in psychological maturity. Thirty is a milestone for individuals in their 20s, whereby there is recognition that the "dress rehearsal" is over.

The breaking point is somewhere around twenty-nine, thirty. There's something about seeing another zero roll up. (Malley, as cited in Sheehy, 1995, p. 52)

Before the shift, men and women feel unable to make clear choices or cope with life's vicissitudes .... After the shift, they feel confident enough in their own values to make their own choices and competent enough in life skills to set a course—even if that course clashes with a parent's wishes. (Sheehy, 1995, p. 52)

Fluidity in Relationships

Flexibility and fluidity characterized the interpersonal relationships of many of the participants. Just as Coontz (2005) has observed that there is increasing flexibility and fluidity with respect to the institution of marriage, there also appears to be increased fluidity and flexibility in relationships prior to marriage. Participants attached significance to having a satisfying career in place and being "complete." Alexis, Marnie, and Raymond spoke to the issue of increased fluidity in relationships.

Alexis: [There is] much more fluidity. There is definitely more of a feeling you can date someone for a while and move on. I don't see that in prior generations. [It probably has something to do with the] post-feminist sexual revolution. No stigma is attached to that, which I think is a good thing.

Marnie: [Previously], a lot more pressure came from your religious affiliation. That was the social network that socially controlled things. The social network is much more fluid, so you don't have people telling you what to do.

Raymond: There are so many different kinds of relationships. People can find companionship in so many different ways, without getting married. I have a lot of nonsexual relationships with girls. It depends on the person. They fulfill some kind of need in you. You can get what you want from many people instead of just one .... I wonder if it has something to do with the sexes being more equal, the breakdown of gender roles.

Increased fluidity was in part driven by economic considerations. The marketplace, driven in part by an information age that redefines existing borders and creates jobs that are more fluid, affects the nature of relationships and the way they are negotiated. Warner (2005) reports that 65% of women in their 20s state that "it's extremely important to be financially 'set' before they marry, and 82 percent [state that it is] unwise for a woman to rely on a marriage for financial security" (p. 22). In addition, commitment to launching a career was viewed by some of the participants as colliding with time needed to nurture intimate long-term commitments.

With increased fluidity, there exists the possibility for increased casualness in relationships. Ken, a 28-year-old participant, contrasts his experiences with those of his parents:

My mother's side relied on her parents to find suitable partners, matchmaking. Today they are much more individual. I think a lot go to bars, Internet dating, and that sort of stuff. My perception is that they are a lot more casual than people in my parents' generation. Well, I guess there isn't as much social stigma, taboo associated with it. If a guy wants to hook up, there is no stigma. It has to do with cell phone, e-mail; you don't make concrete plans because you can change them 20 minutes before. [There is] less formal dating. My parents dated more formulaically. They dated one-on-one, and now it is in groups.

Experimentation Associated with Minimization of Risk

Having a range of interpersonal experiences tended to be valued and viewed by the participants as helpful in defining and consolidating one's identity. Committing to marriage without prior experimentation could be "risky," and experimentation was associated with mitigation of risk. Participants aspired to an identity that felt coherent and integrated, that allowed for entering a relationship "complete." Fear of divorce informed views and concerns related to long-term commitment and marriage. In turn, individuals experimented with a range of individuals. They tended to value difference in their relationships, in part to ascertain goodness-of-fit with a potential life partner, and in part to address concerns related to averting financial loss associated with a poor choice of a life partner. Ron, Steven, and Sergio speak to these concerns:

Ron: [The] biggest mistake my generation has seen is high divorce rates, making the wrong decision at an early age. They [my generation] want to have fun, not settle down. [They want to] hang out .... They're chasing more of a social agenda. Individuals are taking more time and care before they commit to someone in marriage, because of the financial implications.

Steven: We are not afraid to make the mistake (referring to marriage). We are educated. People are waiting longer, they are having more time to hang out with different personalities, to figure out what they don't fit with, what they clash with, and don't clash with.

Sergio: I would like a few solid relationships, five or six long-term relationships so that I have a good idea of what I like in a woman that I want to marry .... I have tried [to be in different relationships], some of which I liked, some of which I did not like, but they have all shaped me as an individual.

Sergio's hope is that by actively experimenting with difference, "People will be happier, more adjusted in our society."

Linda, 27-years old, currently in a master's program in fine arts, expresses a need to explore a variety of relationships with men, so that she can better position herself to assess the degree of "balance" in her relationships. Moreover, she expressed skepticism regarding long-term commitment and marriage:

Almost nobody I know is getting married in their early 20s. Some are in long-term relationships for a while—a few that have been [in long-term relationships] have recently gotten out of them .... I think there is more of the idea, you have to see what is out there before you settle. [You might think] this was my first boyfriend, and I am not sure he is the perfect match, because I have not been with other people. I think some people think of it as the [search for the] perfect man, perfect woman. I think of it as [the search for] someone who would be a good balance for you .... People are more skeptical [regarding] what it means to be with someone your whole life, and they don't trust it. They see marriage as a real compromise, and not in a good way. Sometimes when I see a man pushing a stroller, a young family on the subway, the parents don't seem to be that happy. I don't want to be unhappy. There is a tone that I sense in their relationship that I don't like. I also know a lot of my male friends think girlfriends restrict the coolness and the laid-backness of their friends.

Macko and Rubin (2004) speak to the concerns expressed by the participants, male and female, regarding risk and divorce:

As a generation, the core story we absorbed about divorce was that it happened most often to couples who married too young, had babies too soon, or just grew up and grew apart. Accordingly, we launched our post-collegiate years armed with a big cultural lesson: The route to marrying the right guy for the right reasons was to focus on ourselves for a while. Unlike past generations of women who married young and assumed they would continue to grow as individuals alongside their husbands, the women we interviewed came to believe that living on their own terms before walking down the aisle was the best way to ensure that a marriage would last .... It's as if, consciously or unconsciously, we've all been after some kind of Divorce Insurance Policy, and taking control of our own lives—by focusing on our careers, pursuing personal passions, and delaying marriage—seemed the right way to get it. (p. 22)

Emily, a 32-year-old participant, validates this concern:

We see our parents worked so hard. Then they get divorced, never traveled. Why not do these things while you are young? You have strength and energy, and start the career a little bit later. Really be sure about it, and start to have the career a little later and have kids later. Our parents graduated thinking that marriage was the greatest thing. We graduated knowing that half of all marriages end in divorce.

Sheehy (1995) suggests that Emily's perspective, reinforced by many of the participants, appears to be adaptive with respect to marital longevity:

. . . marrying later and even more selectively also bodes well for their personal security. The one preventive measure against divorce that holds for every generation is this: The older we are when we marry for the first time, the less likely the marriage is to end up on the trash heap. (p. 52)

Emerging and young adults, mindful of the alarming divorce rates associated with their parents' generation, were motivated not to replicate their behavior. One approach to mitigating risk includes discussion, prior to marriage, of roles and responsibilities. Many emerging and young adults appeared to be on a mission to try to avert failure in their personal lives.

The Process of Negotiation: Let's Make a Deal

Although the pursuit of passion informed work-related behavior, many of the participants spoke of their personal relationships with forethought and deliberation. For example, Thea, a recently engaged 29-year-old woman working in human resources, states:

I think, in my parents' generation ... a lot of things were assumed, not talked about. In today's generation, there is a lot of conversation, a lot of conversation before one gets into a relationship, a lot of negotiation. I guess, one partner says I need this and this, and the other partner says I need this and this, and they try to mix and match .... It is not just a relationship where I like you, and you like me .... It is more that it is beneficial to both people .... Almost like a business relationship, pragmatic.

[Your personal and work life are] interrelated. The priority is career and self-sufficiency, so to make any relationship work, you need to state that up front. [You choose] people who are similar with similar goals, you give this, you give that, and that is how to make things work.

The benefits [to this approach] are open conversation, sharing everything, nothing is assumed, especially roles. However, the bad part is there is no passion. It is more like a business contract. Very very few people take risks. More calculated in some ways.

According to Thea, one enters into a contract, a business transaction that will be mutually satisfying and beneficial to both parties. Clarity regarding roles and responsibilities is key to the process of negotiating a long-term relationship. Thea forged ahead in her relationship and became engaged, only after participating in a difficult negotiation process. The process included rationally and systematically exploring the viability of the relationship, particularly with respect to day-to-day realities.

In listening to Thea and others, the author had a sense that the question being asked among many emerging and young adults considering a marital commitment is, "Can we make a deal?" A children's rhyme comes to mind: "First comes love, then comes marriage, then comes [female name] with a baby carriage." Perhaps the rhyme needs to be reconceived to capture the experiences of the participants: "First comes love, then comes the question can we make it together in a marriage, and if so, most likely a baby carriage," captures the process more accurately. If each member of the couple can agree on how the relationship will work on a day-to-day basis, then marriage may be considered a viable option. Negotiation is built into the process, and is taken quite seriously by both parties. The rules as described by Thea, are such that both partners enter the negotiation process in good faith, honoring a process that can lead to resolution of differences.

Alexis, a 30-year-old investment banker who works an average of 80 to 85 hours a week, is currently in a ten-year relationship with a woman who is attempting to build a career in the arts. In the context of a serious and loving relationship, Alexis speaks of their combined priority in ensuring that career goals are met for each individual in the relationship. The goals for Alexis's personal life with her partner are a direct outgrowth of the goals both she and her partner have for their respective careers. In response to a question posed to her by the author regarding long-term goals, Alexis states:

In ten years, I will still be with my girlfriend, but I'm not sure .... I don't know if we will have kids. We are in a holding pattern on the relationship side. At some point, we will get out of it. Our personal relationship is tied to our careers. Both of us want to get to a career point that we are both happy with. That is why we are in a holding pattern.

Adam, a 34-year-old entrepreneur, talks about the possibility of marriage in the future:

I am single, unfortunately; eventually, yes, I would like to be married. I wouldn't say tomorrow, when you have had employees, sometimes it does not work out. Made me very careful entering into agreements with people. You don't want to jump into anything that is difficult to undo; you have to do your homework; you have to be careful; there are a lot of steps. You are being foolish, if you don't do the steps, the downside is so bad .... have to minimize your risk because the downside is so bad. You have to have the patience to follow the right steps.

You got to find the right person, you got to have the right priorities. It will not happen by chance. [It is] painful to fire someone. You have to have your eyes wide open; it's foolish if you don't. And it's risky; it's so much more risk than you want.

Technology and its Influence on Relationships

Participants spoke to the influence of technology on relationships, that is, availability of e-mails, cell phones, instant messaging, and Internet dating. Although no unifying threads linked the discussion, participants acknowledged the importance of technology and its influence in their day-to-day lives. They focused on the ability of technology to inform and titrate the natural course of relationships. More specifically, technology was associated with: (1) facilitation of human connections despite the physical distance, (2) increased availability and potential for immediacy of response, and (3) the ability to build additional communities based on mutual interests via the Internet.

Advances in technology facilitate one's ability to be casual in relationships, increase or decrease the speed and intensity of a desired relationship, and overall provide for increased flexibility in terms of entering and sustaining a relationship. Technology tended to be viewed by many of the participants as a tool for controlling desired distance in a relationship. Linda, Ed, Meghan, and Christie allude to the impact technological advances have had on their personal lives.

Linda: There are all these amazing technology advances that are going on and being developed. My friend is in Africa. I just chatted with him this morning. You can chat with people instantly. I had a conversation on the computer with my friend in Africa this morning!

Ed: There seems to be more contact between people in their 20s and 30s, usually through technologies, e-mail, chatting online, text messages, not personal contact. It fosters longer-term relationships, no matter what the contact is. It continues to keep that person in your life.

Meghan: Technology has changed relationships. Technology and travel—airplanes and cars. Connections and contacts happen at a speed when there is no face-to-face contact.

With e-mail, you can respond an hour later. It increases the intensity just because of the rate of interaction.

Christie: It was more difficult to meet through a personal ad before, a lot easier to post something online and there seems to be endless amount of people to choose from, whereas with personal ads you only had 20.

Linda expresses awe in relaying her ability to keep in touch with a friend from college, a relationship that provides her with continued support and adds meaning to her life. Ed, Meghan, and Christie acknowledge Linda's perspective with respect to the ease of staying in touch via technology, as well as gaining access to potential new relationships. On the other hand, technology enables one to be less committed and planful in relationships. Tools such as e-mail and instant messaging provide possibilities for increased intimacy, as well as increased anonymity, as discussed by Jones (2006), and confirmed by Deidre, Justine, Mark, and Christie.

Jones (2006) in a column written for the *New York Times* on February 12, 2006, summarizes his observations related to the downside of technology and its impact on relationships:

In pursuing love, electronic communication allows us to be more reckless, fake, distracted and isolated than ever before .... [M]en and women are more apt to plunge into love affairs via text message, cut off by PowerPoint, lie about who they are and what they want in forums and blogs and online dating sites, pretend they're young when they're old and old when they're young, ignore the people they're physically with for those who are a keystroke away, shoo their children off their laps to caress their BlackBerrys.... Has electronic communication officially become the most seductive mistress of all time?

Deidre, a 32-year-old participant, speaks to the commodification of the individual as well as the dehumanization that occurs in the process of developing relationships via the Internet:

People don't take relationships that seriously any more, not a lot of personal connection. You can meet someone on the Internet, they can be best friends, you will never meet that person. I do think it is pretty common. It is easy. You don't make time to call them. You can just type up an e-mail, or chat online.

For me, I meet most of my friends at church, also at the workplace. It is very common to go to speed dating, spend three minutes with someone; what kind of impression can you make? I grew up in a conservative family with traditional values. [They are] fast food relationships. I don't think the outcome will be very good. With speed dating, I guess they see the date for three minutes; if it does not work out, they move on to the next person. For me, it does not work. It is like [you are treating the person like] a commodity. Like old clothes, if it does not fit, you get another one. It gives you that kind of feeling.

Justine expressed a different perspective with respect to use of the Internet and dating, "It makes it fun, because you are anonymous. You can remain anonymous for as long as you want to. When people are anonymous, they become more playful or bold, willing to take more risks. There are no rules."

Mark speaks to the influence of technology on rules of social etiquette and day-to-day interactions. Although on the one hand technology may facilitate interaction for those individuals who are shy and introverted, technology may also compromise skillsets acquired in day-to-day relationships and interactions:

People who are introverts have an easier time adapting in this particular environment. People who are extroverts cannot derive the kind of energy they need from an existence that is electronic.

Christie suggests that an important venue for sharing one's life—letter writing—has been rendered obsolete due to advances in technology:

I think what bothers me is that people don't write letters any more. The art of the letter is lost. People write quick e-mails. They have caller ID and choose not to answer their phones. We make communication easier, talking to people in Australia. We're isolating ourselves in some respect as individuals. When people wrote letters, they would talk about meaningful things .... When you check your e-mail it is not the same. Ask anyone how they feel about getting a letter, puts a smile on your face, something special about it.

A few of the participants alluded to the importance of having a virtual community, based on mutual interests. As a result, the meaning of community has expanded. Sergio and Jeff speak to the importance of having a venue for exchanging ideas and "belonging to a community:"

Sergio: To talk to different people that are in the same boat that you are in—you exchange opinions; you have their experience of different situations; they have yours. Online forums, online communities have a lot to do with it, belonging to a community, online or not, where you exchange ideas is a good idea.

Jeff: Because people are learning to adapt to live in this abstract information world, many people not only have a physical manifestation, but also this abstract mark. They have no idea what I look like, my personality, my race. I take up considerable real estate in the world that is totally electronic; I have a presence .... There is a me that is completely divorced from my body. This generation, in order to survive, has to learn a completely different set of skills for interacting. What comes after, I am not sure.

An alternative view of community, consistent with the writing of Cote (2006), is articulated by Erica:

These social networks like Friendster, they become your group. There is a lot of passion about changing the world and making it a better place. You don't see outside of it. You are righteous about it. Your world is a bigger world. It has a larger focus. It is sort of a collaborative interactive narcissism. You always have your finger on the pulse of your friends, political blogs; these things are all me; even my friends are me. Friends who blog, have blog readings, and they organize, do different things outside of work. They are different kinds of affiliations.

In summary, participants alluded to the presence of technology in their lives, and spoke about technology vis-à-vis their relationships in interesting and at times contradictory ways. The advent of technology has assisted emerging and young adults to engage with one another in a multitude of ways, some of which create distance and/or misinterpretation, whereas others promote intimacy and closeness. A prevailing view expressed by the participants is that technology provides individuals the ability to sustain relationships in a global world. Access to technology enhances one's ability to regulate affect in relationships, slowing relationships down or stepping up the tempo, that is, amplifying the intensity of the interaction. It enhances one's ability to modulate desired intensity and intimacy, and can promote time for recovery if an infraction has occurred. Participants overwhelmingly endorsed the view that technological tools such as e-mail and the Internet have become critical in understanding the communication styles of emerging and young adults, particularly with respect to the way they negotiate their personal lives.

Friendships

The majority of the participants considered friendships key to living a balanced, meaningful, and enriching life. Friendship provided stability and support in a highly fluid and mobile work context. Alexis, a high-powered investment banker, speaks of the significance of friendships in her life:

I think friendships take the place of relationships. You have a network of friends that is more like a family. A network you lean on. People have networks of friends in [different] cities. I think it is a replacement to the extent you don't choose a more traditional path, getting married and moving along that trajectory. It is an alternative, more blurred boundaries, maybe a focus on a delayed adolescence. Your friends are more important.

Colette, Frank, Sergio, and Christie, all in their mid to late 20s and unmarried, echo the importance of friendships in their lives:

Colette: Friends are very very important …. Friends and relationships are one and the same. You inherit a group of people you will see at least once a week …. Going back to the mid '90s, it is all about friends.

Frank: I definitely lean on my friends a lot. I talk to my friends from college almost every day. We always talk about what gets on our nerves. He lives in Los Angeles. Different friends offer different things. I may be relying on them too much.

Sergio: Maybe adults [referring to his parents' generation] have a harder time trusting their friends. People in their 20s and 30s trust their friends. It has to do probably with what they have gone through in their life. Adults have gone through tougher times. Living in a more peaceful time you can have the freedom to trust your friends. It has to do with your experiences.

Christie: I feel very very close to a lot of my friends. I have great friends. They know everything about me. [It is] very important to me. I'm not sure my parents have that. They have each other. I just have me. I don't know how intimate they are with their friends. It seems that the level of relationship is different with my friends. My parents are into perceptions. They care about what other people think. I know my friends are going to love me no matter what. We share everything with our friends. They are my friends. They will not judge me.

Colette, twenty-six years old, alludes to television programs such as *Friends* and *Sex and the City*, which resonate with her day-to-day life experiences. According to Colette, friendships provide the sustenance needed to navigate one's emotional and professional life:

It is all about your friends. Even if you have boyfriends, you go out in groups. Are we mimicking the show *Friends*? It is like group dating. For me, going out with all of my friends is more fun. When you go out, it is like a party. Let the good times roll when you go out with your friends. When you go out one-on-one, it is less fun and more serious. [There is] less pressure to be funny and brilliant in groups. You do not have to monopolize the conversation, the more the merrier. Going out one-on-one can be kind of boring, unless you are in the first stage of a relationship when you think he is wonderful, and then you get past that at two or three months. And then you want to be with all of your friends.

In speaking about co-ed friendships, Paul speaks to the flexibility, diversity, and variability in his friendships:

I do not want to be dependent or commit to one person. A number of guys I know don't want to commit. It is a lot easier to have friends. It may have to do with immaturity and not knowing what they want in their lives.

A minority position expressed by a participant suggests that friendships interfere with commitment to a life partner: "I think it makes things difficult, it keeps people from committing and settling down until later in life."

Several of the married men and women expressed regret with respect to not having the time to cultivate their friendships. However, the men did comment on their ability to readily re-engage with their friends. Frank, an employer of emerging and young adults, also in his 30s, and married, focused on gender differences and friendships:

From my own experience and from my male friends, the men tend not to stay in contact as much. They will visit with friends every so often, and no one is upset about this period of time where there has been this lack of communication. I can pick up with my male friends exactly where I left off. Can be once a year or even longer than that, once every several years.

In my experience the reason the relationship has gone off into the ether is either distance, people not living local anymore, or preoccupation with something else. What resparks the communication is usually some common interest that occurs. One of my friends likes wine. I think of the Boston wine expo, call him, hey we should get together. Or you get together, if you are visiting the town they are in. Women are generally in contact more frequently, and if they are not in contact, it is much harder to establish a relationship that has been broken off.

Karo (2005), a comedian and writer, echoes the ease in which males engage and re-engage with one another:

Twentysomething males often refer to their guy friends as "my boys." … I started with a group of friends in elementary school, gained a few in high school, added several recruits during college, and all those guys remain my boys to this day. Moving to Los Angeles last year was difficult, but whenever I get a text message from one of my boys back East … I feel like I never left. All my boys have an understanding that they will endure vicious but good-natured verbal abuse from one another …. Guys bond by making fun of each other. As twisted as it seems, I think that constantly demolishing each other's self-esteem ensures that no one ever gets too big a head …. My boys in 1996 are my boys in 2006 and will be my boys in 2016. And that really does make my soul feel good.

Watters (2006) extends Karo's depictions to females and likens friendships in one's 20s and 30s to belonging to a tribe. Tribes are guided by unspoken roles and hierarchies, and tribal members think of themselves as "us," and the rest of the world as "them" (p. 87). The tribe is bonded together, much like a family, and is self-protective, particularly during times of duress. Members of the "tribe" hold each other responsible for their actions: "Tribal behavior does not prove a loss of 'family values.' It is a fresh expression of them" (Watters, 2006, p. 88).

Watters argues that although tribe membership may delay marriage, it may also enhance the institution of marriage in that it may assist emerging and young adults in understanding what they need in a mate. He concludes:

What a fantastic twist—we "never marrieds" may end up revitalizing the very institution we've supposedly been undermining…. Those of us who find it hard to leave our tribes will not choose marriage blithely, as if it is the inevitable next step in our lives, the way middle-class high-school kids choose college. When we go to the altar, we will be sacrificing something precious. In that sacrifice, we may begin to learn to treat our marriages with the reverence they need to survive. (pp. 88–89)

A minority of the men and women, married and/or with children, tended to express regret related to not having sufficient opportunity to see their friends. The demands of a family as well as a career interfered with their ability to remain connected, although e-mail provided them with an invaluable tool.

For a minority of the participants, friendships were sacrificed due to very heavy work demands. Chris, a married 32-year-old engineer, laments the fact that he does not have the time to pursue relationships in general, including friendships: "[There is] less commitment to relationships. We're so driven by getting ahead that we sacrifice personal relationships."

Daniel, a 31-year-old married computer consultant, attributes his nonsocial existence to the fact that he has relocated with his wife to Seattle, and spends most of his workday on the phone, troubleshooting with customers on issues related to technology:

At the moment, I work from home. I have few social connections. It does not upset me. It is just a way of being for the moment. It is a byproduct of my professional arrangement for the moment. There are plenty of things I can do. Like Friendster, log up with people of similar interests. [I] have not felt compelled to do that. That is not to say that at some point I might.

Amanda laments the fact that she does not have time to nurture her friendships. She wishes she could carve out time to have a moment for herself and her friends. Her friendships are suffering due to overwhelming responsibilities at home and at work:

It's really hard. I don't have much of a personal life. I have so many responsibilities. Sometimes I feel like I don't have a life; like getting together with girlfriends, I just don't do it. There is not enough time. The way I feel right now, I feel like I am really missing out on life. I am working so much, trying to make ends meet for my family. And I don't have any time to do anything else. I'm up very early in the morning and I go to bed late at night. The majority of the time I don't take any time for myself. Maybe I could paint my own nails or something.

Overall, participants in both cohorts tended to view friendships as an important source of sustenance and support, a finding that is reinforced in the literature (Oswald & Clark, 2003). Linda, a 26-year-old fine arts student, and Martha, a 28-year-old nursery school teacher and part-time physical trainer and waitress, speak to the importance of friendships, focusing on the significance of the current environmental context with respect to informing their friendships.

Linda: In the previous generation, people were creating family units a little younger. In our generation, we are trying to create families outside of our families. You don't really have the stability of that kind of unconditional support. You want that closeness. Everybody wants to have people that love them no matter what, reserving judgment. We try to do that for each other, me and my friends. [We are living in] unstable environments. No one I know lives in the same town that they grew up in. Many people don't live even in the same state. I think friends want to help each other and take care of each other. They sometimes cross the line in telling you what to do.

Martha: In my family, there is the Catholic guilt. You always look out for your family and your friends even if you don't like them. For the younger people, we have such open communication. [Via] the Internet, we have such a large group of friends. I feel we can be pickier. Kids today don't have a lot of time. I can't be spending time with someone I don't like.

We did not have time. We were conditioned not to have as much time, whereas they (referring to her parents' generation) played with every Dick, Tom, and Harry in the neighborhood. Because our parents drove us to practice, I did not know my friends till I met them. When my parents were kids, they played with kids in the same neighborhood .... [My experiences] taught me to reach out and build a wider net of friends on my own, and my parents made friends with the neighborhood kids. And that adds to the guilt factor. I knew your parents when I was young; that means you have to hang out with them. If I go to school and make friends on my own, I am more self-actualized in terms of what traits I want in a friend. My mother did not have that choice. She has to have friends from a neighborhood. You get told to have friends, as opposed to finding out what you like in a friend.

Participants tended to report increasing differentiation with respect to selection of friends over time, a finding consistent with the literature (Collins & van Dulmen, 2006). Adena, a 28-year-old educator, states:

I think I am looking for longer-term friends these days compared to when I was younger. I seem to get along with people who have similar interests. Before I used to talk to everyone; now I tend to be selective about friendships. Before, I did not know who I wanted to hang out with.

It is important to note that with age, "Affiliations with friends, romantic partners, siblings, and parents unfold along varied and somewhat discrete trajectories for most of the second decade of life, then coalesce during the early twenties into an integrated interpersonal structure" (Collins & Laursen, 2000, p. 59).

Overall, friendships tended to be organized around similar interests and values and an appreciation of the other. Some of the participants reported a greater degree of openness and trust in their relationships with friends when compared to their parents' generation. In addition, participants observed that friendships continued due to a common purpose. Over time, an increasingly important component that was identified by the participants included reciprocal support. As Daniel describes below, each individual in the friendship could count on the other for emotional and tangible support:

Friendship starts with things in common. They develop from general attraction of personalities, similar to love. I don't know if that has really changed. Friendships formed differently may not be friends. They may be mutually beneficial arrangements, business relationships, but friendship is based on people liking each other.

Too Many Expectations—A Female Concern

Too many expectations, too many things we want, so nothing is ever perfect, nothing is ever good enough.

(Colette, 31-year-old participant)

Female participants were prone to feelings of inadequacy and vulnerability, independent of their objective accomplishments. Many in their late 20s and early 30s reassessed long-held assumptions and aspirations for their professional and interpersonal lives. The process entailed acknowledging limitations, and wrestling with prior cherished beliefs that included limitless possibilities. There was recognition by many that the goal of "having it all" was illusory, and for many participants in the affluent cohort, it became evident that they were not likely to sustain a lifestyle they experienced as children.

Participants encountered an inflexible job market that was not responsive to their expressed need for balance. A sense of limits, within a context of limitless possibilities, defined them (Warner, 2005, pp. 198–199). They worked hard, tried to live up to the expectation of limitless promise, and felt discouraged by barriers encountered. Embedded within a historical context, Macko and Rubin (2004) capture the angst and frustration of many of the female participants:

Thanks to the efforts of Friedan and her contemporaries, women of our age are now facing a radically different set of collective questions and concerns. Ironically, part of our generation's new and ambiguous but omnipresent dilemma stems from a shared sense of inadequacy for failing to live up to the dreams and expectations those inspiring women defined.

Bestowed upon us [was] the belief that anything was possible in our futures. But when rapid-fire decisions about marriage, children, and career converge on the compressed timetable at or around 30, otherwise calm and competent women find themselves at the precipice of panic. Even those with the most impressive life resumes feel that they are failing to live up to the Anything is Possible opportunity for achievement and the work/life symmetry implied by that promise. (p. 14)

Christine captures the collective angst related to unrealized dreams, based in part on the mandate, "I can do-anything-and-be-anything" (Warner, 2005):

We need to learn to be more sure of ourselves and who we are. Women, we have this vision. We have to reconcile that we did not get the guy of our dreams, the job of our dreams. And we do not know how to reconcile it, and still feel good about ourselves. (p. 121)

Rachel, a 32-year-old single woman, expresses angst related to unmet expectations and "having it all," questioning the goal, as well as herself, "We still try to model ourselves. At this age we expect the house, the kids, the fence, and we're all confused about why and when it is supposed to happen."

Jill reviews the choices she has made related to her professional and personal life. She has a successful career in publishing that she enjoys. Her personal life, although rich, does not include a significant other. She describes herself as working hard and playing hard, and generally content with the way her life is unfolding. However, at the same time, she expresses a strong wish to be a mother in her 30s, and although she is very "ambitious," she would consider herself a "failure," if she were not a mother within the context of a loving marital relationship:

You see I am conflicted, my whole existence conflicts with some of the values I grew up with. I am hopeful I will have a lot of relationships and a lot of fun. I feel like people are instantly self-gratifying themselves. Divorce is so high. I am an ambitious person. I don't think I will be fully satisfied with the status quo, nor will I be complacent. I always look for opportunities for self-improvement. My goal absolutely in ten years is to start a family. I would consider myself a failure if I had not done that.

Most of the female participants aspired to having a professional and personal life that did not include "settling" in either domain. They expressed a desire to be the best, and they frequently found themselves in environmental contexts that reinforced the pursuit of excellence and perfection. They were not willing to enter marriage for marriage's sake, nor were they willing to consider compromising their values and standards with respect to the maternal role. Jones (2006, p. 23) captures the dilemmas of the participants with respect to marriage:

I realized that all the things I expected marriage to confer—male companionship, close family ties, a house—I already had, or were within reach, and with exponentially less drama. I can do bad by myself, I used to say as I exited a relationship. But the truth is, I can do pretty good by myself.

Susan mirrors the sentiments of Jones (2006):

People are more idealistic about who they will marry. It is not good enough [just to get married]. It has to be someone better than a single lifestyle, which is not so bad. People look at marriage as not better than nothing; it has to be better than a single life which is pretty good.

Jones (2006) notes that the "structure of white families is evolving in the direction of black families of the 1960's" (p. 23). In 1960, 67% of black families were headed by a husband and wife, in comparison to 90.9% for whites, however, a shift was reported in 2000, indicating that 79.8% of white families were headed by a husband and wife. Births to unwed white mothers shifted significantly as well: 22.5% in 2001, versus 2.3% in 1960. Although traditional ideas regarding marriage and children prevail, women are "less likely to settle for marriage to a man who doesn't bring much to the table" (p. 23). Female participants spoke of the difficulties inherent in juggling their multiple roles and responsibilities: wife, friend, mother, and daughter. Those who held perfectionistic strivings in every arena of their life were particularly vulnerable. Some "opted out" of one of their multiple roles and responsibilities, Wendy, Daria, Jennifer, and Christie speak to the difficulties encountered:

Wendy: Pressure, we are imposing it on ourselves. We studied, we got our degrees, and we are wasting it. Finding that balance is really hard. You are going to get a critic from both sides .... Women have come so far. On the flip side, women have gone too far. We want it all, and the pressure of wanting both the successful professional life and family life is great. I do think we are struggling with how to get that balance.

Daria: When I started working for my boss, I worked late, I worked on weekends. There are a lot of people they can hire. They would rather have someone who can give everything. They cannot get enough out of you.... I went to a good school. I am still at a point that is not totally satisfying, and I will probably leave next month and it is frustrating. I am thinking I will focus on my son for one to two years, and not go back to financial services. And I will be at a place where I am building something from nothing.... I think it sucks.

Jennifer: With men, we are taught to be beautiful, nice, accommodating, and it is hard to be all these things, and find our way .... Women above all, before all other goals, need to please people.

Christie: A lot of people in my generation are doing too much; they think they can do it all but they can't do it all at the same time. Women especially are doing a lot. Raising a family, trying to be the best girlfriend, mother, wife. Trying to do it all and I don't think it is possible, all at the same time.

Hewlett, Luce, Shiller, and Southwell (2005) note, "opting out" of the role of working woman is an option for only a few, given that only relatively privileged women can afford to quit their careers. Some of the female participants chose to delay the decision to have children. Others chose to be single for the time being, and focus on their careers and friends, and a minority of the women interviewed entertained the possibility of single parenthood.

The costs for "opting out" professionally, albeit for a limited period of time, are considerable. A report by Hewlett et al. (2005) entitled *The Hidden Brain Drain: Women and Minorities as Unrealized Assets*, provides insights with respect to understanding the alarming exodus of highly qualified professionals (those with a graduate degree, a professional degree, or a high-honors undergraduate degree). A total of 2443 women (older women aged 41 to 55, and younger women aged 28 to 40), and a much smaller comparison group of 653 highly qualified men were surveyed.

Results revealed that professional women are currently twice as likely to leave their respective companies, in comparison to men. Nearly four in ten women opted to take time off from work (43% for those with children), in contrast to 24% of highly qualified men. Reasons given for opting out were different for males and females. Whereas the top five reasons cited by women included: (1) family time (44%), (2) earn a degree/other training (23%), (3) work not enjoyable/satisfying (17%), (4) moved away (17%), and (5) change careers (16%), the top five reasons cited for men included (1) change careers (29%), (2) earn a degree/other training (25%), (3) work not enjoyable/satisfying (24%), (4) not interested in field (18%), and (5) family time (12%). Interestingly, results showed that the 93% of the women currently "off-ramp" wanted to return to the workforce. Although nearly half of the women (46%) cited a desire to have "their own independent source of income" as a reason for their desire to re-enter, 43% cited a desire to reconnect with what they perceived as satisfying careers that offered them "deep pleasure" (p. 45). Twenty-four percent of the women reported that they were motivated by "a desire to give something back to society," and were seeking jobs that allowed them to "contribute to their communities in some way" (pp. 45–46).

Hewlett et al. (2005) concluded that "once a woman has taken one [off-ramp route], on-ramps are few and far between—and extremely costly" (p. 46). Women lost an average of 18% of their earning power when they took an off-ramp route. It is important to note that these women had been off-ramp for an average of 2.2 years. Only 74% of the off-ramped women were able to become employed, and among those women, only 40% returned to full-time professional jobs. Twenty-four percent assumed part-time jobs and 9% became self-employed. The percent reduction in salary upon return was 11% for those out less than one year, and 37% for those out three years or more. Lester Thurow, (as cited by Hewlett et al., p. 46) an MIT economist concludes:

These are the prime years for establishing a successful career. These are the years when hard work has the maximum payoff. They are also the prime years for launching a family. Women who leave the job market during those years may find that they never catch up.

According to Hewlett et al. (2005), the solution to addressing the retention problem and the resulting brain drain in corporate America is not to treat women as "men in skirts" (p. 50). Rather, it is to create pathways, via changed policies, practices, and attitudes, that permit women to re-enter the workforce without being marginalized. Specific solutions include creating reduced-hour jobs and flexible work arrangements that include opportunities to telecommute during the entire "arc" of one's career (p. 52). One such example is currently being adopted by Booz Allen, a program known as a "ramp up, ramp down flexible program." The program "unbundles standard consulting projects and identify[ies] chunks that can be done by telecommuting or shorts stints in the office" (p. 52). By providing the much-needed flexibility that women and minorities are seeking, the current brain drain problem can be averted and/or significantly minimized.

A minority of the women interviewed chose to "opt out," and become full-time mothers. Jennifer, influenced by a fractured relationship with her own mother, takes pride in her maternal role. She observes the prevalent restlessness and dissatisfaction among mothers she meets on the playground who have also "opted out:"

Everybody seems to be looking for something else. They like staying home, but they feel there should be something more. I have a very interesting breakdown of duties in this household. I am not a housewife. I am a stay-at-home mother. He comes home and cleans up after dinner. The other mothers I talk to believe they should be doing that [cleaning up after dinner}. There is no joy in all these things. They think there must be more, so they are looking for a job. I don't feel like that. I just feel like what I do at home is the best of what a stay-at-home mother does …. I wish I could have a conversation with someone who could stimulate me. What I see, are mothers not getting support from their spouses. They may not be asking for it because sometimes they think they don't deserve it.

Married female participants as well as single-parent participants expressed angst and concern related to their multiple roles and commitments. Most of the participants viewed working as the only option they had, and were actively trying to meet the needs of their families as well as the needs of their work settings, trying to do their personal best in both domains. As Amanda, a participant in the study articulates, the need to spend time with themselves and with their friends was compromised, with an accompanying sense of regret and sadness: "I would definitely spend more time with my friends. Carve out time to do maintenance things for myself to have a moment. Where I am not changing someone, doing dishes, maybe I could paint my own nails or something."

Philanthropy and the Need to Make the World a Better Place

A commitment to philanthropy was evident in a significant minority of the participants. Despite lives that included demanding jobs, commitment to friends, significant others, and/or family, a significant minority of the participants chose to engage in philanthropic volunteer activities. "Giving back to the community" was incorporated by the participants and appeared to be an internalized mandate. For many who were not engaged in altruistic activities, there was an acknowledgment, and for some, guilt, that they were not "giving back to their community." They tended to view their generation as "philanthropic," although those who strongly identified with the need to give back to their communities, commented that they wished that more of their peers would do so. Rachel, a married 27-year-old woman with a demanding career, speaks to the importance of "giving back," and the personal fulfillment she receives: "I enjoy my life, the things that I do. I really enjoy the volunteer work. I enjoy the people who do the work with me." She then proceeds to list three activities she engages in that are substantive in terms of the mission and scope of her responsibilities, all in the capacity of a volunteer.

Claire, currently working as a press secretary, and previously working as an administrator in mental health, states:

The most difficult thing for me was leaving the mental health field. There was guilt .... It is almost a sellout. With what I do, I still look at it as helping people. I spend a lot of time with my grandmother at a nursing home; I still have a philanthropic personality. I plan on lobbying for adolescents in need of mental health services at some time in the future.

Raymond, a 27-year-old single male, laments that some of his friends do not appear to share the same philanthropic values he upholds:

I am always disappointed in how much my peers don't put themselves out there. I put myself out there. I do a lot of things for a lot of people. I honestly think that this is healthy. [Maybe] this is a time they need to focus on themselves, and maybe later they can focus on other people when they are financially in a better place.

Dean and Jeff both feel ambivalent about their peers who are not engaging in philanthropic work:

Dean: I try to do things that are socially rewarding, I am tutoring to help inner-city kids to get into college. I have consistently done that, makes you feel good. I am one of the few people who does these things. Everyone I know is out for themselves and I am guilty as well. You've got to do what is best for you. We don't know where we are going. How can you get at these answers without thinking about yourself.

Jeff: Well I guess I've chosen a very specific task, the Wall Street corporate thing. Caretakers of the earth, giving back to the community, we are probably the least contributors to the community [referring to his Wall Street community]. There are truly amazing people who are doing wonderful and amazing things for others. Working in the Peace Corps. I don't do anything that helps anyone. For every jerk like me, there are other people who do make the world a better place. There are a lot of people who are committed to improving the world we are living in, and they have a lot of great ideas.

Amanda uses her job as a venue for contributing to the world, hoping to have impact on others and contributing to their betterment:

I feel like I am at the tail end of my crisis (referring to her emerging adulthood crisis), figuring out what I want my legacy to be…. I am here for a purpose and I want to do something significant with my life. What did I contribute? For me, that quarter life crisis started with my trying to figure that out. Thinking about my mom, my mom passed away. I mirror what my mom did. People talk to me about my mom. She was a daycare person. Everyone who knew her loved her. They have such nice things to say about her. Working with teenage girls who are pregnant, that is what I have committed my days to, wanting to have an impact on someone's life.

Jill, born into wealth, provides tutoring and pro bono tennis lessons and states:

When you are wealthier, you have more choices, more choices, more expectations, more pressures. Having grown up in an upper-class environment … If I don't do something great, I will be a failure because I have been given every opportunity. My parents are philanthropic. It is the values I grew up with. If I don't do it, who will? A lot of my friends are struggling to pay the groceries. Worrying about paying for grocery bills, that puts everything in perspective.

A significant minority of the participants in both cohorts demonstrated a desire, if not a commitment, to helping those in need, a finding that is inconsistent with the literature on emerging and young adults (Draut, 2005). They spontaneously talked of a need to give something back to their respective communities. Draut (2005) provides statistics that suggests high school and college-age individuals are engaging in a greater degree of volunteering activity, when compared to their elders. However, their volunteer behavior does not persist over time. Although 40% of high school and college-age individuals reported that they had volunteered within the last year, a statistic that is double that of a decade ago, a closer analysis reveals that context is critical in understanding volunteer and philanthropic behavior. Students in high school and college are "incentivized" to participate in organized civic activities, in part motivated by the need to strengthen their resumes (p. 203). One-third of high schools in the United States require students to do community service to meet graduation requirements. The rate of volunteer activity drops significantly once individuals are no longer in high school or college. Draut suggests that volunteerism is not viewed as a "way to address social or political problems" (p. 204). Despite a "flurry of volunteer behavior, these altruistic behaviors lack 'staying power'" (p. 205). Based on the responses of the participants, a significant minority do indicate a commitment to continued philanthropic activity, despite demanding schedules and competing interests.

Conclusions

Participants spoke eloquently, providing a window to their rich and textured social lives. Common threads emerged attesting to the complexity of their interpersonal worlds. The majority of the participants followed a pathway that included "identity-before-intimacy," having a career in place before launching a formal committed relationship. Participants tended to value experimentation and diversity in their relationships, and were hesitant to rush into what they viewed as premature marital commitments. Committing to marriage without prior experimentation could be "risky," and experimentation was associated with mitigation of risk. Participants attached significance to having satisfying careers in place and being "complete." They tended to view investment in a self that was differentiated as increasing the likelihood of a successful marriage and/or long-term commitment.

Participants overwhelmingly expressed traditional goals regarding marriage and children. A preponderance of the participants expected that their spouse or partner would work and assume joint responsibilities for their child(ren). However, there was diversity with respect to the timing of marriage. Among the minority participants who chose to formally commit to one another by age 25, one or both of the partners tended to be focused and launched in their career path(s). The age range of 30 to 35 seemed to be an important developmental marker, albeit a flexible one, a yardstick for determining whether participants were launched personally and professionally. For women, the biological clock and the choice to have children influenced their assessments.

Participants spoke to the issue of technology and its impact on their relationships in interesting and at times contradictory ways. Technology provided emerging and young adults the ability to sustain relationships in a global world. Access to technology enhanced their ability to regulate affect in relationships, slowing relationships down or amplifying the intensity of their relationships. The use of e-mail and the Internet has had a profound influence on the way they negotiate their personal lives. The following chapter addresses the issue of choice in the lives of emerging and young adults.

References

Collins, W. & Laursen, B. (2000). Adolescent relationships: The art of the fugue. In C. Hendrick & S. Hendrick (Eds.), *Close relationships: A sourcebook* (pp. 59–70). Thousand Oaks, CA: Sage.

Collins, W. & van Dulmen, M. (2006). Friendships and romance in emerging adulthood. In J. Arnett & L. Tanner (Eds.), *Emerging adults in America: Coming of age in the 21st century* (pp. 219–234). Washington, DC: American Psychological Association.

Coontz, S. (2005). *Marriage, a history: From obedience to intimacy, or how love conquered marriage*, New York: Viking Adult.

Cote, J. (2006). Emerging adulthood as an institutionalized moratorium: Risks and benefits to identity formation. In J. Arnett & L. Tanner (Eds.), *Emerging adults in America: Coming of age in the 21st century* (pp. 85–116). Washington, DC: American Psychological Association.

Draut, T. (2005). *Strapped: Why America's 20- and 30-somethings can't get ahead*. New York: Doubleday.

Dyk, P. & Adams, G. (1990). Identity and intimacy: An initial investigation of three theoretical models using cross-lag panel correlations. *Journal of Youth and Adolescence*, 19, 91–111.

Hewlett S., Luce, C., Shiller, P., & Southwell, S. (2005). *The hidden brain drain: Off-ramps and on-ramps in women's careers*. Cambridge, MA: Harvard Publishing.

Jones, J. (2006, March 26). Marriage is for white people. *The Washington Post*, Outlook; B01.

Karo, A. (2005, January 31).Ruminations [Weblog entry.] *Monkey Business*. (http://www.aaronkaro.com/issue.php?id=36). Retrieved May 3, 2006.

Macko, L. & Rubin, K. (2004). *Midlife crisis at 30: How the stakes have changed for a new generation—And what to do about it.* New York: Plume.

Oswald, D. & Clark, E. (2003). Best friends forever? High school best friendships and the transition to college. *Personal Relationships, 10*, 187–196.

Sheehy, G. (1995). *New passages: Mapping your life across time*. New York: Ballantine.

Straus, J. (2006). *Unhooked generation*. New York: Hyperion.

Twenge, J. (2006). *Generation me: Why today's young Americans are more confident, assertive, entitled—And more miserable than ever before*. New York: Free Press.

Warner, J. (2005). *Perfect madness : Motherhood in the age of anxiety*. New York: Penguin.

Watters, E. (2006). In my tribe. In C. Amini & R. Hutton (Eds.), *Before the mortgage: Real stories of brazen loves, broken leases, and the perplexing pursuit of* adulthood (pp. 86–89). New York: Simon Spotlight.

6
The "Tyranny" of Choice: A Re-Examination of the Prevailing Narrative

We are living in a time of choice (for some emerging and young adults more so than for others). Unprecedented affluence, in the context of an array of advances in technology, has resulted in an expansion of choice selection (Arnett, 2004, 2006; Sheena & Lepper, 2000). For example, our TV viewing patterns reinforce the possibility of limitless "on demand" choices. The supermarket experience, replete with choice, is stimulating at best, and at worst, leaves the consumer questioning his or her judgment and capacity to select the "best" for the lowest possible cost. The current college experience barrages individuals with abundance of course selections and offerings:

> Today, the modern institution of higher learning offers a wide array of different "goods" and allows, even encourages, students—the "customers"—to shop around until they find what they like. Individual customers are free to "purchase" whatever bundles of knowledge they want, and the university provides whatever its customers demand . . . . They [students] go to a class, stay ten minutes to see what the professor is like, then walk out, often in the middle of the professor's sentence, to try another class. Students come and go in and out of classes just as browsers go in and out of stores in a mall. "You've got ten minutes," the students seem to be saying, "to show me what you've got. So give it your best shot." (Schwartz, 2004, p. 16)

Although choice emerged as an important theme, the experience of choice for the participants representing the two cohorts appeared to be qualitatively different. In keeping with the stated goal of a careful and systematic analysis, one that incorporates and integrates the full range of diversity of experiences of emerging and young adults, this chapter addresses the rich and textured experiences related to choice. The literature related to choice in a context of abundance is reviewed, followed by a discussion of choice and risk as experienced by the participants in the study. The lives of four emerging and young adults are presented to capture the diversity of experiences with respect to choice.

Choice: The Prevailing Narrative

The prevailing literature eloquently speaks to the paradox inherent in choice selection in a context of abundance. Schwartz (2004) questions many assumptions related to choice. He argues that the cumulative effect of abundance of choice causes "substantial distress," especially "when combined with regret, concern about status, adaptation, social comparison, and perhaps most important, the desire to have the best of everything—to maximize" (p. 221). According to Schwartz, individuals negotiate choice selection using a variety of approaches, including maximizing and satisficing. In maximizing, one seeks and chooses to accept only the best and seeks to verify that he has chosen the best possible option. "As a decision strategy, maximizing creates a daunting task, which becomes all the more daunting as the number of options increases" (p. 78). All options are researched thoroughly. Satisficers, in contrast, select an option that is good enough. One has standards, and stops the search when those standards have been met, in contrast to expending additional time and energy searching for the best possible option. Satisficers are not satisfied with mediocrity. "A satisficer may be just as discriminating as a maximizer. The difference between the two types is that the satisficer is content with the merely excellent as opposed to the absolute best" (p. 78).

One's approach to choice is domain-specific (Schwartz, 2004). Nobody is one or the other at all times (satisficer or maximizer). There is a dynamic interplay between maximizing and the social context of abundance. In an affluent society, characterized by an abundance of goods, individuals seek products that are inherently scarce. The more the competition for inherently scarce goods, the strategy of good enough is not good enough. Maximization is most likely to be utilized in times of abundance, which in turn may create undue pressure. For example, upon discovering the wide range of choices available when selecting a pair of jeans, given the availability of options, standards for buying jeans are "altered forever" (Schwartz, 2004, p. 9). In contrast, an individual who is unaware of the number of choices available, may enter a store, buy a pair of jeans within a short time framework, and fail to engage in the search for the best possible fitting jean.

According to Schwartz, in a context of abundance, choice increases the likelihood of making mistakes, increases the amount of effort that needs to be expended to make a decision, and makes the psychological consequences of mistakes more severe (p. 74). Given the range of options, an important distinction made by Schwartz is the notion of being a picker versus a chooser. A chooser thinks about the options available to her and then makes a selection. A chooser reflects on what is important to her vis-à-vis the decision to be made, what's important about the decision, and what the short- and long-term consequences are of the decision. In contrast, a picker makes selections based on what is available to her and hopes for the best.

Schwartz (p. 4) suggests that we subscribe to faulty assumptions regarding choice:

1. The more choices people have the better off they are.
2. The best way to get good results is to have very high standards.
3. It is always better to have a way to back out of a decision than not.

In response to "the dark side of choice," he presents the following counterintuitive prescriptions:

1. We would be better off if we embraced certain voluntary constraints on our freedom of choice, instead of rebelling against them.
2. We would be better off seeking what was "good enough" instead of seeking the best. (Have you ever heard a parent say, "I want only the 'good enough' for my kids"?)
3. We would be better off if we lowered our expectation(s?) about the results of decisions.
4. We would be better off if the decisions we made were nonreversible.
5. We would be better off if we paid less attention to what others around us were doing. (p. 4)

Although Schwartz (2004) does not specifically address the developmental period of emerging and young adulthood, he provides a framework for understanding choice and how it applies to this population (i.e., choosers versus pickers, maximizers versus satisficers). Many emerging and young adults may be picking rather than choosing, maximizing rather than satisficing, in a way that may be counterproductive in important domains of their lives. Hassler (2005) mirrors concerns related to choice raised by Schwartz (2004), speaking specifically to the pressures emerging adults face in their attempts to navigate a plethora of choices. Many emerging adults are burdened by the perceived need to make optimal choices in all domains of their lives, in a context of high expectations (Hassler, 2005):

One twenty-four-year-old says she feels tremendous pressure to make choices that will give her the best education available or affordable, the perfect job that pays four times more than it would've paid my mother, the perfect husband, the perfect house in the new and upcoming area and the perfect family, including the dog, while still maintaining [a] full-time perfect job and figure. (p. 67)

Schwartz offers a cartoon that appeared in the *New Yorker* in 2001, as a possible frame for navigating the terrain associated with emerging adulthood (p. 236). In a fishbowl, clearly contained by its natural boundaries, a parent fish offers advice to the child fish: "You can be anything you want to be—no limits" (p. 235). Schwartz suggests that

[L]iving in the constrained, protected world of the fishbowl enables this young fish to experiment, to explore, to create, to write its life story without worrying about starving or being eaten. Without the fishbowl, there truly would be no limits however; the fish would have to spend all its time struggling to stay alive. Choice within constraints, freedom within limits, is what enables the little fish to imagine a host of marvelous possibilities. (pp. 235–236)

Schwartz (2004) argues that in a context of abundance, creating fishbowls that are protected, which allow individuals the freedom to explore and experiment with choices within safe confined boundaries, may be a strategy that best serves individuals who are barraged with choice. It is important to note that the literature on choice and emerging and young adulthood is underdeveloped, and is relatively silent with respect to issues of diversity (Blustein, 2006; Cote, 2000; Flores & Ali, 2004).

Diverse Narratives: Analysis of Choice Responses

Participants in both cohorts recognized and affirmed freedom associated with choice. They tended to be united by common beliefs regarding the value of choice, especially as it pertained to freedom of choice. Choice was associated with autonomy and individuality. Participants tended to believe that individuals ought to be free to choose on their own terms. They also spoke of the challenges associated with negotiating a wide range of possibilities.

Many participants alluded to the downside of choice, the limitless possibilities that can be experienced as overwhelming and stress inducing. Alexis, when asked what she finds most difficult about living and negotiating these times, states, "I guess making choices. I am constantly questioning, and it is immobilizing in some ways." On the other hand, when asked what she finds most satisfying about living and negotiating these times, Alexis states, "The sense of possibility, the flip side."

Alexis captures the coexistence of immobilization with the freedom of possibility. Meg captures the complexity of negotiating choice in her life as well. She contrasts her experience of choice with the experience of her father trying to negotiate his 20s:

My father states how lucky we are to have options. When he was my age, it was not the case. It is hard not to agree that choices are wonderful, yet sometimes it seems that navigating through life would be easier if there were fewer choices. Or maybe a set of directions that explained what you had to do . . . so that you could attain your dream job, and ease the feeling of uncertainty. Unfortunately, this is not the case, and that is why we may appear to be floundering. Yet in reality, we are just testing the many options that are out there.

Susan, a 28-year-old participant, discusses the nature of choice in her work life as she experienced difficulty landing a job, despite her stellar credentials. She required financial and emotional support from her parents for approximately two years before securing employment in her field of studies. She states:

I have the space to do it [referring to spending the past two years pursuing a job in her chosen career] because my parents are supportive, helping me out. But I think because I have the option to do it, I am trying to do something I really want to do. A lot of friends, they want there to be a purpose behind their choices, versus the need to make money for the moment.

Although the prevailing narrative for the more affluent cohort included ambivalence related to overwhelming choice, for the less affluent cohort, a narrative related to risk and risk management emerged. The economic context informed choice selection and perceptions related to choice. Greg, a 30-year-old black single father of an 11-year old daughter, is trying to find his way as an entrepreneur. When asked how he would rewrite the story of his life to date, Greg states, "I guess I would have stepped outside of my comfort zone, maybe moving to a new location, being more open-minded about career choices and taking more risk . . . . I would have traveled the world, living abroad overseas."

When asked what advice he would give to someone about to embark on his or her career path, Greg speaks to the importance of taking risk:

I would tell them to take risks and understand that failure is part of the journey of becoming successful.... What is helpful is having enough choices. I think a lot of young people feel like they don't have a lot of choices. Maybe they don't believe there are enough choices to make the right decision.

Adam, growing up in a more affluent family context, echoes the importance of taking risks as articulated by Greg, yet his approach toward risk-taking is characterized by self-assurance, optimism, and a sense of opportunity. He provides the following advice to individuals about to embark on their career paths.

I would say to have reasonable expectations. Don't think you will have one job; there is no shame in changing careers. If you change course, you are not a failure. The bad experiences are where you learn a lot, and become who you are. You have to have some tolerance for risk, and not everyone does, and that is fine. Easy for me to say go ahead and take risks, it would be different if I did have a family.

If they are not risk takers and insecure, it [risk] paralyzes them. If you are not optimistic and feel that there is opportunity, if you don't feel that way, your work life will be more difficult. No one wants to hire someone who gives off negative vibes. I never feel like you have no options, not for college-educated people; how can you feel you have no options.

For some people it takes so much longer to figure out what is their place.... In the old days you did not question it as much. You would stay with an unhappy job. People want more from life. People's expectations are higher.... What I am trying to say, is that the idea got out, that there is a big world out there, a lot of fun things to do, interesting things to see. Goes against the idea of being satisfied with a great life, but a limited life. People know there is more out there, and they want to experience it.

Discussion related to the experience of choice was qualitatively different for many of the participants in the less affluent cohort. For some, there was a perception of scarcity of choice. Navigating within more limited degrees of freedom, that is, greater restrictions on one's ability to maneuver and take risks, seemed to be the more pressing concern for many of the participants in the less affluent cohort. The need for a safety net limited choice selection. Michael, an employer of emerging and young adults, eloquently captures the tensions related to choice and risk for those emerging and young adults who are struggling with lack of sufficient economic resources:

[With more limited economic resources] they have to be risk takers. If they don't take risks, they are more inclined to be locked in. [However] they have to think about safe risks.... They need to take risks, but it is risks that are calculated; they are not mindless risks.... The affluent person [going with one's gut] trying out options, can do so without negative consequences. He can simply go with his gut. No matter what happens and what he does, when he takes paths that involve risk, he will be safe.

Calculated risks, according to Michael, involve:

Making decisions that involve a careful analysis of the pros and cons, carefully weighing the pros and cons, and keeping an eye and focus on the prize. [Economic constraints impose a scenario where] the margin of error that is allowed is less. Kids in affluence have a much larger margin of error. Race and class influences people's choices, narrows their ability to take the risks they have to take. In order to be responsible, they cannot take risks as freely [in part] because of commitment to other people in their lives. I think it is helpful to be thoughtful about what the consequences of choices [that one makes] are. Having someone to talk to, people who will not ridicule you, will stand by you regardless, being willing to make use of confidantes, can help a lot with margin of error.

Frank, a young adult himself, currently a supervisor of other emerging and young adults, echoes the sentiments expressed by Michael, specifically the need for caution in navigating risk:

In this economic climate, individuals do not have the luxury, the freedom to take a chance and fail. It would be devastating and have repercussions throughout their 20s and 30s. For example, individuals who have recently graduated, trying to set up shop, if their credit is okay, the bank will extend them a loan. [However, they are at significant risk] if they overextend themselves, and if they don't have finances and the safety net of the family. This is where caution comes from. [Emerging adults need to be] more cautious about how they go about their business.

. . . It is so hard to maintain status quo these days, never mind getting ahead of the game. To have the ability to extend credit, and have to deal with the reality of extending cash, the risk is greater for those on their own. Once you fall behind, the system is set up in a way [that will increase the probability of failure]. It makes it so that you will stay behind, with finance charges and penalty costs. The system is setting people up for failure, and that is where the caution is coming from. The ability to fail is so apparent and so easy to trip into. This is particularly true for individuals who do not have that safety net financially from their family. Yet, one needs to be proactive, self-motivated, in this environment. Those are the people we hire, who take advantage of the system.

Both Frank and Michael speak to the difficulties emerging and young adults face in a context of limited financial resources. Although on the one hand, assuming risk is critical to the process of navigating the terrain of emerging and young adulthood, the consequences of experimentation and the ability to recuperate appear to be increasingly compromised in a context of scarcity. Errors made along the way can be far-reaching, especially with limited safety nets. Subsequent ability to engage in experimental risk-taking behavior, a process critical to this developmental stage and times, is stifled.

Apter (2001) and others conclude that emerging adults are negotiating a context of "decreasing social capital" (p. 267), a context that privileges those with safety nets:

Today young people need continuing support as they find their footholds in the adult world. As their futures appear before them more like a maze than a set of paths, they need others' focus and involvement. During this passage, young people are more or less forced to become navigators who negotiate opportunities and risks. Those who succeed in tolerating risks and change, and navigating this passage successfully are those who continue to have a parent's responsive care, attention and support. (pp. 261–262)

Emerging adults, according to Apter (p. 264):

Crave a supportive forum in which they can explore possible solutions to present impasses and paths to their futures . . . . Over and over, they expressed a wish for more personal guidelines and safety nets .... [T]hey crave acknowledgment of their hopes. This acknowledgment can be expressed by helping them develop plans to realize their hopes .... [They] benefit from parents' wisdom and experience in aligning their ambitions with their current choices .... Research repeatedly shows that young people who are able to see their ambitions through and recognize opportunities spend a significant amount of time with their parents discussing actions and strategies to help them reach their ambitions.

Being an adult, according to Apter, does not mean standing alone. Apter proposes that there needs to be a revision of our concept of "real adult" and what he or she does in the role of adult. According to Apter, the "real adult" knows how to be responsive, knows how to use his or her knowledge and practical skills to help others. "We help ... by setting a good example of how to behave toward another family member, how to show continuing care" (p. 265).

Many of the participants who were constrained by economic limitations and family obligations showed fierce resolve to overcome adversity. They were able to assume adult roles, and honor their commitments to others. However, at times their need to follow their dreams had to be deferred or reconsidered. For example, Denise, a 27-year-old participant, expressed a desire to pursue graduate school, but given financial and family responsibilities has chosen to defer resuming her education. The meaning of choice as it relates to emerging and young adults needs to be contextualized to include and integrate experiences related to a scarcity.

Sharon, Brad, Denise, and Greg each struggled with choice. Their narratives represent a diversity of experiences, and raise interesting questions related to the prevailing narrative with respect to choice. The remainder of the chapter focuses on the experiences of the emerging and young adult participants with choice, and specifically addresses the interplay between choice and available resources during the developmental period of emerging and young adulthood.

Sharon

Sharon, a 25-year-old single female, articulated a life plan, "a vision" she developed that includes the pursuit of three sequential careers: (1) account planning in advertising (a career she plans to pursue during for the next four to five years), (2) teaching elementary school age children (a career she plans to pursue in her 30s while perhaps raising children), and (3) developing and growing a small business (a career she plans to pursue in her 40s). Sharon encountered significant difficulties executing the first phase of her plan, due to what she perceives as a highly competitive, saturated marketplace. She engaged in a job search for two years, and has just recently procured employment in her field of study, advertising. She remains guardedly optimistic about her chosen career stating: "Hopefully I held out for something I want to do." In speaking about choices, Sharon reflects on her college experience and states the following.

We had a lot of choices, a lot of emphasis on it being okay if you did not know what you wanted to do. We were allowed to pick a lot of subjects and like all of them. We did not have to commit too much. We could take classes in acting, writing, philosophy, psychology, all over the place, and that was seen as a good thing. I think ultimately it is a good thing. But, you now have to pick something, and you are not prepared for it as well as you could be. There is so much possibility and choices.

Sharon shares her ambivalence regarding her career choice, speaking to the difficulty she has experienced entering the field, and the culture of the industry as she perceives it. Although she understands that company loyalty to employees is scarce, she also associates a dearth of loyalty with the creation of an environment that encourages one's personal best:

Clients are not particularly loyal to the industry [and that is reflected in the way employees are treated]. You become a commodity. They trade employees like they trade baseball cards. I think it makes it exciting. Every one is competing to be the best, and it creates very high standards, which makes it a challenge. All things being equal, it is nice to work in an industry that is constantly adapting, and tries to make it better. That said, that's why I only want to work in advertising for four or five years. And then I will be a teacher, and I will be able to breathe a little more.

At age 25, Sharon feels that she has been raised to believe that she is lucky to have choices in her life. Her parents have supported her quest for fulfillment, both financially and emotionally, providing a safety net that enabled her to endure her grueling search of two years for the current position she holds in advertising. Sharon feels ill-equipped to deal with the sheer number of choices available to her. She has selected three careers to pursue sequentially during her 20s, 30s, and 40s. Each is informed by Sharon's passions, selected in part to coalesce with a lifestyle choice that Sharon views as consistent with what she anticipates will be her needs at different developmental junctures. Sharon's view of work is an interesting one, a product of the times, and her experiences growing up in an affluent community. "Work is like a jigsaw puzzle that has boundaries. It is more a mosaic jigsaw puzzle, and you're basically the artist. You are the artist and you have to fit the pieces so it looks right to you."

The mosaic jigsaw that Sharon constructs requires patience, perseverance, and skill. Sharon views herself as the solo agent responsible for developing her career, an agent who will make the pieces fit in a way that is optimally pleasing to her. She laments the fact that she did not have sufficient experience with making choices during her childhood, choices that include experience with loss. Sharon, a maximizer in most domains in her life, states that she is barraged with choices on a daily basis, but feels ill-equipped to rule out possibilities.

Sharon describes a weekly family ritual of going to a candy store with her mother, a ritual she associates with fondness. Her wish for an excessive amount of candy routinely resulted in her mother selecting her weekly allotment of candy, in essence making the choice for her. The process of choice selection would reoccur the following week, with her mother assuming responsibility for narrowing and making the choice selections for Sharon. Looking back at the experience, Sharon would have much preferred to make the initial selection herself, creating oppor-tunities whereby she would need to deal with choice, including prioritizing and excluding possibilities. She states that the opportunity to do so would better position her to engage with the process of choice, feel more secure about her choices, and empower her to feel more self-assured in her pursuit of creating a mosaic jigsaw puzzle designed to meet her needs.

Sharon laments the lack of opportunity to practice and work through the skill of coming to terms with not being able to have it all, and having opportunity to prioritize and narrow her selections in a wide array of domains. It is interesting that she has a life plan, at this moment in time, which includes planning and prioritizing what she anticipates will be her developmental needs at future junctures in her life. With respect to her personal life, Sharon makes it clear that she would consider long-term commitment and marriage, but only under certain conditions, which include meeting the "right" person to share her life. She remains open to a range of possibilities in her personal life, including the option of having a child and not being married.

Brad

Although Sharon appears to have a life plan that includes three careers, and the possibility of a spouse as well as children in her life, Brad is encountering difficulties conceiving a life plan that is suited to his needs and interests. Brad is a 27-year-old male currently working within a university setting in the field of fundraising. He is struggling with what he perceives as an abundance of choice. He attended an Ivy League school in the northeast, graduated with distinction, and has been in his current work environment for the past four years. He is dissatisfied at work (rating his overall satisfaction 5.5 on a scale of 10). Although he has had a promotion and excellent overall performance evaluations, he feels stymied and stuck in his current position:

I know that my skills are underutilized. I graduated with honors and my job is pretty easy comparatively. I want to be helping society a little more. I don't know what that quite means yet, and I feel like I will have a greater sense of fulfillment . . . . This is not my calling, what I am doing now.

When asked how he would rewrite his story, he states, "I would have known in school what I want to be, follow the appropriate route, take classes I needed to take."

He laments his current predicament and wishes that he could take a path similar to many of his friends. His friends have gone on to secondary degrees, and although he knows he has the "capabilities," he does not know what it is that he "wants right now." He remarks, "Once I figure what I want to do, the drive [I have] will come to play. I just don't have my sights on it yet." In describing his current situation, Brad seems stuck:

I am still hoping lightning will hit in the middle of the night and it will come to me as an epiphany. But more realistically, I may have to put myself out there, and apply for different things and maybe that will help me figure out what I want to do.

...My life is like an open book, ahead of me the road is like a blank slate, nothing is written in concrete. I can still go anywhere right now.

Brad does not want to close off possibilities. He seems to take solace in the view that he has not closed any doors. He describes his personal life using the following metaphor, "Sort of like a safe harbor, everyday is safe; I am in a routine socially and every other way and I know what is going on. Stable quite stable."

He is afraid to take risks, choosing stability, a safe harbor, from which he sees a vista of limitless possibilities. The perception that he has not closed off any options or possibilities, seems to be consoling to Brad, and provides him with a sense of safety and consolation:

There are so many options, that it is stifling. I think life would be a lot easier if [I had a model whereby] my dad worked in the factory and I knew that I would work in the factory, and that was all to it.

He views himself at a disadvantage in comparison to many of his friends, who have a vision and are at various stages of implementation. People who "know the track they want to be on, can pursue it with gusto. People who know what they want are advantaged in the marketplace."

Barraged with possibilities, informed by his desire to make the world a better place, Brad describes himself as conflicted. On the one hand he uses denial to curb his potential "obsessive" inclinations, and worries about "what the future holds," but he is concerned that he is not taking sufficient action in terms of "figuring it out:"

It might be helpful [to deny less], because it would motivate me to change. Denial is easier. It is an easy way out. It is easier for right now. I don't know. Something will happen, and I will figure things out. But now is not the time; so because I can't figure things out, it is easier not to think about it. Taking the easy way out is taking a random job and making money. I don't feel like doing that. I feel like I can benefit society. I am a smart guy. I can get an MBA but I don't want to do that. I don't know what to do with all these options.... With all the opportunities open to us in terms of careers, it is hard to make a decision.

...When I was a teen I was very pressured, I did so many extra-curricular activities, here I am in a delayed state. As a teen, [I had the feeling], look what I can do; that is what I am trying to find, that kind of work ethic and motivation again. I even had it in college.

Maybe I felt I had to and maybe I am slacking more now. I would not like to think that. The road was clear in high school; it was very prescribed. Now it is not; there were people pressuring me. It was more cause and effect in high school. Once, people were telling me what to do and I did it; now it is up to me. I think I am still capable of that, [capturing that level of motivation and engagement].

I might be able to self-motivate more, instead of the need to be motivated by external factors. I did not learn the art of self-motivation; I need to do this. [The external road map] it is not there, or my motivation is too vague. I know I need more money. That does not translate how to get things done.

Brad states the following with respect to what he finds most difficult about living and negotiating these times:

Indecision. It is satisfying that there is a world of possibility out there, and I don't feel I have to settle. I have so many options. I can find something I love to do and that is exciting. However, it is also difficult to make a decision given all these options.

He is inspired by his peers pursuing careers that have "impact," where they can help society, not only locally but also globally. He expects to find a career that inspires him, one that is consistent and compatible with his intellectual capacities, evolves "from his heart," and that engages him. He states, "I have the luxury of not working to survive, I am hoping to work so that I can be fulfilled."

Although Brad hopes to commit to a career by the age of 30, it is not clear how Brad will navigate the choices available to him. Questions arise as to whether he is sufficiently experimenting with choice. Is Brad taking too much solace in the fact that he has not limited himself, that there are endless possibilities open to him, and that to date he has not closed off any options? Are there alternative strategies and action plans that would serve his needs to a greater extent? He has ruled out possibilities, that is, pursuing degrees in medicine, law, or business. However, is his need to view himself as having options and limitless opportunities within his grasp, also paradoxically immobilizing him?

Denise and Greg describe their experiences with choice somewhat differently, using a different frame to describe the process of being on their own. Whereas Brad and Sharon know that their parents would support them financially (and emotionally) should the need arise, Denise and Greg talked about responsibilities and constraints imposed upon them based on fiscal and emotional realities. Both Denise and Greg, single parents in their teens, wished for experiences that exposed them to a wider world, but at the same time expressed gratitude for being able to take care of themselves and their families, having learned invaluable life lessons along the way. Their evolving skillsets are a direct outgrowth of their valued experiences as parents and professionals in the workforce. The role of mentors was particularly salient for Denise and Greg.

Denise

Denise is a 27-year-old black woman, recently married, with two daughters, ages ten and one. She is currently working as a supervisor of parent trainers, providing workshops designed to assist parents in their roles as advocates for their children. Denise presents as an articulate, determined, and focused woman.

Denise recently completed her college degree, a degree that took her eight years to complete. She became pregnant at the age of 16, raised a daughter as a single mother, assuming multiple full-time jobs along the way, many in social service, to help support herself and her daughter. Denise is currently married with a second child. Although she is very responsible in all domains of her life, she regrets that she does not have the time for "much of a personal life." Her life is very "hectic," whereby she juggles her multiple responsibilities as a working woman, wife, and mother:

Sometimes I feel like I don't have a life. Getting together with girlfriends, I just don't do it; there is not enough time. The way I feel right now, I feel like I am really missing out on life. I am working so much trying to make ends meet for my family. And I don't have any time to do anything else. I'm up very early in the morning and I go to bed late at night. The majority of the time, I don't take any time for myself.

Denise brings a sense of purpose, curiosity, and determination to all domains of her life. She articulates a life plan that includes moving to the South with her family, and opening a business with her husband. This move is a calculated one, and includes possibilities for home ownership, as well as a less hurried and harried existence, and one that allows for greater time for friends and family.

Denise brings a maturity that belies her chronological age of 27. In fact, she states that she feels as though she is 40 years of age, due to her level of responsibility. Although she is in her 20s, she talks about her legacy:

Figure out what I want my legacy to be. I want to start early, figure out what I stand for. I am here for a purpose and I want to do something significant with my life. I want to contribute.

I want to have an impact on people's lives. I had three teachers who stuck by me, and if it were not for them, I don't think I would be where I am. I still maintain relationships with them today.

Denise is of the opinion that many emerging and young adults have not had sufficient experience being on their own, and make choices on their own:

My mom taught me how to take care of myself and my business. I might have been evicted. I don't think I would be as together [if it were not for my mom]. I don't think they [emerging and young adults] have had enough life experience to make them ready; they have had no experience being on their own, and all the responsibility that comes along with that.... What makes me happy is a sense of accomplishment, the personal gratification I get, that makes me feel good.... I have been able to secure a position that sustains my family. I have been able to compete in the world.

In reflecting on her career, Denise states that one should not feel comfortable with the status quo:

When you sort of get stuck, do not hinder yourself from seeing what is out there in the world. If the door is closed, I want to know what is behind it. I am curious.... I have always been curious, wanting to know about what is outside, what I see, what I know. I lived in Boston all my life. Just because this is all I have known, does not mean this is all I want to do.

Denise wants to create a life for herself and her family that is beyond her current experiences, one that includes greater possibility and choice. She includes home ownership and growing a business as possibilities she would like to pursue. She is also contemplating going to graduate school, once she has sufficient economic resources to do so.

Like many in her cohort, Denise laments that she has not had opportunity to travel, to see and experience a larger world, the ability to experience a "larger fishbowl." However, she states that with the advent of the Internet, "You can go anywhere you want all over the world."

Denise does not speak to the issue of abundance of choice. Although she is highly aware of a world of possibilities that may be available to her at some time in the future, she is focused on providing possibilities and abundance of choice to the next generation, her daughters. She communicates to her eldest daughter that "education is key. You can do whatever you want, whatever makes your boat float is what I want for you." Denise envisions a world of possibility and choice for her two daughters, fueled by passion and a sense of purpose. Currently she assesses that her responsibilities as a supervisor, wife, and mother preclude experimentation with choice; her energies are channeled toward doing her personal best in what she describes as an overly scheduled life that does not allow for spending time with friends, cultivating new relationships, and spending time in activities that focus on her needs exclusively.

Greg

Greg is a 30-year-old male, a middle child in a family of seven children. In the past, he has assumed responsibility for helping his mother, a single parent, emotionally and financially. Greg, himself a single parent, resides with his 11-year-old daughter. After working in education for four years, Greg is trying to develop his own business, selling food products on the Internet. He joined the air force when he completed high school, and took six years to complete his college degree. Referring to his college courses, he states:

I wish I knew back then what I know now . . . . I would have taken more risk. I would have traveled the world. I guess I would have stepped outside my comfort zone, maybe moving to a new location, being more open-minded about career choices and again taking more risk. Challenging myself more. You need to believe in yourself, challenge yourself, and expect more out of life.

Like Denise, Greg focused on wishing that he had allowed for more diverse experiences in his 20s, experiences that incorporated risk taking. He laments missed opportunities to travel, and wishes that he had challenged himself intellectually as well as emotionally.

Greg is challenging himself in his current career as an entrepreneur. He has sought the help of two mentors, one who provides him guidance in the spiritual realm, and one who provides him guidance in his career as an entrepreneur:

I have a couple of mentors. I have a spiritual mentor, a gentleman in my church. I go to him for advice in terms of everyday things; I deal with my mentor as a Christian: relationships, temptations, personal conflicts. Someone I look up to . . . . My second mentor is an entrepreneur. He gives me some advice about my business. He teaches me wealth strategy techniques For me, to have a mentor, somebody you look up to, who is successful, who is already where you want to be, is important. The true meaning of mentors came through when I got involved in e-commerce. I see now how important it is for me to have mentors. It makes sense to listen to people who already have been there, who are invested in you.

When asked to provide a metaphor for his worklife to date, Greg states:

A rat race. But I think a rat race with optimism. What I mean is that even though I realize I might be in a rat race, there are opportunities to get out of the rat race. I just have to make a plan and work my plan.

Greg strives toward balance in his personal life. He comments that individuals have lost perspective in their life. He is concerned that too much energy is going into work, at the expense of a future generation of children, as well as at the expense of relationships and family:

What is helpful is having enough choices. I think a lot of young people feel like they don't have a lot of choices. Maybe they don't believe there are enough choices to make the right decision.... What is helpful is if they have a strong support system, friends, teachers, mentors.

Conclusions

Choice emerged as an important theme for both cohorts, although the experience of choice appeared to be qualitatively different for the two groups. Although limiting the size of the fishbowl seemed to be an apt and insightful possibility for those emerging and young adults who struggled with abundance of choice, expanding the size of the fishbowl, within the confines of a safe harbor, seemed to more accurately characterize the experiences and wishes of the cohort of emerging and young adults who encountered a context characterized by limited economic resources. The prevailing narrative as it is represented in the literature appears to represent the diverse voices of those emerging and young adults who live in relative affluence. For those individuals with fewer economic resources and safety nets, a different narrative emerges, one related to risk and risk management. Participants in the less affluent cohort may prosper from an environment that exposes them to a wider range of possibilities, one that includes provision of a larger fishbowl in which to swim.

References

Apter, T. (2001). The *myth of maturity: What teenagers need from parents to become adults*. New York: Norton.

Arnett, J. (2004). *Emerging adulthood: The winding road from the late teens through the twenties*. New York: Oxford University Press.

Arnett, J. (2006). Emerging adulthood: Understanding the new way of coming of age. In J. Arnett and J. Tanner (Eds.), *Emerging adults in America: Coming of age in the 21st century* (pp. 3–19). Washington, DC: American Psychological Association.

Blustein, D. (2006). *The psychology of working*. Hillsdale, NJ: Lawrence Erlbaum.

Cote, J. (2000). *Arrested adulthood: The changing nature of maturity and identity—What does it mean to grow up?* New York: New York University Press.

Flores, L. and Ali, S. (2004). When will we start fertilizing the brown spots? An urgent call to vocational psychologists. *The Counselling Psychologist, 32,* 578–546.

Hassler, C. (2005). *20 something, 20 everything: A quarter life woman's guide to balance and direction.* Novato, CA: New World Library.

Schwartz, B. (2004). *The paradox of choice: Why more is less.* New York: Harper Collins.

Sheena, S. I., & Lepper, M. (2000). When choice is demotivating: Can one desire too much of a good thing? *Journal of Personality and Social Psychology, 79,* 995–1006.

7
Parental Voices: "Adjustment Reactions to Children's Adult Life"

I thought I child-proofed my house but they still get in.

(Author unknown)

A clinical case analysis of Ben appearing in the March/April 2005 edition of the *Psychotherapy Networker* provides a window to one of the many quandaries parents of emerging adults face as they attempt to adapt to a new set of realities. Ben, a recent college graduate, feels depressed and embarrassed about moving home. He is worried about being "a failure." He has held no job to date, has college loans to repay, and needs his parents to bail him out of credit-card debt. Ben and his parents are seeking family therapy to help with existing tensions at home.

David Waters, an invited consultant on the case, asks the following question in relation to what has transpired in the therapy. Are Ben's parents and his therapist Linda Gordon "coddling" him? Parents of individuals in their 20s, particularly those who are privileged economically, are facing questions such as the one raised by Waters on a day-to-day basis. Waters (2005) concludes that Ben's family, as well as his therapist, are indeed "coddling" him:

I believe that when kids return home . . . they need to hit a bit of a wall: the situation is different, the rules have changed, and we have to negotiate something substantially different than what we had. It needs to be palpably uncomfortable and strange for a while, lest everyone slip back into the old way of doing things. I often find myself engineering collisions with families in this situation to get to the underlying question of what the new rules need to be, and magnifying, not easing, the discomfort . . . . I'd have liked her [the therapist] to respond to the family . . . [and say] what the hell are you doing? (p. 76)

Underlying the discussion related to "coddling" raised by Waters (2005), is the concern that "coddling" reinforces irresponsibility, dependence, and that parents may be hampering growth of their "adult" children (advertently or inadvertently). Parents are frequently functioning without an anchor, inventing the wheel without historical precedent. Aquilino (2006) states:

Tensions and contradictions in the parent–emerging adult relationship result from the child's having adult status in many domains while still dependent on parents in some ways.... [M]ost still need some measure of parental support to thrive, which thus creates a contradiction between society's granting of (legal) adult status and autonomy while economic realities often necessitate a lingering dependency on parents. (p. 195)

Clara, a parent participant of a 27-year-old daughter, raises a related issue concerning financial support. Although she perceives her daughter as responsible, she is "conflicted" about financially supporting her daughter's "life experiences:"

I am very conflicted. I don't want her to be spoiled, but I don't want her to miss out on life experiences. My parents would have said, "Now is the time to earn money and save for your future. You have the rest of your life to have those experiences." Do you say, "Sure, go to Switzerland, go to London? You will worry about the house and the down payment later?"

How do parents navigate in a way that reinforces autonomy, minimizes alienation, and does not compromise the possibility for mutually satisfying relationships between parents and their "adult" children? Experience and collective wisdom is sorely lacking given the environmental terrain their adult children are navigating. Ways of parenting that have worked in the past do not seem to apply. "Radical changes in the economy" have changed the dynamics (Hargrave, 2006, p. 81). Adjusting for inflation, "Minimum wage—and higher wages as well—are only worth 75 percent of what the same amount of money was worth 30 years ago" (Hargrave, 2006, p. 80). What is clear is that parents cannot turn the clock back and function under rules that are no longer relevant. They need to parent in ways that match the complexity of the times (Aquilino, 2006; Elkind, 1998).

Many questions surface for parents of emerging and young adults, and they are frequently unsure of how to proceed in their new role:

1. How do I define my new role? What are my responsibilities? What are my "adult" child's responsibilities?
2. How much support—instrumental, emotional, financial—should I provide? How much of a safety net should I provide?
3. How do I ensure and reinforce mature, responsible, independent behavior in my "adult" child?

Lack of "strong normative expectations" as well as lack of "strong cultural expectations" regarding how parents and adult children may optimally negotiate this developmental period allow for greater variability as well as greater tensions among parents and their adult children (Aquilino, 2006, p. 212).

In this chapter, the findings of interviews conducted with parents of individuals ranging in age from 25 to 35 are presented. Included is a discussion of their experiences and the meaning they attribute to their parental role. Thirty parents, all of whom were volunteers located in suburban communities of Boston, were interviewed (a more detailed description of the participants can be found in Appendix A). Identified themes include: (1) high expectations, paucity of opportunities; (2) negotiation of finances; (3) standing by, letting it be, and letting go; (4) finding balance, the "delicate dance"; (5) acceptance of the other, co-creating a "new" relationship; (6) having faith; and (7) solicited advice. First, a discussion of the current environmental context parents are encountering.

Contextual Considerations

As discussed in Chapter 2, developmental markers have shifted. Normative expectations are less clear and rituals acknowledging developmental markers are lacking. In the past, emerging adulthood was associated with getting married or being in a long-term committed relationship, having children, and finding a job with stability, promise, and economic independence. The current context is such that 65% of adult children expect to live at home either after college or between jobs (Trunk, 2005). Fields and Casper (2001) report that 56% of men and 43% of women ages 18–24 live at home with one or both of their parents. Individuals are marrying and having children at a later age (Arnett & Tanner, 2006). Emerging and young adults have fixed costs—rent, college loans, and insurance premiums—all of which are rising faster than wages. Yet, they have expectations for work that are high,"It should be fulfilling, fun, [and] accommodating to a substantial personal life" (Trunk, 2005, ¶ 15). In addition, an overwhelming number of emerging and young adults feel the need to be passionate about the work they are doing, and are fearful that they will be stuck in dead-end, nongratifying jobs. Those raised in affluence are anxious about the possibility that they will not be able to replicate the lifestyle of their parents.

Given that many emerging adults are uncertain about their future and are unable to support themselves financially, parents are confronted with a new set of realities that require reassessment and readjustment. Their "adult" child's room may have been reconfigured into a study or guest room, a move that formally acknowledges that the family is "moving on," seemingly ready to embrace the next phase of the family lifecycle. The guest room or study may need to be reconfigured once again, this time into a bedroom (albeit on a revolving-door basis). The family is faced with the process of reincorporating their adult child into the family system. The rules are unclear, and family members are frequently ridden with anxiety. The process requires negotiation, and "grappling with these tasks will lead to fundamental change in the nature of parent–child interaction" (Aquilino, 2006, p. 196).

The anxiety many parents express may require a period of waiting that includes recalibration of developmental time lines. The following statistics provide insight and clarity with respect to this developmental period.

1. It takes emerging adults approximately five to ten years to make the shift from their parent's home to their own place of residence. There are an increasing number of young adults who return home with the intent of moving out within a relatively short period of time, "Using home as a base for their first career steps." The shift does occur, but on a protracted basis (Apter, 2001, p. 22).
2. The majority of young adults do marry and/or commit to a relationship. On average, they do have children by age 35. Furthermore, these realities apply to

similar global sociopolitical contexts. Women in the United States are similar to their counterparts in Canada and Germany. Although women in the United States are delaying leaving home, they are not delaying as much as women in Italy, nor are they leaving home as early as women in Sweden (Apter, 2001, p. 22).

3. Seventy-three percent of emerging adults report being satisfied with their current job. Those individuals in their late 20s report that they have found work they want to do for the "long run." (Arnett, 2004, p. 152).

High Expectations, Paucity of Opportunities

The expectations of emerging and young adults have increased. "Today's 'ambitious generation' expects a great deal from adulthood. They want to have jobs that are satisfying, well-paid, and prestigious. They want to live comfortably, have friends, and lots of fun" (Apter, 2001, p. 256). Clara, a parent of a 27-year-old son, speaks to the issue of choice, possibility, and expectations:

The message is that there is choice and that the world is completely open, and that you can do whatever you want and become whoever you want to be. As opposed to when our generation was in college, the message was that upon graduation you would know exactly what your entire future would look like . . . . My husband is a perfect example. He was told to be a doctor. He became a dentist. He had so many interests he wanted to pursue, but he did not have the time because going to dental school was a 12-hour-a-day experience. Now he looks back and he feels he missed out.

Many parents perceived a dissonance between expectations and work opportunities. Janice, a mother of a 26-year-old daughter, speaks of high expectations and the "illusion" of choice:

A lot of choices, but reduced opportunity. A reduction of opportunities and a sense of a lot of choices. [There is] an illusory sense of there being a lot of choices. [There are] different avenues to consider and yet the jobs are not really there. A lot of fields, but you don't have a sense that there are a lot of careers . . . . They are not just spoiled and indecisive. The world and shrinking opportunities in the world coupled with high expectations, and just looking for jobs. They are looking for real personal fulfillment. Expect their jobs to do so much for them. It is not just a way of making money. There is a discordancy between reality and expectations . . . . Children grew up with one set of expectations, expectations about how we live. Expectations are higher than the world can deliver.

Kevin, a father of a 28-year-old son, and Brit, a mother of a 29-year-old daughter, echo concerns raised by Janice regarding dissonance between expectations and workplace realities:

Kevin: Their expectations are that when they get out of school, especially when they studied something specific, that they will be able to get that job. But it is much more difficult than they anticipated. [Employers are] hiring entry-level people for fairly menial jobs . . . . All the structure is gone.

Brit: There is too much competition, and there are too many of them [emerging and young adults]. The resources have decreased. Even if they are fit, they will have to be fitter. Survival of the fittest.

Both parents and emerging and young adults expressed disappointment related to marketplace opportunities available to individuals in their 20s and 30s. They expected that the marketplace would embrace them, and value their energy, talent, and credentials. Concordance between parents and emerging and young adults with respect to their views of the work environment was evident. Parents and emerging and young adults tended to view the workplace as insufficiently embracing of the potential and actual contributions of emerging and young adults.

Negotiation of Finances

Parents identified management of finances as an ongoing issue with respect to their adult child. Consistent with reports in the literature, parents expressed confusion and concern regarding economic support to their adult children who are struggling financially. Aquilino (2006) reports that fewer than half of American parents of emerging adults felt obligated to support their adult children. However, a qualitative study conducted by Hamon (1995) suggests that parents who view children in need (i.e., divorce), are more inclined to provide money for everyday living expenses, ranging from mortgage payments to attorney fees. Payment for education tends to be less laden with conflict for parents, particularly if parents associate the investment with better work outcomes (Semyonov & Lewin-Epstein, 2001).

Parental financial resources determine the amount of financial support available. The greater the financial resources, the fewer the siblings, the more likely parents are to assume responsibility for college payment. Parents are also more likely to assume financial responsibility for educating their children if they hold greater educational aspirations for their children (Steelman & Powell, 1991), in part driven by a reality that the labor market increasingly favors those individuals with greater education and skills (Hill & Yeung, 1999). Given the above finding by Steelman and Powell (1991), and given Aquilino's (1996) findings with respect to financing of room and board, it appears that American parents are willing to finance their adult children if they perceive that they are supporting movement toward autonomy and independence, a finding that was evident in the interviews conducted with parents of emerging and young adults. Michael, a parent of a 30-year-old son, and Ron, a parent of a 27-year-old son, offer a majority position, whereas Sheila, a mother of a 31-year-old daughter, offers a minority position with respect to management and allocation of finances.

Michael: It's fine to give them the confidence that if financially they need help you are there, but make it clear only if they have shown that they are responsible. We see kids being irresponsible, and their parents just keep covering their tracks. They need to have a comfort level that they can take some risks and their parents are there to back them. I am comfortable doing it. I don't feel comfortable if they have been irresponsible.

Ron: Financially, you can always ask me for money. If I have it, I would always give it to them. But somehow, they know that it was important that if they have a financial problem, that it is important for them to figure it out on their own.

Sheila: I think things are so precarious financially for this country that we do have to sort of be there for them if we can. What else do you have to spend your money on besides your children?

Parents may confuse being responsible with being independent, and financial indulgence with emotional support (Apter, 2001). Responsibility is best taught in the context of emotional support. The following guidelines are offered by Apter (pp. 224–237):

1. Work out the specifics of the source of conflict (financial arrangement) and explain it carefully.
2. Acknowledge the difficulty and challenge of learning how to manage money, rather than focusing on perceived "irresponsibility" or "immaturity."
3. Whenever possible, provide opportunities for the emerging adult to suggest possible solutions to the conflict.
4. Reinforce efforts of autonomy and mastery.

Above all, the spirit of the message is critical. It is important to assume a nonblaming stance that reinforces a problem-solving approach that is respectful and supportive. The message conveyed is critical. It is important to determine the intent of the messenger and how the message is being heard. Are adult children hearing the communicated message, "You are inadequate," or are they hearing the message, "How can we solve this particular issue?"

Standing By, Letting It Be, and Letting Go

It is hard not to be in control and to let them go their own way. You have to shift emotional gears. You need to shift from being in the role of protector and making things happen for them, to standing by. Who is good at it? I think the people who are less overly involved and less intrusive, they have a better perspective. I don't know anyone who is sailing through it. All my friends are having issues.

(Kim, mother of a 26-year-old daughter)

I think we don't give young people enough credit. They have been given the freedom to choose. If you give them the freedom [to choose], you have to give them the opportunity to work it out.

(Peter, father of a 25-year-old son)

Parents allude to the importance of viewing this developmental period not only from their perspectives, but also from the perspective of their "adult" children. Being empathic and "standing by" are particularly difficult, given that the developmental experiences of parents interviewed differed significantly from those of their children.

Parents speak of coming to terms with their adult child, accepting him or her and the "new world" which they inhabit. Specifically, they acknowledge the difficulty inherent in establishing perspective, particularly given the perception that their children may not be ready or competent to navigate the marketplace. They found it challenging to provide their adult children with the space to be, including the space to make their own choices. In creating the space for their adult children to be, parents may be giving themselves the space to be as well, including the ability to tolerate difference and imperfections in each other (Karen, 2001, p. 268).

Janice, Dorothy, Clara, and Kate speak of the difficulty of letting go of their old ways of being. Janice, a mother of a 26-year old daughter, acknowledges that parenting at this developmental juncture is a learning process. Dorothy, a mother of a 25-year-old-son, speaks to the difficulty of "letting go" of her "version" of her son.

Janice: It is a process. They need to be their own people. We did not give them too much to rebel against. They were comfortable. She is still trying to challenge me, but still seeking approval. She makes choices that I would not naturally approve of, yet comes back for approval.

Dorothy: I can hear myself contradicting myself. Fun thing [referring to her son pursuing activities in the service of fun] drives me crazy. Yet it is all right to make a mistake. I have to resolve these contradictory feelings or live with them at any rate. I know it is better for him to find autonomy, better for him to be in charge of who he is. Yet some of his views and activities drive me crazy. That is letting go. I need to let go of my version of him. You go there by finding meaning in your own life. Children can provide some of that meaning but it can not be that . . . . I am not there yet.

In the service of moving on in the relationship, acceptance is integral to the process of co-creating a relationship based on new assumptions. The process of identity exploration and commitment is facilitated when parents provide a secure accepting base from which emerging and young adults can explore and define themselves (Bartle-Haring, Brucker, & Hock, 2002).

The importance of taking a more accepting stance was emphasized by Clara, a mother of a 26-year-old son, and Kate, a mother of a 27-year-old son:

Clara: My child is trying to work on his future. In the process, mistakes will be made. I need to remind myself that it is important to accept that he made a mistake and move on in the relationship.

Kate: It is possible to come to terms with the existing realities, accept them as a truth, part of history, and then decide how to proceed. Accept that he makes mistakes, and you move on—coming to terms with it.

Parents spoke of the importance of observing what is occurring not only from their perspective, but also from the perspective of their "adult" children. "As we move away from the tendency to make other people play in our own internal dramas, we are freer to see them for who they are" (Karen. 2001, p. 174). The ability to empathize, "see," and come to terms with "who they are," facilitates the process of acceptance.

For some parents, there exists either an implicit or an explicit reference to the importance of the ability to view existing tensions from multiple perspectives, letting go of the notion of one "correct" perspective, and experiencing empathy for the other. Marie, a mother of a 32-year-old daughter, speaks to the issue of letting go:

Letting go means allowing yourself to acknowledge how you feel, but understand it in terms of all people involved. It's about realizing that everyone does things for a reason, and if you can put yourself in another's shoes, its easier to not feel so victimized.

In talking about the process of letting go among college students, Coburn and Treeger (2003) remind us that letting go is critical to the parenting process. Parents revisit issues associated with letting go at key junctures of their child's life:

Young men and women ask for little more at this time than a steady and rooted home base to return to, just as they had many years ago when they hurried back from their adventures across the playground to find Mom and Dad sitting on the park bench where they left them. To provide this sanctuary and still stay out of the way is an artful balancing act. It requires sensitivity to the often confusing dynamic of separation. (Coburn and Treeger, 2003, p. 210)

Brit, a mother of a 29-year-old daughter, speaks to the importance of evaluating one's actions and recognizing that parents may be "holding back" their adult children:

Brit: Young people are running around. Everything was structured for them by their parents. It is the first time that they are accountable for their own activities. They were never left alone to play in the sand dunes. They had no coping mechanisms to structure anything for themselves. We never let them do anything on their own. Every child had a mother structuring their day. They could not even play with each other. Once they were out of their structure, they can't do anything, and we wonder why they can't do it. It is hard to let go of that as a parent.... These kids feel like complete failures sometimes. They have not added anything to themselves.... Well, you learn to let go when you know that by not letting go, you are keeping them behind. There are age-appropriate behaviors, plus or minus two or three years. You let go when you know you are holding someone back.

Finding Balance, the "Delicate Dance"

We stumble through it. A fallacy is once they are launched, you don't worry about them. You worry about them more, because you don't have any control over them. You just help them where they are willing to be helped and supported. And you use your instincts about pushing them when they need to be independent. Finding that line between support and helping, and them being independent, maybe forcing their independence. It is also about life skills. What do you do when you have a car accident? What do you do when the landlord does not return your security deposit? . . . Helping them learn to be capable. How do you deal with a bad boss?

(Fran, mother of a 26-year-old son)

Fran assumes that the process of becoming an adult is a gradual one, and that adult children learn best when they perceive their responsibilities to be manageable and within their grasp of competency. Steven, father of a 32-year-old daughter, echoes Fran's concerns related to worrying about one's adult children, implying that balance, understanding, and judgment are needed:

Emotionally, you never let go. You are always involved, connected, worried, concerned. It is just the degree that it occupies your level of consciousness . . . . Let things flow naturally. [I] don't force interactions. [I] make contact but don't overdo it. [I] don't have lots of expectations, demands.

Debbie, Rona, and Brit also speak of the difficulty in finding balance between fostering adult children's capacities to "lead their own lives," while continuing to provide parental support.

Debbie: Communication is huge. Learning how to do enough, how to stay close. And on the other hand, not doing too much. It is a balance. It is hard for parents. You want them to lead their own lives and not be accountable to you for everything. I think it is real important that parents continue to be parents, but the balance. You have to be careful not to step over the lines, the boundaries . . . . I think just knowing when to be involved, when to ask, when to tell, when not to tell . . . . I think that it is really hard. Unless it is the laundry of course. They still want you to be that person.

Rona: I vacillate from doing too much and doing enough. I cannot find that happy medium of guiding them that feels mature and responsible, without babying them . . . . Doing enough to guide them without babying them. Pushing them from behind, rather than pulling them by the hand. Pushing them to fly.

Brit: Give them slack and be harsh other times. Try to understand their mood swings and honor and appreciate that. Reality checks, keep that in mind. It is a volatile period. You need to be tender and also harsh, like a chemical solution. A little bit of acid, a little bit of alkaline to get a perfect titration. [It is] not stable. That is why it is a lot of work. It changes every day.

I Am Not My Adult Child: Co-Creating a "New" Relationship

The process of co-creating a new relationship is facilitated by the ability to transcend the moment, and view the larger context. The larger context often includes acknowledgment that statements about one's adult child are not statements about the self. Caroline, a parent of two adult sons, 26 and 29 years old, and Janice, a mother of a 26-year-old daughter, spoke to the issue of differentiating one's self from one's adult children.

Caroline: I did not take responsibility for their strengths as children. I do not take responsibility for their shortcomings as adults.

Janice: They have a capacity to grow. They are growing. Whatever worries me now, it is reasonable to presume that they will mature in a way I don't see right now. The mantra, it is them not me; it is their life. You have to let go of the idea that it is a reflection of you. You want to brag about your kid. They don't own this to you. They do not need to enrich my life, embellish my life. They are not a statement of who I am. They are a statement of who they are.

Marcia (2002) eloquently addresses the quagmire parents of adult children experience. Although he aims his remarks at parents of adolescents, his insightful observations apply to parents of emerging and young adults as well. Marcia argues that although parents realize that they need to provide "care, guidance, forbearance, and appreciation," they can also "overdo intimacy," confusing their own issues with the issues of their children. Parents are vulnerable to overidentifying with their children, and depending on them for meeting their own unresolved issues and needs (Marcia, 2002, p. 204):

On the one hand, [they] need our care, guidance, forbearance, and appreciation. On the other hand, we as adults, need some validation . . . in our own struggles to achieve and maintain a sense of generativity . . . . [T]he growers also need to be confirmed in their generativity by the growing. However, we can overdo our intimacy with them, confusing our issues with theirs, and we can undermine our own integrity by identification with and dependency on their meeting our needs for generativity.

Many of the parents interviewed cited the ability to see beyond the immediate and view the larger context as helpful to the process of co-creating a new relationship, including a renegotiation of boundaries and roles. Emerging and young adults may:

Rebuff parental advice, but they will appreciate acknowledgment of their distress—a listening ear that doesn't judge even if he/she disagrees, a sense of confidence that doesn't crumble when they do, an adult anchor who provides perspective on the predictable but often painful changes that young adults are bound to experience as part of the process. (Coburn & Treeger, 2003, p. 31)

Michael, a parent of a 30-year-old son, and Brit, a mother of a 29-year-old daughter state the following.

Michael: Don't be surprised if they ask for your advice, but don't bother taking it.

Brit: We had to figure out how to interact with each other. If you are not coming home, give me a call. Coming to some understanding that she would call me because she felt like calling me, not because I demanded she call me.

Having Faith

In listening to participants speak about their parenting experiences, "evidenced-based" parenting did not seem to be a helpful stance to take vis-à-vis one's adult child. What did seem to facilitate positive interactions was a faith-based parenting approach, having faith in their adult children, regardless, and perhaps in spite of the immediate evidence.

Mary: Say your child wants to move to Latin America. Although that will give me pause, just sitting back and believing in him helps. I am not in a position to not let him do it. I need to try to get into it, and not interfere and let my worry interfere with his planning. I have to let him go and have faith in him.

Susan: I think that she will figure it out. I do have faith that she will figure it out herself. That is not to say it will not be rocky or that she won't stumble. You cannot lead them. There is no other way to do it.

They just have to do it. Some of it is personality. My son will ponder, consider all the possibilities, does not get paralyzed. Then he makes a decision and it is his decision. My daughter has a hard time putting a stake in the ground. The underlying basis is that he is sure he is going to be okay, no matter what he decides. He is confident. He thinks he will be happy no matter what he decides. She really doubts herself, doubts whether she is doing the right thing. Does not trust herself the same way he does. Some of it is developmental, they're not integrated. Different parts of themselves that don't fit into an integrated person yet. Life experiences help the integration process.

Michael: If you hang in there, kids go through phases, and if you hang in there, they will work it out. I lost them in their teenage years. They sort of came back to me in their 20s. They are communicating again. That has helped me a lot with my other two kids. I have learned to trust them more. They seem not to need as much help as I thought they would . . . . Have confidence in them . . . . Back them up, support them, but also allow them to get the independence they need for the rest of their lives.

Parents may expect that at some magical juncture, their adult child will become autonomous and independent. Graduation from college may serve as a marker for parents that their children have crossed the threshold, and are ready to assume a new role marked by adult responsibilities. However, Robert and Beverly Cairns (1994), based on their study of young adults, conclude that it is "misguided" to think that parents can remove themselves from the responsibility of parenting at some "magical" time period. Parents may espouse beliefs that lead them to binary dichotomous thinking: "Today a child, tomorrow an adult." More often than not, this belief is coming from a loving place, a place of concern.

According to Robert and Beverly Cairns (1994), emerging adults who experience their parents as highly supportive, are most likely to successfully navigate this developmental period. Apter (2001) suggests that there is a threat that emerging adults may become more isolated and alone. She is particularly concerned about the "shortfall of social capital" and its impact on emerging adults (p. 268). Apter suggests that close family ties and frequent communication can serve as a buffer in terms of the dearth of social capital that is characteristic of the contextual realities emerging and young adults are navigating.

According to Apter, the vision of continued care and responsibility is threatened by "the maturity myth," which denies the need for social capital. Depriving emerging adults of help does not foster "true" independence. To "let them go" just at a time in social history when there are fewer and fewer networks outside the parent/child relationship does not appear to be a reasonable option. Instead, we must perform that delicate dance between moving close and giving room:

It is mandatory that parents see helping their daughters and sons across the threshold to adulthood as their responsibility . . . . [This proposal] simply makes use of the love and concern that is already in place. Instead of clinging to our ideals of independence and maturity, we can respond to our children's needs. If we listen and learn, we can foster their slow-growing spirits . . . . In so doing, we will establish a richness of relationship that will last a lifetime. (Apter, 2001, p. 268)

Solicited Advice

The following are words of advice conveyed by parents of emerging and young adults.

Kate: You can't tell them what to do. You have to watch them make what you think are mistakes. Don't give feedback unless asked . . . . Create a space for your kids to create their own life, not being overinvolved and not being underinvolved.

Caroline: Build some kind of continuing process for discussion . . . in your life together. Set up time to explore these issues. Be careful what you say about stressing the importance of finding deep personal satisfaction. Because that is a concern of your 50s, and you have the luxury of thinking about it because you have already been working for 30 years. I have been bitten on the fanny because I have had my children say, "Mom you've made choices that constrained your earning potential and work hours, in order to be personally happy and satisfied. I want to do that too." But it is too early for them. They basically have reminded me of this repeatedly. They are in search of balance before they are entitled to balance. Young people typically are supposed to be out busting their fannies.

Barbara: The one thing I wish I could do all over again is help them from a very young age to make decisions independently, age-appropriate decisions. As a mother I wanted to make things better, to fix it, even if it is a minor dilemma. My temperament is a compulsive one. I start suggesting solutions. I analyze the issue that she may or may not have thought about. I am getting better. I now say you will figure it out, but it is an effort.

What we have found useful is to ask them to seek the advice of at least one adult that they view as having good judgment, if there is a presenting issue that is difficult to resolve among us. We need to all agree that this adult has good judgment. It diffuses the tension. And it usually leads to good outcomes, but not always.

Susan: Try not to be reactive. Do not be reactive to what your kids are doing. Respect the difference, that your child is not you.

Perry: I found that it was helpful to involve another party when things got very intense. Like a three-legged stool. You need a third leg for balance and perspective . . . . It helps with the intensity of the conflict.

Ralph: Ultimately it is their life. They will do what they want to do. Don't impose your ideas. Have open communication. Your child may still listen to you. Important not to impose your will.

Max: You got to let them be their own people, ongoing from the time they are little. When they are little you have more control. If they make mistakes, you have to let that happen, knowing that you can't run interference for them. You have to be in a supportive role. You are not always going to approve of all their choices and that is okay because you are not living their life. They are living their lives for better or for worse.

Beth: You've got to let them make some mistakes. And then you can't say I told you so. You have to stand back and more or less help them understand what they can understand from those mistakes. Guide them through it. You can say so much and then they have to be responsible for making their decisions.

Karen (2001) states:

Given that we are living in a time of complexity, complexity in relationships is a natural outgrowth. Acknowledging complexity allows parents and children to view themselves as individuals, capable of experiencing a range of feelings. The parent–adult child relationship frequently calls upon both parent and adult child to engage in the emotional struggle of holding simultaneously contradictory feelings, accessing and expressing the loving aspects of the relationship, without stifling and expressing negative affect. From that place, clarity and growth within the relationship can occur.

Coming to terms and acceptance of the other, separate yet interconnected, was identified as key to developing and sustaining a gratifying relationship between adult parent and adult child, a finding consistent with the literature (Aquilino, 2006). Specific "skillsets" identified by parents of emerging and young adults included mastering the process of "standing by" within a supportive context, finding balance, accepting difference, and having faith. The co-creation of a relationship between two adults that is historically rooted, and requires major shifts in one's roles and responsibilities, is challenging at best.

Conclusions

Parents of emerging and young adults are negotiating new terrain. Given lack of experience with (1) existing environmental contexts, (2) changing developmental markers, (3) lack of clear expectations, and (4) fewer available support networks outside the parent/child relationship, tensions between emerging and young adults and their parents are perhaps inevitable. The anxiety many parents expressed may require a period of waiting that includes recalibration of developmental time lines. "Evidenced-based" parenting did not seem to be a helpful stance as experienced by parent participants. What did seem to facilitate positive interactions was a faith-based parenting approach, having faith in their adult children, regardless, and perhaps in spite of the immediate evidence. Coming to terms and acceptance of the other, separate yet interconnected, was identified as key to developing and sustaining a gratifying relationship between adult parent and adult child. The process of co-creating a new relationship was facilitated by the ability to transcend the moment and view the larger context.

References

Apter, T. (2001). *The myth of maturity: What teenagers need from parents to become adults.* New York: Norton.

Aquilino, W. (2006). Family relationships and support systems in emerging adulthood. In J. Arnett and J. Tanner (Eds.), *Emerging adults in America: Coming of age in the 21st century* (pp. 193–217). Washington, DC: American Psychological Association.

Arnett, J. (2004). *Emerging adulthood: The winding road from the late teens through the twenties.* New York: Oxford University Press.

Arnett, J. & Tanner, J. (2006). *Emerging adults in America: Coming of age in the 21st century.* Washington, DC: American Psychological Association.

Bartle-Haring, S., Brucker, P., & Hock, E. (2002). The impact of separation anxiety on identity development in late adolescence and early adulthood. *Journal of Adolescent Research, 17,* 439–450.

Cairns, B. & Cairns, R. (1994). *Lifelines and risks: Pathways of youth in our time.* New York: Harvester Wheatsheaf.

Coburn, K. & Treeger, M. (2003). *Letting go: A parents' guide to understanding the college years.* New York: Harper.

Elkind, D. (1998). *The hurried child: Growing up too fast too soon.* Reading, MA: Addison-Wesley.

Fields, J. & Casper, L. M. (2001). America's families and living arrangements: Population characteristics. *Current Population Reports: United States Bureau of the Census.* Retrieved May 30, 2006, from http://www.census.gov/prod/2001pubs/p20-537.pdf

Hamon, R. (1995). Parents as resources when adult children divorce. *Journal of Divorce and Remarriage, 23,* 173–183.

Hargrave, T. (2006). Case studies: Failure to launch: The struggle to leave home in the 21st century. *Psychotherapy Networker, 30* (July/August), 79–86.

Hill, M. & Yeung, W. (1999). How has the changing structure of opportunities affected transitions to adulthood. In A. Booth, A. Crouter, and M. Shanahan (Eds.), *Transitions to adulthood in a changing economy: No work, no family, no future?* (pp. 3–39). Westport, CT: Praeger.

Karen, R. (2001). *The forgiving self: The road from resentment to connection.* New York: Doubleday.

Marcia, J. (2002). Adolescence, identity and the Bernardone family. *Identity, 2,* 199–209.

Semyonov, M. & Lewin-Epstein, N. (2001). The impact of parental transfers on living standards of married children. *Social Indicators Research, 54,* 115–137.

Steelman, L. & Powell, B. (1991). Sponsoring the next generation: Parental willingness to pay for higher education. *American Journal of Sociology, 96*(6), 1505–1529.

Trunk, P. (2005, May 15). Believe it or not moving back is now in. *Boston Sunday Globe,* BostonWorks, G1.

Waters, D. (2005). Adultescence: Helping 20somethings leave the nest. *Psychotherapy Networker, 29* (March/April), 73–76.

8
Voices of Employers: Overlapping and Disparate Views

Management of emerging and young adults has become "one of the hottest topics in management training" (Trunk, 2006, ¶ 1). Emerging and young adults bring different mindsets to the workforce that may baffle their older employers. Although employers and emerging and young adults tend to agree that the work terrain has changed, assessments regarding how to best navigate the changing terrain may diverge. In an environment where the rules are in flux with no absolutes, difference in points of view may bring new tensions to the workplace as well as possibilities for misunderstanding and resentment. In response, "... [B]aby boomers are sitting in seminars for hours trying to demystify the alien ways of the new workforce" (Trunk, 2006, ¶ 1).

This chapter focuses on the perspectives of employers, specifically with respect to their experiences with emerging and young adults in the workforce. Thirty employers, representing a diversity of fields, including but not limited to medicine, education, engineering, law, advertising, nursing, marketing, retailing, graphic design, physical therapy, and social service were interviewed. Each of the participants supervised a minimum of five emerging and young adult employees within the past three years (please refer to Appendix A for further description of the sample of employers). In speaking about their experiences as employers of emerging and young adults, common themes emerged. They include: (1) entitled, self absorbed, self-focused; (2) technology and its impact; (3) mentoring; and (4) work–home balance. First, here is a brief summary of the prevailing descriptions provided by employers of emerging and young adults and the work contexts they are navigating.

Prevailing Depictions of Emerging and Young Adults and Their Work Contexts

Despite diversity of representation of employer participants, there tended to be unanimity in their perceptions of the work environment as: (1) highly competitive and (2) lacking loyalty. Marie, a 59-year-old manager in accounting, and Fran, a

39-year-old manager in advertising capture the environmental context emerging and young adults are negotiating:

Marie: The rules have changed and the young get it. The loyalty bond between employer and employee was broken in 2000 forever, and they go wherever is best for them for their careers.... [T]he employers move people around today like assets, and sometimes they don't even know what your skillsets are. They put you where they can use you, need you. Operative word is use. You are a commodity.... I am nothing more than a paid contractor. And ... with benefits. That's the difference between a contractor and an employee. I am an employee at will. I just get paid benefits. It is the needs of the corporation, so why should I not go where it is best for me.

Fran: Corporations are driven by profit and not by loyalty to employees and [there is] no sense of how companies play a role in culture. Companies change direction all the time, pursuing financial gain, not looking at the big picture. Things are supposed to be more certain if you work hard. Things are supposed to fall into place. That rule is not working.

In addition, several employers noted that emerging and young adults face a marketplace with fewer opportunities because older employees are not leaving at retirement age, in part due to economics, and in part due to overidentification with work, as noted by Denise and Tom.

Denise: They [emerging and young adults] have their challenges. Every generation has different challenges, getting appropriate work opportunities. Us baby boomers are not letting go over our power in the workforce.... They have been brought up thinking they can do anything, and then they look for a job, and meet limitations. As long as I can talk, I can work, thus minimizing opportunities for a younger person. We can do what we can do, and we are holding onto our power. We are looking at retirement in a different way.

Tom: I don't think we are getting out of the pipeline when we should get out. People are working in their 60s and don't want to give up their jobs. I think it is part economics. In our generation, it is an identity factor. People have to identify in a way by the work they have. Some of it is security. It is an identification of who you are.

Employers communicated complexity in their depictions of emerging and young adults in the workforce. They observed delays in the actualization of career paths, stating that the developmental shift to adulthood occurred approximately at age 30, observations confirmed by emerging and young adult participants. Jenine, an employer working in marketing, and Harvey, an employer of chemical engineers, spoke of the significance of age 30 as a developmental marker.

Jenine: I have to say this, some of them ...[as] they get to a 30-year marker, they start to reassess. You don't see that in their 20s. They are still evaluating the situation.

Harvey: In their 30s, [they] are beginning to put pressures [on themselves]. More relaxed in their 20s, and then there are pressures once they hit the big 30.

Although most employers viewed emerging and young adults as bright and hard working (particularly under conditions of praise and appreciation), they also described them as impatient, entitled, and not willing to invest the necessary time and energy required for advancement ("arrogant" and/or "rushed"). The prevailing descriptors included: bright and knowledgeable, tolerant, open, flexible, experimental, adventurous, passionate, acquisitive, arrogant, lack of respect for hierarchy, materialistic, mobile, self-focused, and low tolerance for frustration.

Employers overwhelmingly tended to view emerging and young adults as intelligent and flexible. However, although intellectually adept, many noted that emerging adults did not bring valued skillsets to the workplace. Their educational experiences, particularly those individuals grounded in the liberal arts, were not viewed as synchronous with the needs of the marketplace. Tom, a 54-year-old manager and co-owner of a public relations firm remarks:

They are seen as somewhat disposable. I think they are also seen as not particularly ready for positions that are above them …. The reality is when you go knocking on the door, they don't necessarily need an art historian …. I don't think it is their fault. They misunderstand what college is about. You need to be able to network with people to figure out what you want to do. Not only about going to class. Colleges need to respond to that. The fact that you love English is wonderful. What do you want to do with this? I don't think this aspect of work is built into college early on. Besides liking this, you need to think about how you will be able to use this in life. Look at how the world is changing, need to have some structure that will relate to the world of work. If you have an interest in international finance, get experiences that will relate. "History of Women" is a great course, but I don't think there is enough consideration given to this. There ought to be if not a four-year plan, a two-year plan.

Employers noted the sense of ease and comfort with diversity displayed by emerging and young adults, a finding confirmed in the literature (Twenge, 2006). Overwhelmingly, employers characterized emerging and young adults as tolerant and respectful of the other, across race, gender, ethnicity, sexual orientation, and disability, represented by the assessments of Tom and Derek:

Tom: I think they are extraordinarily tolerant of alternate lifestyles, not a big deal if you are gay, transsexual, not a big deal.

Derek: We are in a transition stage. Their perspectives on race, class, and disability is different from previous generations. It does not mean that there are no problems. It is very different interpersonally …. Now there are problems with smaller systems. They marry between races, cultures; it is much more accepted. It causes problems for the older members of the society.

Carmen and Alisa spoke of the materialistic acquisitive behavior they observed in emerging and young adult employees, a point of view that was reinforced by emerging and young adult participants:

Carmen: One of the things I notice, this new group wants to maintain a very new car, hefty car payments, [they] want the bells and whistles. Sacrifice factor is not there. I am not going to give up my nice car. The expectation to have it all is higher. I'm not going to give up these nice things that I am used to.

There is just one person [at work] that has the discipline to save anything. The rest of them are operating by the seat of their pants doing what they want. [It is] curious to me that they do not want to give up anything and they are determined to not give anything up.

We had a young man from China, 25–30 years of age. The same group of people could not understand why he needed to pay for a car, TV, etc. He was not raised with debt. It does not even feel normal to them when people sacrifice. They could not understand why he was doing it. Getting a car payment, it is the American way …. His clunker would break down, he would ask them for a ride, and they would start to get annoyed.

Alisa: The materialism is a very sad part of our society. The amount they need! Living for today, not being able to defer gratification. I have to have this today. I may not be here tomorrow. Everything could change so I might as well spend it all, get it all, experience it all now.

In the context of a materialistic acquisitive society, a minority of employers depicted emerging and young adults as concerned with not being able to replicate or surpass their parents' lifestyle. Alisa, a supervisor of educational personnel, notes the following.

In the past, it used to be, I can exceed what my parents had. Hard for them to envision this. They cannot afford to live where they grew up. There is much more competition out there. Sometimes competition can breed passivity. People who are not confident retreat. If I don't try, I can't lose.

Kim, a 62-year-old employer in the automobile industry speaks of these concerns and brings a historical perspective to the discussion:

They [emerging and young adults] do not remember their parents struggling, they think they had it all and want from work what their parents are articulating in their 50s, not what they were articulating in their 20s.

Some employers noted a difference in attitude toward hierarchy in the work environment. Brad, a 62-year-old manager of emerging and young adults in a social service agency states:

Most [emerging and young adults] don't really expect there to be a hierarchy in the same way that there was. They expect you to have a work relationship with them. And if you don't have one, they are gone. Thirty years ago, there was a thing called frustration tolerance, but that does not exist any more. If you had less opportunity, you did not make the shift [referring to his generation in a context of greater job scarcity]. So losing the job was a real problem. This is much less the case now.

A majority of employers commented on emerging and young adults' propensity to change job settings frequently (every year or two), represented in the following comment by Alisa, a 42-year-old supervisor of teachers in an urban school setting, and Juanita, a 31-year-old supervisor of nurses:

Alisa: There is more jumping around from job to job. They probably are more apt to take risks. [On the other hand] people are getting married later and have less responsibility than in the past [so] that they can do those things. There is a lot of creativity and experimentation and that is good. Even though they are struggling more [it is] better in some sense than pigeonholing yourself too soon.

Juanita: They are all going to leave; they will be good and they won't stay. Everybody does it [they] move around a lot. It is not like in the past where people looked down at it. I think that although people are looking out for themselves and what employers can do for them, they also need to consider what they can give back. Their employers are investing a lot to train them and they need to consider that they should give something back before they move on.

Increased mobility creates difficulties for some organizations. Juanita speaks of recent strategies developed by her organization to address a high turnover rate. She notes that although a significant amount of money and effort is being expended on training, turnover remains an issue for her organization. According to Juanita, the expense of training personnel and not being able to reap the rewards are problematic from an organizational and fiscal perspective:

We are telling them how important training is, and what we are giving them, and that we expect them to stay for a minimum of two years. We don't know if it is working, just started it. To have them understand, you would not be getting this [next] job, if it were not for us. To stay a little bit longer and repay that debt. I hope it will work. It is our hope that they will stay longer.

Fran, an employer in the field of marketing, notes that the shift toward changing jobs more frequently, in some cases, appears to be unplanned and unfocused:

There is a great deal of luck that some of these kids capitalize on. They fall into things. In being flexible, they sometimes hit the jackpot. It is not what they planned to do in going to school. There is lots of opportunity. Sometimes you get lucky. It is not because it was scripted and planned. It is not because they were focused and had a long-term plan. It is almost falling into things .... By not having a long-term plan, they had the flexibility that brought them around to that. I am not saying they are passive. They were adventurous, taking chances, trying new things. I don't know if the workforce will incorporate it. It is not a grand scheme of how to.

Fran is describing a pattern whereby emerging and young adults "try out" jobs to obtain a greater sense of themselves in terms of their talents and skills. According to Fran, it is unclear whether the strategy of moving from job to job on a yearly or bi-yearly basis, is an optimal strategy.

Greater clarity and understanding is needed regarding the processes by which emerging and young adults negotiate their career paths, including understanding of adaptive and nonadaptive strategies. Some emerging and young adults follow productive career paths by actively experimenting and searching for a good fit, however, others appear to be floundering, particularly in the context of experimenting in low-paying and low-skilled random jobs that do not appear to be informed by purposefulness and/or planfulness.

The key according to Schneider and Stevenson (as cited in Hamilton & Hamilton, 2006), is to understand how to best position emerging and young adults to "make choices that will leave them with more good choices to make in the future rather than with narrowed and unrewarding options" (Hamilton & Hamilton, 2006, p. 273). It is important to differentiate purposeful and directed behavior from premature foreclosure of options (Hamilton & Hamilton, 2006). A thoughtful approach is needed to address this important issue (Blustein, Junthunen, & Worthington, 2000; Csikszentmihalyi & Schneider, 2000).

Entitled, Self-Focused, Self-Concerned?

Employers alluded to entitlement as a problematic issue as it relates to supervision of emerging and young adults. Although many employers tended to contextualize feelings of entitlement, others tended to link entitlement with a self-orientation, a "what can you do for me orientation," that may be in conflict with the needs of an organization. Denise and Diane, supervisors of physical therapists and sales personnel, respectively, capture the complexity of the observations related to entitlement with respect to emerging and young adults:

Denise: They have [this] feeling I am owed this. I have to have this. I deserve this. I don't have to work hard for it. [On the other hand], they have a hell of a world to deal with. It is very complex. I see a lot of wonderful people out there and that gives me hope.

Diane: They are somewhat more entitled. They expect more out of life, more out of relationships. We elevated the standards as parents for the life we wanted our children to have. We wanted our children to be better off than we were emotionally, economically, but the difference is that we had more resources and more options especially as women.

Marnie, a director of pupil personnel services in an urban school system, speaks of a "me generation." However, her observations are grounded and informed by a broader context:

Employees, they want to know what the job can do for them, versus how can they get this job. They had it a little easier than when we were younger. Parents protecting them more, but in a lot of ways the world is more stressful. Maybe it is a combination of we don't know what tomorrow will bring …. This generation is definitely more about me. What can this job do for me? What is in it for me? They do not feel a need to be pinned down, pigeonholed. I am going to have my fun now, travel, relationships, and then I will be tied down to all these things, and that is acceptable. Now we kind of encourage people to take some time off because we are afraid that it won't last. In a way, we have encouraged delaying choices, because we have seen so many not work out …. So many divorces, people our age get into careers they don't like. We brought up kids to be less and less responsible, so they feel they need [a] longer [time] to be responsible.

Although employers described similar behavioral patterns with respect to entitlement, they attached different meaning to the behavior they described. For example, Carmen, a human resource manager, while acknowledging that some workplace behaviors appear to be entitled, also suggests that an entitled stance may be understood in the context of negotiating a difficult marketplace. "Blustering through," as she frames it, may be adaptive, given the complexity and challenges of the times:

I think they are looking to find what will satisfy them, rather than going into a prescribed career, prescribed life. [However] I also see in the workplace entitlement that has not been earned yet. Part of the nature of the 20s [is thinking you know everything]. I thought I knew everything. Maybe you cannot make it through your 20s unless you think you know everything. Maybe you have to bluster your way. If you don't, you get buried by how scary it is …. It just takes some sheer courage to make it through.

Tom views entitlement as driven in part by unmet expectations. He concludes that "self-concern" is triggered by a work environment that is difficult to negotiate:

> I think they are self-concerned, not self-absorbed. [They are struggling with] how come their life is not turning out the way they thought it would be, the way it is supposed to be.

Cathy, a supervisor in the field of publishing, views entitlement as a self-protective stance and links it with arrogance and "specialness:"

> Essentially, they have more of an arrogance about their position. If the company does not treat them right, does not give them their vacation, then who cares. They can get their job from somewhere else .... Some of them experienced, in their personal life, parents getting laid off, and then also some of their college education reinforced the fact that you are more special than other people.

In summary, employers alluded to entitled behavior on the part of many emerging and young adults. Although some employers tended to view entitled behavior in a broader context, others spoke of entitlement as a "what can you do for me orientation," an orientation that tended to conflict with the culture of the organization.

Technology and Its Impact

Employers focused on the impact of technology, specifically as it relates to the changing dynamics of procuring and maintaining employment. Abundance of choice was linked to advances in technology. Brad and Mark, employers of emerging and young adults in the fields of biomedical research and social service, both focused on the Internet and its impact on one's ability to engage with the search process, allowing the individual greater mobility, freedom, and choice.

> Brad: What is particular to the current era is the enormous fluidity that has been created in communications, especially the Internet. Young people can look for a job, explore jobs online, and really pursue a job 24/7. They can explore the different options in much greater breadth and depth. So that they can really understand the numerator and the denominator for job options in the way they never could before. The denominator is the total sum of all jobs they might be potentially interested in, informational seeing of the lay of the land, understanding what the scope is, and the numerator is what the actual job options are at any given point in time.

> There is also an interactive element to the denominator as the young person explores job opportunities on the Internet; there is an interactive component. They may learn about hybrid opportunities that they never knew existed.

> Mark: People don't feel that the job they have now is the job they will have later. The letter of commitment is different from 20 years ago. You can figure out what jobs are available in Seattle, San Francisco, or London, without a problem. The number of possibilities is so much greater in terms of decisions. So it changes the whole paradigm.

Both Brad and Mark associate access to the Internet with increasing choice. However, they also allude to the difficulties inherent in navigating the Internet, specifically with respect to the risk of "information overload." How to best navigate opportunities, including exposure to "hybrid fields" is challenging at best. Brad uses a food metaphor to describe the challenge:

Brad: The concern is that there are so many choices and they are so inundated with information, that they will be misled, or will not have the presence of mind to really carefully consider what is the right fit for themselves. It is a matter of information overload. That can be distracting. They need guidance [in terms of] how to temper that. Like someone who goes to a wonderful ice cream shop with lots of choices and eats themselves sick rather than choosing a few flavors they truly love. They will need to slow down and think about whether things are a good fit for themselves.

Brad states that support may be needed to help emerging and young adults navigate the abundance of choice, due in part to advances in technology. Bernice, a 55-year-old employer in textile design, echoes Brad's concerns related to technology, specifically with respect to "information overload."

Bernice: They [emerging and young adults] over-bombard themselves with the information, because of technology. Try to block out all the information, and try to stay true to what you want to do. One of the young moms knew she was coming back to work. By the time she was done researching [childcare options], she was distraught in terms of what she had to do .... [T]his book said; this Web site said; it does at times make it more difficult to navigate.

Mike, Fran, and Charles, employers, all in their late 30s, allude to skillsets, particularly in the interpersonal realm that are not being nurtured in an information economy heavily reliant on technology:

Mike: What is happening is that this information economy is creating a subset of a generation that is ill prepared to interact with real people and to have a working knowledge of things that previous generations took for granted. Having a conversation with the barber at the barbershop, going next door to talk to a neighbor about nothing in particular, to understand how to do anything without consulting Google. Our generation has displaced the capacity of our knowledge to the oracle of Google.

Fran: E-mails and lack of communication. [They are a] blessing and a curse. So efficient. This is a generation that does not know how to come up to a senior person and have a conversation and have a healthy dialogue. They hide behind their e-mail. They don't have to talk to anybody. I used to have to talk to people that I was afraid to talk to. They could send out notes. I don't think their communications skills are the strongest.

Charles: Their ability to read emotions is just hideous. It's e-mail. I think it is difficult to read the affect and intent in e-mails. As a result they don't have enough practice. They don't read body language. No affect in reading an e-mail.

Work–Home Balance

The pursuit of work–life balance was identified by a majority of employers as responsible for creating tensions in the workplace. A survey conducted by Spherion (as cited in Cleaver, 2006) concluded that work–life balance is one of the three primary factors that affect retention. The report indicated that 32% of employees reported dissatisfaction with the work–life balance they were maintaining.

Despite existing tensions, employers overwhelmingly noted that emerging and young adults brought their personal best to the workplace. However, they provided clarity about what they were and were not willing to do in the service of a job. Nura, a lawyer and supervisor, and Carmen, a director of human resources, observed that many emerging and young adults, particularly those with children, set clear boundaries, while simultaneously committing to and giving their personal best to their work:

Nura: Almost uniformly, they are careful about having more balance in their lives, balance between work and their personal life. We raised them that way, to think they are free enough to respect their personal life, and they want to avoid the pitfalls of the previous generation, to have to work so hard.

I see a significant difference between my mindset and the mindset of people I supervise between 25 and 35. One of the most significant things that I find real interesting [is the mindset of] I am going to do my best every day. I showed loyalty. My approach differs greatly from how they think.

Carmen: Today's kids are separating their home life from their work life much better than our generation. The contract was broken, so they put into the job their professional best, but save a much greater percent of their emotional energy for home …. [They are] much more open about talking about kids at work. Much more committed to their kids. My generation had to hide [talking] about their kids. They choose not to hide. I am not going to tell them they are wrong.

They know how to set boundaries with their professional home life. Very good at it. Much better than I was at their age. I'm not sure where it comes from, but I do know that they do care much more about balance. An example would be, a working mom [an employee] was asked to work later with a 15-month-old baby. She says "I'm sorry, my day care will charge me more. I'm not willing to do that." [There are] no consequences. She draws the line. I've done my best and now I am leaving. I don't care if that has to go out tomorrow. Falls on someone else in the department. One of us will pick up the slack.

… The young men in their early thirties, they will go to a trade show; they have worked nonstop. [They say] okay I am taking this time off. I have given you my whole weekend, give me Friday. They come into the position saying this is work; this is home life, clearly drawing the line.

… They make it clear from the start. I need to leave by 5:30 every day. There is respect associated with openness. When we review the candidate as a group, we appreciate knowing upfront where they are coming from. It makes our life easier.

As people come into new companies, in this age group, they will also say you are offering a little less in salary, I want balance and I am willing to take a little less money to have that balance. I am going to give the company 110 percent while I am here, but I am not going to let it rule my entire life.

Dora, an employer of emerging and young adults working in information systems links the need for work–life balance to the "pace of change." Individuals are being barraged with an ever-changing work environment, which in turn leads to unease and lack of "comfort:"

The pace of change is so fast that you can never adjust to the actual change, never get a chance to adjust to it. [It] means you don't get comfort from work. Never in a comfortable position. You separate the treadmill of work from life. It is what you do to live. People don't identify the same way with their work as they used to. Your job is not your life. It is a much healthier thing. It does not define you as a person.

Denise, on the other hand, in speaking about the need for balance, associates the pursuit of work–life balance with delay. She suggests that the need for balance interferes or competes with the pursuit of other activities, such as marriage and children:

My children and my employees constantly need to set priorities to keep a balance between personal life and career. Therefore, they have had to give up some aspects of maturity in favor of others, for example, postponing marriage and children for training for a career.

This finding is confirmed by a 2005 survey conducted by Spherion (as cited in Cleaver, 2006):

[Previously] baby boom moms largely worked out the details of flexible hours, telecommuting, and the like with their bosses one at a time, behind closed doors, for fear of setting an apple-cart-upsetting precedent. Their daughters, now mothers of young children, put their expectations squarely on the table. Employers can respond with "flexwork" options, or they can look for someone else (G6).

Prioritizing balance can create tensions, feelings of resentment and ambivalence, as evidenced by the following observation by Carmen, a director of human resources:

Maybe because I have an old-school work ethic, without worrying about the circumstances. They are taking advantage of the company. Makes me take a step back. When I was up and coming, you tried to accommodate both [referring to home and work demands]. [As opposed to the stance] this is very important to me to be at my child's game. I won't be at work. I cannot stay. I sort of feel who am I to judge. I have a lot of respect for people who are at this age. They have good decent positions. They are talented and intelligent and they have things clearly defined coming into the workplace. I'm not sure if there is harm. When raises come around they get the average raise. I have not seen anything that has hindered them professionally for being this way. As a sidebar, they are reliable and responsible.

David, a supervisor of physicians in training, in his depiction of work contexts with shifting commitments and needs, presents a complex picture. The meaning of patient care has changed, as well as the players negotiating the terrain:

Medicine is different. There is a delayed maturational process because of the structure by definition. One can argue that maybe a byproduct of the change in work hours [is] that maybe people will spend more time in terms of maturational stuff than before. Too early to tell. In 10, 15 years, we will have to see the next generation of doctors. Are they more content, more balanced in their life, better parents. [The] previous generation were great doctors, but they did it at the expense of their family life. You have far more two-career families and that has changed. That puts a new slant on family life.

… They [physicians in training] need to be honest about the different competing forces in their life. Potential conflict about location between wife and husband needs to be negotiated.

… The change in medicine is that people in the old days, they chose a job [and] the intention was that it will be their practice forever. Now, [it is] I will try something; if it does not work out, I will try something else. Not so sure [that] it is necessarily bad. People out in practice move around a lot more than they have before. Changing structure of medicine, work for an HMO. Turnover in docs can be 25% a year. People view it as a job; don't bring in the same sense of commitment; some of it may be because they are an employee, not in their own practice. What is the cart, what is the horse? If you know you're not going to be in control of your environment, you do approach it differently. If you are not on a salary, your attitude is a little different.

All the stuff going on with regulation has put a slant on people's view of the job. More of a job rather than a calling. All this shift mentality and people not taking ownership for what they do. They do not have the same dedication to taking care of patients.

Employers overall expressed ambivalence related to their employees' attitudes toward work–family commitments. On the one hand, they respected their abilities to set boundaries and viewed emerging and young adults bringing their personal best to their respective worksites ("110% while on the job"), but they identified a difference in terms of their own work attitudes. Many employers, in contrast to their perceptions of emerging and young adult employees, viewed themselves as committed to doing what needed to be done in the service of their respective work settings.

Mentoring

Mentoring was identified by employers as helpful and empowering in assisting emerging and young adults to adapt and advance in the workplace. According to Allen, Poteet, and Russell (as cited by Casto, Caldwell, & Salazar, 2005) mentoring is a relationship in which a less experienced individual is nurtured, trained and "shown the ropes" by a more experienced person. A divergence of views was expressed with respect to mentoring availability. Assessments made by Derek (supervisor of mental health personnel), Serge (supervisor of technology consultants), Alisa (supervisor of educational personnel), and David (supervisor of physicians in training) represent the diverse views expressed by participants with respect to mentoring availability.

Derek: Mentoring is not structurally available. We are asked to mentor but no one has time for that. Way too busy to help someone. Only way we can structurally do it is through internships. It is costly.... It is not structurally available. What structure is available in corporate America? The idea of a mentor selflessly providing a service is important, but everything needs to get paid for.

Serge: I think mentoring is very important. I do agree that it is not the easiest thing. It is easier if you are a goal-directed person. If you are not, it is harder to get mentored .... I think a lot of mentoring is available and goes unused. The kids don't know how to access it and are kind of embarrassed to admit that they need it. I wish that the college experience included a lot of mentoring. Not something that you had to seek out, something you had to go through.

And the last piece of that is that it requires good social skills to tap people of another generation. Kids have lack of social skills. It is missing for a lot of kids, what we call home training. I understand that our generation is so task-oriented and busy.

Alisa: I don't believe that it is that difficult to find mentors. [It is] difficult for individuals to reach out to the mentors. It has to do with the thought [that] they will be blown off, made fun of, pushed away, when in fact a lot of people are very happy to assist people and give guidance. You don't know how they will respond. A lack of understanding of how people are actually. Here is this adult above them, an authority they have to deal with, and that is intimidating. I know how difficult my career path was, and if I could make it easier for someone I would be happy to do that.

David: [Mentoring is] problematic in our profession. It is hard to mandate mentors. Like any relationship there needs to be a certain chemistry. You have to promote an environment where people are able to seek out mentors. The problem in medicine [is] a lot of people who are viewed as role models are not the most happy or content.

The bottom line is that in medicine [doctors are] dealing with pressures that they never dealt with before. [It has] caused disillusionment, anger, which sometimes gets translated down to people that they are mentoring.

The importance of emerging and young adults reaching out to potential mentors was emphasized by Marie (supervisor of sales personnel). Embarrassment and shame were thought to inhibit emerging and young adults from reaching out to mentors.

You need to reach out. People are very open to sharing and that holds true for me professionally. I am always happy to share a profession that I have enjoyed with someone that is younger.

Overwhelmingly, mentoring was valued by employers and viewed as helpful in launching and sustaining careers. The views expressed regarding the positive aspects of mentoring are supported in the literature. Employers interviewed tended to agree with the perspective that good mentoring provides opportunities for individuals to ascertain how to best maximize their talents (Csikszentmihalyi & Schneider, 2000) and that positive mentoring experiences provide opportunity to demonstrate career commitment, a finding that is particularly relevant to women and minority groups (Russell, 1994). Women who advance to senior management are more likely to report having mentors, in comparison to men (Russell, 1994). In addition, women who do not reach senior managerial positions are more likely to attribute lack of support and instrumental help from supervisors as one of the essential factors responsible for lack of advancement (Burke, 1994).

With good mentoring, emerging and young adults are better prepared to negotiate complex work scenarios including acquisition of skillsets in the interpersonal realm (i.e., office politics), as well as skillsets related to knowledge-based expertise of the industry (Casto, Caldwell, & Salazar, 2005). Key functions that mentors provide particularly for marginalized populations include: (1) recommendations for promotions, (2) encouragement to strive for higher goals, (3) advising mentees on their worth and enhancing their self confidence, (4) helping them cope with others' resentments and discrimination, as well as deal more effectively with their coworkers, (5) pointing out their positive attributes to others, (6) helping mentees overcome discouragement, (7) inspiring mentees to be more creative, (7) keeping their performance visible to senior management, and (8) giving them credit for their work (Russell, 1994). Good mentoring has been identified as particularly helpful to women and other minority groups with respect to advancement (Allen, Proteet, & Russell, 2000). Mentoring assists individuals to "combat feelings of isolation and marginalization" (Casto, Caldwell, & Salazar, 2005, p. 333).

Based on interviews conducted with emerging and young adults, a difference between the views of employers and emerging and young adults was identified with respect to mentoring. Many emerging and young adults tended to view potential mentors as pressed for time, pressured to produce within tight deadlines, and not adequately "incentivized" to mentor. Given recent cuts in middle-management personnel, there was also the perception by some emerging and young adult participants that there existed a paucity of available mentors. Despite a work context that may not support mentoring relationships (given time pressures and lack of financial compensation), a majority of employers interviewed tended to view mentoring relationships as available, if appropriately sought out by emerging and young adults. Participant employers urged emerging and young adults to "reach out" to potential mentors, and to overcome feelings of possible embarrassment or shame. Fiscal concerns associated with the mentoring role were also raised by employer participants. Employers interviewed were volunteers which may account for the enthusiasm expressed regarding mentoring, and their assessments may be overly optimistic.

Advice Offered by Employers

Passion was identified and reinforced as an important driver of career choice and behavior. The most frequently given advice by employers and emerging and young adults related to the importance of the pursuit of passion. Employers and emerging and young adults are allied with respect to the value of passion. Brad, Ellen, and David describe emerging and young adults as passionate, and provide the following advice.

Brad: I would say that the most important thing to me [is that] they should only pursue something that in their hearts is exciting to them. But, I often say to people who are doing research, if you wake up in the middle of the night, and all you think about is the science, that is a good sign. I think they need to follow their hearts, not just their heads. They need to think about it in a quiet moment, unencumbered by influence of parents and close friends. What really excites them. The irony is that the only way to find your passion is to give yourself the time to find it. And that is okay.

Ellen: I always advise [emerging and young adults] to follow your passion. It is where your gifts lie. It is where you take risks; intuitively you know when you can take risks …. Follow your passion, not completely blindly. Focus your passion where there is opportunity. You will really make a difference in the world. When we follow our passion, we can create a better world. We cannot, as a society, do everybody's job. You create a healthy society when you follow your passion because your passion is where your gifts are …. Fundamentally, you are happier and that has its own rewards.

David: Follow your passion. You have to be happy doing what you are doing, and if you are happy you will do a good job at it. Choosing your career, you have to objectively look at not only what turns you on, but objectively look at what your strengths and weaknesses are.

The system has been set up at too accelerated a pace. Kids don't have time to assess where they are going, to sort out all the different career options. These kids for instance, they feel like they get caught up in a roller coaster. Easy to feel the pressure .... No need to rush into something. Take your time and you will have a better sense of what is best for you.

They may take an extra year before applying for a fellowship. The vast majority need to realize that there is nothing wrong with that. All the stuff going on with regulation has put a slant on people's view of the job. More of a job rather than a calling.

Employers advised against premature foreclosure. They urged emerging and young adults to honestly and realistically assess their skillsets and determine how they interface with the marketplace. In addition, employers argued for colleges and educational systems to take a more proactive stance in preparing students for the world of work, a recommendation reinforced by Arnett (2006).

Existing Tensions, Expressed Concerns

Some employers identified a difference in orientation toward work between baby boomer employers and their employees. Existing tensions associated with personal beliefs about responsibility to oneself versus responsibility to an organization were identified. Ellen, a 44-year-old manager working in the arts, relates an experience with an employee taking time off to "grieve" to be emotionally available to a friend, an action she views as irresponsible:

We had an ambitious clear plan how to turn around a Web site. The art director was out for a week, unable to work on the project for two weeks. She [an emerging adult employee] did not have a sense of responsibility for it. She felt she had to go through a grieving process. It was more important for her to be part of this grieving experience with her friends. She was not obligated to her work responsibilities. For the 20–30 generation, for them work is a nice thing if it fits with their agenda. What is more important is their emotional state, pacing their life according to what their needs are, rather than fitting into an organizational structure's needs. She [the employee] knew the person who died peripherally, and nevertheless she chose to be a support for her close friend who was grieving the loss .... [They have] been catered to all their lives. Everything in their lives has been organized around them, for them, around their needs.

In contrast, Ellen's experience of herself, as well as others of her generation, is in opposition to what she observes:

[We] tended to organize our needs around the needs of others at times .... They seem to be emotionally needy. [They] come from a place where they are more catered to, they are used to having [attention], and they demand more attention to their emotional needs. They are not as focused on work—it is more about what work can do for them personally. They resonate with work as a personal journey. I viewed myself as falling into an organizational structure. I am not used to putting my emotional needs before the needs of an organization. I viewed myself as needing to sacrifice for the organization.

Drew, a 37-year-old manager of emerging and young adults working in the automobile parts industry, echoes Ellen's sentiments:

Talking from my own personal work ethic ...[they need] to understand that they need to be patient and take their time, and to respect personal responsibility. I think that people I supervise, in general, they don't feel as accountable, and therefore not as reliable. Follow-through is poor. I see it more out there, coming from the expectation that they don't need to be accountable.

Tensions between emerging and young adults and employers are a natural outgrowth of existing generational diversity in the workforce. Sixty percent of employers report that "their workplaces suffer from tension between the genera-tions" (Twenge, 2006, p. 217). The following exchange described by Moses (2005) captures generational differences at work.

Baby boomer employers: Get real. All you care about is getting to the gym or hooking up with your friends after work. When I was your age, if my boss asked me to work late, I did. It's part of the deal, if you want to get ahead. (¶ 17)

Emerging and young adults: Don't hold yourself up as a model. You're out of shape, grumpy, never see your family and your boss doesn't appreciate you. (¶ 18)

A comparison of advice offered by representative experts in the field—Twenge (2006), Moses (2006), and Trunk (2006)—sheds further light on existing ten-sions. Twenge (2006, p. 217) offers the following advice to employers supervising emerging and young adults.

The best thing you can do is realize that this generation is not "spoiled" and does not "have it easy." Gen Me has been raised thinking we were special and getting lots from Mom and Dad, but when we hit young adulthood we face an enormous mismatch between what we expect and what we actually get. Before you say, "Poor babies," realize that the inflated cost of housing and the ultra-competitive market for college and good jobs would be difficult even without our high expectations. A boss who understands this will have a much easier time connecting with young employees. Young people are unlikely to change overnight and berating them isn't going to do any good.

... This generation is not motivated by feelings of duty—working hard is not virtuous in itself, but it is worth it if they are singled out and recognized .... They appreciate directness rather than abstraction. They do not have automatic respect for authority and will feel free to make suggestions if they think it will improve things. You may have to earn their respect rather than receiving it simply by your position in the company.

Moses (2006), an organizational career management expert, acknowledges that both employers and emerging and young adults wish to engage with meaningful stimulating work "in a pleasant environment where efforts are recognized while still allowing time for a life" (p. 1). In attempting to appeal to employers' desire to attract and retain emerging and young adult employees, Moses offers the following descriptions.

1. The "effort/reward ratio is out of whack" with not enough focus on employees and too much focus on productivity. In a toxic environment, employees show "an erosion of interpersonal skill, conflict with team members, petty resentments, growing rudeness and crankiness" and that affects the bottom line. In order to function optimally a collegial environment is needed. (p. 1)

2. They have high expectations that their feelings count, they should be happy all the time and they should be treated with the nurturing care that their parents and teachers showed them. They also want their work to be fun and to interact with other young people. And they are ambitious. (p. 1)

In response to the descriptions offered, Moses (2006) offers the following prescriptions.

1. Understand their desires for collegiality, treat them with sensitivity, and provide lots of learning opportunities. And provide them with high-profile assignments, and lots of feedback and recognition. (p. 2)

2. Accept piercings, tattoos. Ten years ago, it was about accepting guys with earrings. Now it's about embracing employees with visible tattoos and metal beyond the earlobes. Many managers have difficulty with this but body ornamentation is a reality they will have to face and, as piercings and tattoos are moving into the mainstream, managers better get used to them. (p. 2)

3. Recognize individual differences in motivation, whether it's belonging to a team, moving up a ladder, being intellectually stimulated, having security, or doing pleasant work that does not spill into personal life. (p. 2)

4. One of the best predictors of employee engagement is career development. Many younger employees received little support in the earlier part of their careers, entering the workplace in the nineties, when overworked managers did not have the time to nurture them. Organizations now need to race to make up for lost time with coaching, mentoring, and leadership training. This will ready a younger generation of workers to step into the shoes of retiring older managers. (p. 4)

Trunk (2006) and Moses (2005) offer the following advice primarily focused on issues related to emerging and young adults in the workforce. They focus on issues related to communication with baby boomer bosses:

1. You need to make sure that your boss understands that you have shorter-term goals and that you care most about issues such as being challenged, learning new skills, and preserving your personal life. Make your priorities clear to your boss so that you don't get sidetracked in areas irrelevant to you .... Make a list of skills and knowledge you want to accumulate in the next two years. Bring the list to your boss and ask which your boss can help you with. (Trunk, 2006, ¶ 7)

2. You might want to say, "Stop talking to me about my career at this company. I'm leaving in two years to start my own." Instead, you will get a better response if you say, "It would be a big help to me if we could focus on what I'm doing this quarter." (Trunk, 2006, ¶ 16)

3. If you do this and you don't get what you want, you should leave. Don't sit in a job with a baby boomer who doesn't get it. Vote with your feet .... It costs companies so much to replace a worker that they will eventually change. (Trunk, 2006, ¶ 18)

4. Recognize that you and your boss look at the world differently. Still, it's up to you to manage your boss. Communicate what personal time you are and are not prepared to

give up …. Show awareness of his or her needs. For example, you may need to pull a few all-nighters for an important project, but it's reasonable to get some free time in return. (Moses, 2005, ¶ 19)

5. If your boss doesn't get it and you don't feel the effort–reward equation is warranted by the skills you are learning, look for another job. If you resent being at work, you are neither happy nor an effective contributor. (Moses, 2005, ¶ 21)

Advice offered by Twenge (2006), Moses (2005, 2006), and Trunk (2006) are representative of the existing tensions between emerging and young adults and their older employers. Twenge, Moses, and Trunk bring an understanding of the complexity of the issues, and each is attempting to constructively address productivity and satisfaction levels. Questions abound whether the prescriptions offered above can be: (1) heard and appreciated by the other, and (2) experienced as helpful to the other. A darker outlook suggests that the interventions proposed may exacerbate existing tensions. What is clear is that there is convergence with respect to the experience of the environmental context. Both employers and emerging adults described the work environment in similar terms. What is less clear is how to best address identified concerns and tensions. Wakefield (2006) concludes that given generational diversity in the workforce and the challenges associated with diversity of views and orientations, it behooves organizations to "find ways to connect the values of each generation" (p. 5).

Employers and emerging and young adults, as well as the organizations in which they function, will need to engage in a process that requires understanding and working with the perspective of the other. As Wakefield (2006) describes below, collectively, the diversity of perspectives between employers and emerging and young adults can serve to enrich and propel progress:

Understanding generational differences can help an organization recruit, develop and retain professionals of all ages. It can also help to promote generational dialogue on topics such as past and current assumptions about issues and their causes, and how these issues have been addressed and how to move solutions forward in the coming decades. (p. 5)

Conclusions

Despite a range of representation of employer participants, there tended to be unanimity with respect to perceptions of the work environment as highly competitive and lacking loyalty. Employers overwhelmingly agreed with the views of emerging and young adults, as well as parents, that the work environment often treated employees as commodities, disposable in the context of changing market conditions. Those emerging and young adults without valued skillsets, typically grounded in the liberal arts, although intellectually adept, were viewed by employers as vulnerable. Employers overwhelmingly noted the flexibility and sense of comfort with diversity emerging and young adults brought to their respective work environments.

Employers observed a difference in attitudes with respect to work–life balance issues. As viewed by employers, emerging and young adults, although hard-working, creative, and industrious as a group, were more likely to set limits in their respective work settings, in particular on issues related to work overload. Employers, viewing emerging and young adult through their prism, tended to experience their emerging and young adult employees as less conforming and less committed to prevailing cultural corporate norms. Although both employers and employees are in pursuit of work–life balance, potential tensions are likely to emerge given a difference in worldviews, particularly with respect to conformity to prevailing corporate norms.

References

Allen, T., Poteet, M., & Russell, J. E. (2000). Protégé selection by mentors: What makes the difference? *Journal of Organizational Behavior, 21*, 271–282.

Arnett, J. & Tanner, J. (2006). *Emerging adults in America: Coming of age in the 21st century.* Washington, DC: American Psychological Association.

Blustein, D., Junthunen, C., & Worthington, R. (2000). The school-to-work transition: Adjustment challenges for the forgotten half. In S. D. Brown & R. W. Lent (Eds.), *Handbook of counseling psychology* (pp. 435–470). New York: Wiley.

Burke, R. (1994). Benefits of mentoring in organizations: The mentor's perspective. *Journal of Managerial Psychology, 9*, 23–32.

Casto, C., Caldwell, C., & Salazar, C. (2005). Creating mentoring relationships between female faculty and students in counselor education: Guideline for potential mentees and mentors. *Journal of Counseling & Development, 83*, 331–336.

Cleaver, J. (2006, July 23). Younger moms are stating their needs. *Boston Globe*, G6.

Csikszentmihalyi, M. & Schneider, B. (2000) *Becoming adult: How teenagers prepare for the world of work.* New York: Basic.

Hamilton, S. & Hamilton, M. (2006). School, work, and emerging adulthood. In J. Arnett and J. Tanner (Eds.), *Emerging adults in America: Coming of age in the 21st century* (pp. 257–277). Washington, DC: American Psychological Association.

Moses, B. (2005, December 15). 20-somethings: The work angst generation. *Globe & Mail*, retrieved October 8, 2006, from http://www.bbmcareerdev.com/booksarticles_articles_detail.php?article=15.

Moses, B. (2006, February 17). Employers: Dangle the right carrots to entice workers, *Globe & Mail*, retrieved October 6, 2006, from http://www.bbmcareerdev.com/booksarticles_articles_detail.php?article=5.

Russell, J. (1994). Career counseling for women in management. In B. Walsh & S. Osipow (Eds.), *Career counseling for women* (pp. 263–326). Hillsdale, NJ: Lawrence Erlbaum.

Trunk, P. (2006, January 22). Managing up means managing a boomer boss. *Boston Globe*, Boston Works, p. G1.

Twenge, J. (2006). *Generation me: Why today's young Americans are more confident, assertive, entitled—And more miserable than ever before.* New York: Free Press.

Wakefield, M. (2006).Our legacy: Honoring the past, connecting to our future. *Counseling Today*, 5.

9
Running on Empty, Running on Full: Summary and Synthesis

A book review by Henry (2006) of *Generation Me: Why Today's Young Americans Are More Confident, Assertive, Entitled—And More Miserable Than Ever Before*, depicts this generation as "the most wanted generation in history" (given advances in birth control) and the most pampered. As Henry (2006) points out, they have learned their lessons well:

Feeling good about yourself is the most important thing in life .... Self-love is not so much a goal as a birthright .... Old-fashioned values like hard work and skill have been cast aside in favor of giving everyone a gold star—because they're good enough, smart enough, and doggone it, people like them! (p. 32)

Ryan, a 26-year-old participant, offers an alternative perspective:

My generation is self-centered for a reason. We never felt that the institutions were there for us. Long-term jobs and pensions are not there. Social security is going to disappear. You know what? I have to take care of myself. I felt screwed in my 20s; the baby boomers are to blame; their gain is my loss.

The two perspectives offer divergent assessments of emerging and young adults living in the United States. The first narrative depicts emerging and young adults as coddled, self-involved, undisciplined, and seeking and expecting immediate gratification as well as unconditional recognition. The second narrative describes dysfunctional and/or vanishing systems that are in large part due to irresponsibility and lack of forethought and planning on the part of the boomer generation. Emerging and young adults face the onerous task of not only having to fend for themselves, but also having to clean up the "mess" left behind.

A nuanced complex narrative emerges from the interviews revealed in the previous chapters. Emerging and young adults are not a monolithic group, and the meanings they attach to this developmental period as well as the paths they navigated professionally and interpersonally are diverse and textured. It is important to note that the voices captured are those of individuals who are college graduates living on the northeast coast, volunteers, ranging in age from 25 to 35, and therefore findings cannot be generalized to other populations. The voices of parents and employers are specific to this subset as well, with the exception of range in age.

This chapter reviews major findings related to the contexts (work and interpersonal) emerging and young adults encountered, followed by a summary of distinguishing characteristics and attitudes of the stakeholders: emerging and young adults, parents, and employers. The pursuit of passion, choice, and lack of structural supports emerged as distinguishing themes for the stakeholders. First, a review of the environmental context emerging and young adult participants encountered, followed by a brief summary of the data.

The Environmental Context: A Review

Many emerging and young adults encountered an environment in which expectation of promise, opportunity, and possibility was not borne out. With increasing freedom, decreasing security, and lack of structural supports, emerging and young adults experienced increasing pressures, a finding confirmed in the literature (Twenge, 2006). Feelings of anxiety, self-doubt, insecurity, self-blame, anger, betrayal, and/or dissatisfaction were expressed. In the process of trying to launch a career, they experienced a significant discrepancy between expectations held and harsh realities encountered in the workforce.

Twenge (2006) captures the overwhelming barrage of demands and realities emerging and young adult participants confront:

Overwhelming ambition is on a collision course with diminished possibilities. College is more competitive and expensive than ever . . . good jobs are fewer and often pay less; the costs of housing, health insurance and child care continue to spiral. Far from becoming millionaire rapper playboys with their own clothing lines, these kids will be lucky to squeak into the middle class. (p. 33)

Generation Me has been taught to expect more out of life at the very time when good jobs and nice houses are increasingly difficult to obtain. All too often, the result is crippling anxiety and crushing depression. (p. 109)

Generation Me has so much more than previous generations—we are healthier, enjoy countless modern conveniences and are better educated. But Generation Me often lacks other basic requirements: stable close relationships, a sense of community, a feeling of safety, a simple path to adulthood and the workplace . . . . As David Myers argues in his book *The American Paradox*, the United States has become a place where we have more but feel worse . . . . [W]e long for the social connections of past years, we enter a confusing world of too many choices, and we become depressed at younger and younger ages. (p. 136)

Emerging and young adults in both cohorts overwhelmingly aspired toward traditional goals (satisfying career paths, marriage, and children). As Apter (2001) and Arnett (2004) report, participants did transition to adulthood status, but on a protracted basis. Having graduated from college, it appears to take approximately five to ten years on average to shift toward independence (it is interesting to note that Americans are living ten years longer, a time period equivalent to the protracted period emerging and young adults are taking to engage in a process of self-discovery to determine the kind of life they wish to lead). The majority of participants had a defined career path by age 30, and were either married and/or in a committed relationship by age 35. Most of the participants aspired to having at least one child by age 35–40, with a majority of the participants hoping to have two children by age 40.

For many of the participants, the notion of not "settling," finding the "right" person, was key in terms of deciding whether to be in a long-term committed relationship or marriage. Although emerging and young adults expressed similar goals in comparison to their parents' generation, journeys taken to realize expressed goals varied. Their paths included a greater degree of experimentation, exercise of personal choice and options, and a greater emphasis on developing the self. Parental concern regarding their children's reluctance to "settle down" does not appear to be warranted. For parents, waiting may be the antidote; their emerging and young adult children are delaying but not forgoing careers, marriage, and children.

The Context of Work

The stakeholders—emerging and young adults, parents, and employers—described the work terrain in similar terms. Lack of loyalty was an important driver of behavior. Participants described a work context that included an erosion of trust among employees, employers, and their respective institutions, in part due to a highly competitive, fluid, global work environment. Emerging and young adults, some of whom directly observed the devastation of job elimination on their parents, were determined to minimize their sense of vulnerability. Stakeholders interviewed tended to view the search for skillsets and/or better jobs as directly related to a fiercely competitive global marketplace, characterized by a paucity of loyalty and commitment to its workers.

There was recognition by employers, parents, and emerging and young adults that the current marketplace made increasing demands for productivity, while simultaneously providing fewer benefits and guarantees for lifetime employment. In response to a highly competitive and fluid marketplace, emerging and young adults tried to grow and direct their careers, believing that they needed to rely on their own resources, in contrast to gentler times where companies helped direct their employees' futures. Most emerging and young adult participants, particularly individuals in their 20s in search of opportunity, subscribed to the belief that changing jobs frequently would better position them to build skillsets, and/or provide them with a venue to gain greater clarity regarding their calling. The notion of disposability and lack of loyalty in the workplace intensified the search for skillsets and reinforced beliefs related to the importance of self-reliance.

The career paths of the emerging and young adult participants were varied. Some were "on track" (directed career paths, professional or graduate schools). Others tested the waters regarding possible career paths, and a minority of the participants chose to "give back" by committing to time-limited, public, service-oriented programs. Many actively experimented with job possibilities, with most of the participants in pursuit of "passion" and "skillsets" to guide their journey. A majority of the participants reported feeling unprepared for the abrupt shift that occurred once they entered the workforce. Many became disillusioned and struggled with jobs that did not utilize their perceived intellectual capacities and talents.

The primacy of developing a satisfying and meaningful career pervaded the narratives of emerging and young adult participants. Most revisited and reassessed career expectations and perceived choices, some with deliberate forethought, others more randomly. By age 30 most of the participants were on a career trajectory. They acknowledged that their career paths might shift over time, given current marketplace realities. The majority spoke to the importance of maintaining a flexible open stance, a perspective that was reinforced by employers and parents.

A minority of employers expressed frustration related to the attitudes and behaviors emerging and young adults brought to the workforce including descriptors such as demanding, entitled, lacking patience, expecting too much too soon, and not willing to put in the necessary time needed for advancement. They also, however, acknowledged that the current workforce is less likely to retire at age 65, "clogging up the pipes" for emerging and young adults. Parents expressed ambivalence toward their children's experimental stance. Although they simultaneously applauded their children's efforts to optimally position themselves in the workplace, they also expressed concern related to the length of time taken to develop career paths and marital relationships.

Questions arise as to whether the delays observed and the accompanying behaviors described are a manifestation of an immature, impatient, and irresponsible, "me generation", or evidence of a prudent generation, learning to adapt and thrive in an environment that views them as disposable, and is not sufficiently supportive of their actual and potential contributions. Although 66% of CEOs identified high-quality employees as the greatest contribution to growth, and recognized that additional incentives and training and development programs are needed, the vast majority of emerging and young adults, particularly those who did not follow a prescribed career path, did not encounter work settings that validated their actual and potential value, a finding also reported by Dvorak (2006). Many felt devalued and underutilized in the workforce. A contract had been broken from their perspective: they worked hard in college and expected to be embraced and appreciated in their respective job settings.

In the context of a work environment that did not provide them with sufficient opportunity and structural supports, many emerging and young adults adopted a strategy of experimentation; some actively pursued skillsets that appeared to build and expand on existing skillsets, and others engaged in a more random process of employment, hoping to find their passion and/or career path along the way. Given the instability in their work lives, in the context of high divorce rates, they tended to delay commitment, although most envisioned a marital relationship and child(ren). As Emily, a 31-year-old participant states:

We see our parents worked so hard. Then they get divorced, never traveled. Why not do these things while you are young? You have strength and energy, and start the career a little bit later. Really be sure about it, and start to have the career a little later and have kids later.

Our parents graduated thinking that marriage was the greatest thing. We graduated knowing that half of all marriages end in divorce.

The Social Context

The majority of the participants followed a pathway that included "identity-before-intimacy," that is having one's career in place, before launching a long-term committed relationship. Having a range of interpersonal experiences tended to be valued and viewed by the participants as helpful in defining and consolidating one's identity. Most emerging and young adult participants were invested in developing themselves before marriage, preferring to have a sense of themselves as "complete," capable of making a commitment to another who is also "complete." Participants attached significance to having a satisfying career in place. They tended to view investment in self as increasing the likelihood of a successful marriage and/or a long-term commitment.

Flexibility and fluidity characterized the interpersonal relationships of many of the participants. Just as Coontz (2005) has observed that there is increasing flexibility and fluidity with respect to the institution of marriage, there also appears to be increased fluidity and flexibility in relationships prior to marriage. With increased fluidity, there exists possibility for increased casualness in relationships. Committing to marriage without prior experimentation could be "risky," and experimentation was associated with mitigation of risk. Participants aspired to an identity that felt coherent and integrated, one that allowed for entering a relationship "complete." Fear of divorce informed views and concerns related to long-term commitment and marriage. Many of the participants experimented with a range of individuals. They tended to value difference in their relationships, in part to ascertain goodness-of-fit with a potential life partner, and in part to address concerns related to averting financial loss associated with a poor choice regarding a life partner.

Emerging and young adults, mindful of alarming divorce rates associated with their parents' generation, were motivated not to replicate their behavior. One approach to mitigating risk included intensive discussion prior to marriage of roles and responsibilities. Many emerging and young adults appeared to be on a mission to try to avert failure in their personal lives. Although the pursuit of passion informed work-related behavior, many of the participants spoke of their personal relationships with forethought and deliberation.

The majority of the participants in the study considered friendships key to living a balanced, meaningful, and enriching life. Friendships provided stability and support in a highly fluid and mobile work and social context. They tended to speak of their friends as "families outside of their families." A significant minority of the participants (particularly those in their 20s who were not married and/or with children) recreated a sense of family vis-à-vis their friendships. Overall, participants in both cohorts tended to view friendships as an important source of sustenance and support. They tended to report a greater degree of openness and trust in their relationships with friends, when compared to their parents' generation. Over time, an increasingly important component of friendship included reciprocal support: Each individual in the friendship could count on the other for emotional and tangible support.

Although friendships were highly valued, participants struggled with lack of stability vis-à-vis their friendships. Many emerging and young adults, given a fluid work environment, experienced friends leaving and reconnecting over time. E-mail, phone calls, and instant messages, although helpful in keeping in touch, did not appear to satisfy or replace the social support received via live, face-to-face encounters.

Perceived timelines for having children created significant tensions, particularly for female participants. Once married, with child(ren), a majority of the married female participants experienced tensions related to juggling multiple roles. They reported feeling pressured, and did not experience their work settings as supportive of their values and goals. In the context of "you should be everything" and "have it all," balancing responsibilities for family and career felt overwhelming for many of the female participants (Warner, 2005, p. 130).

Distinguishing Themes

The previous chapters identified themes that were specific to each of the stake-holders: emerging and young adults, parents, and employers. This section focuses on common themes that emerged for the various stakeholders, and their implications: (1) pursuit of passion, (2) choice and its impact, and (3) lack of structural supports.

The Pursuit of Passion

Employers, parents, and emerging and young adults spoke to the importance of finding passion, meaning, purpose, and significance in one's work. A minority of emerging adults, particularly in the affluent cohort, expressed a desire to not only find passion in their work, but also find meaningful work that was fun and engaging. High expectations related to work were expressed by emerging and young adults (more pronounced in the affluent cohort), as well as parents. However, for many emerging and young adults, particularly for those without clearly delineated career paths, expectations were in conflict with the realities they encountered.

A minority of emerging and young adults interviewed were disheartened or burdened by their inability to either identify or find passion in their work. Hassler's (2005) assertions regarding the role of passion in our work life is illuminating, given the emphasis on the pursuit of passion by the various stakeholders in this study. Most individuals in their 20s, according to Hassler, are not adept at identifying their passions. Whereas for some, careers fulfill a need for purpose and passion, for others, the process of finding passion in one's work may be a more elusive process. Furthermore, for many emerging and young adults, as has been reported in the literature and confirmed by the interviews conducted, work has taken center stage with respect to identity development. The degree of investment in work, superimposed by the mandate of finding passion in one's work, may leave some emerging and young adults feeling very pressured and vulnerable.

Although a majority of the stakeholders subscribed to the importance of passion in guiding one's work, the author did not ascertain meanings attached to the pursuit of passion. A range of personal meanings associated with the pursuit of passion can be implied, but were not specifically assessed. For example, the pursuit of passion may include (1) finding "flow" (Csikszentmihalyi, 1997); (2) finding something of one's own that satisfies needs for autonomy, independence, and self-expression; or (3) finding meaning, purpose, or significance in one's work. Is the pursuit of passion a manifestation of the idealism or high expectations espoused by emerging and young adults? A darker view related to the pursuit of passion includes the notion that passion is an acceptable "buzzword" that perpetuates and frames the search for the "perfect life," and may inadvertently legitimize avoidant behavior.

The quest for passion may co-occur with the quest for the perfect job, perfect spouse or significant other, or the perfect life. Not "settling" in one's personal or professional life appeared to guide the decision-making processes of some of the participants, particularly those in the affluent cohort. Some subscribed to the belief that there is one "right" job, one "right" significant other, and that it is their responsibility to "figure it all out." To pursue a job that is not "the right one" suggests that one is settling for less. For emerging and young adults who strive for both passion and perfectionism in their work and personal lives, confusion and angst frequently followed.

The Dark Side of Passion: Implications

Hassler (2005) suggests an alternative, potentially freeing, strategy that may minimize the burden associated with the goal of pursuing one's passion, particularly for those emerging and young adults who are unable to identify their passion(s). She suggests the following: identification of one's "dream jobs," juxtaposed with a realistic assessment of one's strengths and skillsets, as well as consideration of marketplace contingencies. Her recommendation can potentially minimize pressures associated with the pursuit of one's passion. In addition, Hassler suggests that it is critical to separate what one does from who one is. The separation assists in minimizing vulnerability associated with the notion that what one does for work can "fill a void or complete us" (Hassler, 2005, p. 272). Work can define us as individuals, at the expense of other domains awaiting further development.

Choice

Choice emerged as an important theme for the various stakeholders. Although the prevailing narrative for the more affluent cohort of emerging and young adults included ambivalence related to overwhelming choice, for the less affluent cohort, a narrative related to risk and risk management emerged. The experience of choice was qualitatively different for many of the participants in the less affluent cohort. For some, there was a perception of scarcity of choice. Navigating within more limited degrees of freedom, that is, greater restrictions on one's ability to maneuver and take risks, appeared to be the more pressing concern for many of the participants in the less affluent cohort. For them, the need for a safety net limited choice selection.

In a context of abundance, emerging and young adults confronted an interesting paradox with respect to choice selection. They welcomed choice and possibility in their lives, but at the same time felt burdened and ill-prepared to deal with the array of choice available to them. Employers and parents also emphasized the difficulty inherent in negotiating what seemingly appeared to be a multitude of choices. Each of the stakeholders spoke to the co-existence of limitless possibilities with limited opportunities.

Schwartz (2004) argues that the cumulative effect of abundance of choice is distress, particularly in the context of regret and aspiration for social status, and wanting to experience the best of everything. He offers a paradigm for understanding and responding to an environmental context characterized by abundance of choice. Limiting the size of the fishbowl appears to be an apt and insightful possibility for those emerging and young adults who struggle with abundance of choice (as proposed by Schwartz), however, expanding the size of the fishbowl, within the confines of a safe harbor, appears to more accurately characterize the experiences and wishes of the cohort of emerging and young adults who encountered a context characterized by limited economic resources.

Many of the participants, constrained by economic limitations and family obligations, showed resolve with respect to overcoming adversity. They were able to assume adult roles, and honor their commitments to others. However, their ability to follow their dreams was compromised. For example, Denise, a 27-year-old participant, expressed a desire to pursue graduate school, but given financial and family responsibilities, chose to consider the needs of her family, and "delay" the resumption of her education. The meaning of choice as it relates to emerging and young adults needs to be contextualized to include and integrate experiences not only related to abundance, but also related to scarcity. The interplay between choice and available resources during the developmental period of emerging and young adulthood needs further clarification and elaboration.

The prevailing narrative as it is represented in the literature appears to represent the diverse voices of those emerging and young adults who live in relative affluence. For those individuals with fewer economic resources and safety nets, a different narrative emerges, one related to risk and risk management. Participants in the less affluent cohort may prosper from an environment that exposes them to a wider range of possibilities, one that includes provision of a larger fishbowl in which to swim.

The Dark Side of Choice: Implications

We worry about making the right choice, and we have no one else to blame when our choices go wrong. Personal freedom, the hallmark of our times, is a glorious thing, but too often we stand alone with our self-doubt about our own choices.

(Twenge, 2006, p. 119)

Unprecedented choice has created an environment rife with potential and possibility, but it has also created a need to "keep things simple . . . to silence the existence of choice in our lives" (Nash & Stevenson, 2004, p. 281). Maximization paradigms are problematic according to Nash and Stevenson (2004) and Schwartz (2004), given that increased choice also increases the likelihood of indecisiveness and exhaustion. Schwartz provides a framework for understanding choice that is potentially freeing. Many emerging and young adults may be picking rather than choosing, maximizing rather than satisficing in ways that may be counterproductive. As individuals age, they are less likely to assume a maximizing stance (Schwartz, 2004). With increasing experience, individuals adapt more realistic expectations, and are more receptive and satisfied with the notion of good enough. Schwartz (2004, p. 5) confirms this view:

The idea of multiple attractive beckoning options is something that is specific to modernity. As adults we have learned (not all too well) how to say no to things we find attractive. Knowing the best way to teach kids how to pass up attractive options would make a real contribution to our understanding of modern parenting and its challenges.

Abundance of expectations and choice has created a unique set of challenges. Satisficing is a difficult and initially painful process to implement in day-to-day practice, particularly in a context of relative abundance. It requires giving up the desire to have the best of everything in every domain of our lives; it requires struggling with loss and "settling" for less. Interventions targeted toward the dark side of choice require a new way of thinking about our expectations and thoughts associated with "just enough." However, Schwartz concludes:

To manage the problem of excessive choice, we must decide which choices in our lives really matter and focus our time and energy there, letting many other opportunities pass us by. But by restricting our options, we will be able to choose less and feel better. (p. 22)

The trick is to learn to embrace and appreciate satisficing, to cultivate it in more and more aspects of life, rather than merely being resigned to it. Becoming a conscious, intentional satisficer makes comparison with how other people are doing less important. It makes regret less likely. In the complex, choice-saturated world we live in, it makes peace of mind possible. (p. 225)

Structural Supports

The stakeholders—emerging and young adults, parents, and to a lesser extent employers—alluded to the lack of available structural support in shaping the experiences of emerging and young adults. Emerging and young adults tended to subscribe to the expectation that they be able to effectively navigate markets for jobs utilizing their own resources. Many were overwhelmed, particularly those with skills and resources that did not meet external and internal expectations. They spoke to the need for increased opportunities in conjunction with systemic support to assist them in successfully negotiating the transition to adulthood.

Apter (2001) concludes that emerging adults in the United States are facing an environment characterized by "decreasing social capital" (p. 267), which privileges those with safety nets. She focuses on the need for greater scaffolding:

> Over and over, they [emerging adults] expressed a wish for more personal guidelines and safety nets . . . . [T]hey crave acknowledgment of their hopes. This acknowledgment can be expressed by helping them develop plans to realize their hopes. (p. 264)

Emerging and young adults, parents, and employers spoke of the difficulties inherent in transitioning from the relatively safe confines of college to the world of work. They poignantly described the abrupt shift that occurred, with many emerging and young adults reporting feeling rudderless and disconnected. The powerful combination of heightened expectations and the perception of unlimited choice (for some), in conjunction with limited opportunities was particularly difficult to navigate. Representative comments by Adena, a 35-year-old participant raised by a single parent on welfare, summarize the prevailing attitudes regarding lack of preparation and lack of support.

> I received absolutely zero guidance as a young adult in high school. Because I had such organization and discipline of focus, no one bothered to tell me about the myriad choices that I knew nothing about. I would have explored much more; getting a journalism degree, public communication, drama degree, interior design. I would have considered many things. The practice of law would have been a much smaller piece of the pie, had I known what I know today.

Adena expressed a moderate degree of regret regarding the meandering path she took both professionally and personally during her 20s. She lacked tangible support at home, as well as at school, and wished that mentors were available to assist her. Although she described her mother as wise, Adena assessed that her mother did not have the skills to help her navigate her career. She did, however, appreciate her mother's wisdom. Adena provides an example: despite significant financial limitations, Adena was given a weekly allowance, an action she associates with responsibility and opportunity to execute choice. It has taken Adena 12 years post college to achieve a sense of stability and satisfaction in her personal and professional life. She has launched her own consulting company within the past year, after multiple careers including law. She is currently in a satisfying marital relationship. Adena has made a deliberate decision not to have children, intending to focus her energies on her career and marriage.

Sergio, a 26-year-old immigrant from Bulgaria, refers to the significant impact Robert Kiyosaki, author of the book *Rich Dad, Poor Dad*, has had on his life. He describes himself as shy and initially unprepared to deal with the cultural differences he encountered both professionally and socially. He recounts experiencing no supports at school, and relied on Kiyosaki to inspire and guide his future career path:

I found it [*Rich Dad, Poor Dad*] very inspirational. I wish [that] I read it a bit earlier. It talks about how rich people and poor people think. Basically before reading that book, I had no idea what I wanted to do with my life. I was basically in school getting a degree to get a job. But then after reading the book, I found that may not be the best path to follow. There are other options out there. Investing, starting a business. Things like that. On top of that, the author talks about even if you work all your life, basically [you are] not guaranteed anything at the end of it. Like pensions . . . . At least the book gave me hope, gave me a direction. Options you never thought about exactly.

I was raised [in a family] where money was not discussed. Go to school, get a degree, get a job, and you are all set. Almost like I did not know anything else. I could not possibly have known about these other choices; like fish in the water, they don't know there is anything outside of water.

Both Adena and Sergio identify the need for individual and systemic support to assist them in the process of transitioning to adulthood. They brought many resources, including intellectual and emotional capital; however, they experienced a paucity of assistance along the way. Thoughtful scaffolding can provide the needed support for emerging and young adults, who like "fish in the water, they don't know there is anything outside of water."

Educational institutions have been remiss in providing scaffolding to offset the tendency toward "privatizing" the plethora of information and potential choices emerging and young adults encounter (Warner, 2005, pp. 162–163). As revealed in the interviews, parents may not have the financial and tangible resources to assist their children. The costs associated with an individualistic, sink or swim, cultural context are significant (Miller, 2006; Twenge, 2006). The increased incidence of eating disorders, substance abuse, clinical depression and/or anxiety, is linked in part to the lack of structural supports emerging and young adults are encountering (Twenge, 2006). Emerging and young adults need assistance with the navigation process, which entails working through a maze of potential choices and possibilities, within a context of limited opportunities for many emerging and young adults.

The problems identified and their respective solutions transcend the individual. A proactive systemic stance is needed, informed by an understanding of the processes influencing the successful transitioning of emerging adults to adulthood. The literature suggests that these skills can be taught. Career exploration, values clarification, and execution of choice are complex issues that require thoughtful comprehensive approaches based on an understanding of human development (Arnett, 2006; Masten, Obradovic, & Burt, 2006; Tanner, 2006). Embedded within a coherent social policy, consideration and provision of equal access and opportunities, particularly for those emerging and young adults at risk is critical. In summary,

Understanding that emerging [and young] adulthood is a developmental period during which individuals benefit from exploring themselves and possibilities in love and work before they make commitments implies that resources should be established (e.g., public policies, workplace initiatives, counseling opportunities) to encourage the developmental and adjustment of all emerging [and young] adults. In this critical turning point in the life span, the years during which adult pathways are established, all emerging [and young] adults should be encouraged to develop a plan and accrue resources that will help them to carry out their plan toward adult self-sufficiency. (Tanner, 2006, p. 48)

Concluding Statements and Case Example

The current environmental context is rife with opportunities to think out of the box, and negotiate possibilities and solutions that are potentially more satisfying. For example, a recent article by Bahney (2006) appearing in the *New York Times* captures an environment of possibility and creativity for emerging and young adults.

Bahney discusses the decision of a 28-year-old man to quit his job and travel so that he can maintain connections and "relationships with people who don't live nearby" (Bahney, 2006, E1). Two weeks of vacation, as this 28-year-old man views it, is "barely enough time to visit [one's] parents for Christmas, go to a friend's wedding and take a long weekend." Similarly, a 32-year-old man quits his job as a software engineer, making a calculated decision that his skillsets are in demand and that he is marketable. He states:

As the retirement age pushes farther back and the finances for that time of life are less and less certain, it was almost unconscionable to not take advantage of the opportunity to travel now, when I had the money and the health . . . . The trick is finding a job that has the balance built in so that I don't have to go off on a grand adventure to recover from work.

. . . [To] be unemployed for six weeks is a healthy thing to help you say I am not defined by what I do. . . . It helps to understand who I am, who my wife is, and that our identity is more important than anything we do . . . . And maybe that's what the younger generation gets that their parents didn't: There's always another job. Having grown up in an era of relative prosperity and upward mobility, it's easy to come to that conclusion (E2).

Each generation navigates the journey to adulthood in its own way, with shared commonalities and distinct differences. Multiple environmental contexts inform the journey and adaptations made. For this cohort of emerging and young adults, the locations in which they reside appear to be particularly salient. Across class, gender, and ethnicity, emerging and young adults are required to navigate the terrain individually, without adequate scaffolding. Within a context of abundance and choice, emerging and young adults are required to demonstrate increased agency, volition, and what Cote (2006) terms "identity capital": self-understanding, self-discipline, and planfulness. Those who lack identity capital are at great risk. They are simultaneously "running on empty" (without adequate scaffolding), and "running on full," negotiating choices in a context of a stimulating environment that is rife with possibilities.

Short- and long-term consequences of the shifting terrain are unknown. For example, will the delays toward establishing careers and long-term relationships result in better choices and increased satisfaction, given increased levels of maturity, cognitive abilities, and overall judgment? Or, will the environmental context described by participants result in disillusionment, decreased productivity, and decreased satisfaction? Will the quality of marital and long-term relationships improve, with perhaps a decrease in divorce rates, or will the delayed commitment to marriage and parenthood result in decreased satisfaction, poorer mental health (in part due to marital status serving a protective mental health function) (Tanner, 2006)? Given the increased level of introspection and experimentation, will the nature of midlife crisis be altered? Little is understood with respect to the long-term consequences of the behavioral shifts reported.

In listening to the voices of emerging and young adults interviewed, what is clear is the degree of complexity and instability emerging and young adults are experiencing. For many of the participants, the navigation process did not include sufficient supports. The majority of the participants approached this juncture with resiliency. Participants, particularly those in the affluent cohort, were confronting issues related to loss. Told that they could do anything and be anything they wanted to be, they actively reassessed and revamped major beliefs and assumptions. The majority of the participants believed in the American dream and their abilities to realize their dreams, despite overwhelming obstacles. Traveling alone, "privatizing" their perceived failures and successes, participants encountered few constants and much debt along the way. Contextually, given the realities described by the participants, and the lack of structural supports available, it is not surprising that over 50% of emerging and young adults phone their parents on a daily basis (Twenge, 2006). Dickerson (2004, pp. 3–4) captures the terrain, particularly with respect to the level of instability in tandem with the level of expectation.

Get a man [woman], have a career, make it on your own, look good, be thin, be popular, leave the nest, follow the rules—do it right and in a timely fashion, even if you're not sure it's exactly what you really want.

The environmental context, on the other hand, is creating opportunities to think out of the box, and negotiate new possibilities that will require individual, community, and societal interventions. Warner (2005) concludes:

We have developed a tendency, as a generation to privatize our problems. To ferociously work at fixing and perfecting ourselves—instead of focusing on ways we might get society to fix itself. This speaks of a kind of hopelessness—a kind of giving-up on the outside world. It's as though we believe that, in the end, we are all we can count on. And that our power to control ourselves and our families is all the power that we have. (pp. 162–163)

Similarly, Jean Baker Miller (2006) concludes that many of the issues emerging and young adults are struggling with require broader and more comprehensive solutions, which are beyond the scope and repertoire of the individual. Miller speaks specifically to the tensions related to thriving at work and at home:

Societies need to build a whole viable context of relationships and arrangements.... We should not and do not need to force women to solve a problem that is insoluble by the individual alone. (p. 16)

When forced to choose between only two options—being a full-time parent or full-time worker—we run the risk of feeling like failures. This is because neither one of the options is good enough. This sense of failure causes despair—a profound lack of hope about the whole thing, as is happening today to some women who struggle with the demands of both work and motherhood. Thus, we are always blaming ourselves and feeling inadequate. We believe it is our own fault. We can find our way out of these forced choices. Society needs to help women, men, and families find new, multiple-choice alternatives today. (p. 17)

Richard a 27-year-old participant, exemplifies the complexity and instability characteristic of this developmental period, juxtaposed within a context that he experiences as somewhat unsupportive and "cut-throat."

Richard

Richard's journey has been unstable and tumultuous. Until recently, he has felt aimless both professionally and personally. Within the past year, he has found his "calling" professionally, and just recently has felt ready to expand his existing social network and resume dating.

Richard was raised in an affluent community, the older of two brothers. Both of his parents are professionals. He speaks of his childhood in positive terms. Nevertheless, he describes his childhood environment as highly pressured academically, a difficult context for him to negotiate, "I was never really a student. I really did not see the big picture when I was younger."

Richard views himself as fortunate, enriched by loving parents who bring different perspectives and experiences, given the diversity of their ethnic backgrounds. He states, however, that although he is enriched by their experiences, growing up in a highly educated affluent community is an experience that his parents will never understand. Each of his parents grew up in a working-class environment surpassing the expectations of their respective parents as well as their extended family networks. When asked to provide a metaphor describing his life to date, Richard responds with the following metaphor, "It is raining outside very very hard. I have an umbrella with many holes, and I don't know how to stop the water from coming down." Richard clearly feels overwhelmed by the demands being placed on him professionally and interpersonally. He views himself as vulnerable, and not able to adequately protect himself. His metaphor suggests that he does not feel capable of controlling external forces that are beyond his control, and feels barraged and deluged by "the rain."

Richard's transition to college was not an easy one; he committed to a technical major, information systems, a major that was not compatible with his interests or his aptitude. Richard dropped out of college after the first year, taking time to reassess his goals and values. During this time, he lived at home and worked as a waiter. His gregariousness and interest in the food industry served him well, and in that context, Richard excelled. Richard left home after two years, choosing a smaller university in which to retest the waters, an educational setting that was in sharp contrast to the large urban university he selected as a high school senior.

During his first year, he made a decision to major in business administration as well as enter a long-term volatile tempestuous relationship with a "troubled" woman, Brenda, a relationship that revolved around a social network that included a fair amount of partying. After completing college, Richard moved back home with Brenda in tow.

Richard and Brenda lived with Richard's parents, ostensibly to begin the process of paying off their respective college debts, and to save for a down payment for an apartment. They worked in their respective jobs in marketing, continuing to do a fair amount of partying. Richard and Brenda's relationship became increasingly tumultuous and conflict-ridden. Brenda "cheated" on Richard, an experience that "devastated" him. Although their relationship endured in college, a relatively protected cocoon, their relationship could not endure the realities of their new life together. Brenda grew up in the South and had a difficult time with a different cultural environment, missed her friends, and overall found her new surroundings stifling and encroaching on her needs for autonomy and independence. Their break-up left Richard "devastated."

It has taken Richard two and a half years to rebuild his life. He is currently living at home, making plans to move out within the coming year. Richard is also beginning the process of re-entering the world of dating. During the past two years, Richard found work unsatisfying, and in response changed jobs on a yearly basis (all of the jobs have been related to marketing). Recently, Richard was offered a job in fundraising and describes a sudden abrupt process, whereby a "light bulb turned on" for him. He is currently highly motivated and is satisfied in his work setting. In speaking about the past two and a half years, he states:

You realize that you sort of don't know where you are going, and what you want to do, and you feel you should. You feel like the whole world knows what they want, and if you don't, you feel lost, and it is scary. I need to move out of my house and start my life over, start from a new slate. I got out of a very very serious relationship. As much as I pulled myself together, because of the situation it left me in, I was not able to fully recover until recently. The next step would be moving out and starting over.

I'm not doing what I want to do. I don't want to live at home. I've already lived practically a married life. I need to get out and start my life over again, and just have a life. I had such a wonderful life. We were an amazing couple. Moving back home kind of killed it all. We realized how different we were; everything started snowballing. We could not do it. We did not want people doing things for us. I'd rather be poor than live off of someone else.

In speaking about his relationship with Brenda, it is evident that Richard carries with him a profound sense of loss. Twenge (2006, pp. 112, 116) effectively captures the impact of loss, in the context of the realities of "modern life."

Most of Gen Me spend their 20s (and sometimes 30s) in pointless dating, uncertain relationships, and painful breakups. Many relationships last several years and/or involve living together, so the breakups resemble divorces rather than run-of-the-mill heartbreak . . . . One of the strangest things about modern life is the expectation that we will stand alone, negotiating breakups, moves, divorces, and manner of heartbreak that previous generations were careful to avoid.

Richard in the process of "rebuilding" his life, has become increasingly focused and goal oriented. For Richard, reconstructing his life occurred suddenly and abruptly. He views the change process as occurring suddenly, an "on-off switch." However, listening to Richard's narrative, the author has a sense that the process of healing occurred over time, a process that also included experimentation. During the interview, Richard mentioned that while Richard was living at home his father was seriously ill, an illness that presented without warning, requiring Richard to assume the role of the "man" in the household. His father's medical problems have been successfully addressed. It is interesting that Richard did not present his father's illness as being related in any way to the light bulb switching from "off" to "on." Richard did not present a textured informed narrative regarding his newfound ability to "see the big picture." Rather, he describes it as a mysterious mystical event that has occurred outside of himself.

The process of rebuilding has included disengagement from friends who are heavy drug users, and experimentation with a wide array of job settings. Richard clearly brings with him social capital (Cote, 2006). His capacities to self-regulate, delay gratification, and execute agency have improved dramatically (Tanner, 2006). Based on the interview, it is unclear how and what has made it possible for Richard to change the course of his trajectory. The research of Masten et al. (2006) as well as others sheds some light, but further longitudinal research (qualitative and quantitative) is needed to understand the processes informing developmental shifts and trajectories.

In reflecting on his drug usage, Richard states:

If I had to do it all over again, I probably never would have used drugs, drunk as much. Would not have partied nearly as much. I would have said no to Brenda. We were together for three years . . . three years seems like 20.

. . . It [drugs] is so embedded in the culture. I would not have done it at such a young age. To get out and get smashed every day. There are other things you could be doing with your time. Our generation, we're the ecstasy, pot kids . . . . It hit us like a ton of bricks. Some of us never recovered. We got it in such mass quantity. Kids were popping pills left and right, every day, and it was turning them into mush.

I don't know that I have recovered. Luckily my body could not physically handle the drugs. If I did use the drugs, I was physically hung over the next day. A case of beer, I'm out two days, like a two-day planning event . . . . Drugs are fun. That's why kids do them now. [It is a] means of socialization. When I stopped smoking pot, your whole circle of friends goes away. Then you see who your friends are.

I just want to have fun with life. I'm still young. [I want to] have my goals set, but not be consumed with just meeting my work goals, my business goals. Having fun is a goal that I think you should have. Life is serious enough as it is. What is the point if you can't enjoy life, have fun?

Richard speaks of his old friends with a sense of sadness:

Sometimes when I see my friends are going nowhere, I get frustrated to see that. The ambition you want for yourself is not in them. You cannot tell someone to think about the big picture. It is something you have to figure out for yourself. They will never strive to grab anything, do anything. There will always be money problems.

Richard refers to an environment that is fast-paced, materialistic, and overly stimulating, one that focuses on the end result, without adequately addressing the process:

We grew up in the computer age, and everything starts to move so fast. [The] pace of life is so fast. Immediate gratification is embedded in our brain. And with public media, as amazing as it has become, all they see is the wealth. They don't see how the wealth was accumulated, how it was gotten. People see Tiger Woods. See an amazing golfer making millions in tournaments. They don't see what it took to get there. The hours spent perfecting his stroke, his game, physically, mentally. All they see is the end result. And that is what all of us are wanting, to get to the end result without working. We see the jewelry. We see the yachts, clothes. All we want is to want. We don't want to earn it. We don't want to work for it. We just want to get it as fast as possible.

...The real world is truly brutal. I'm learning that now as we speak. You have to work hard to make it. It is the only way. The cream always rises to the top, and that is how it is always going to be. I find life is hard. You are not given anything. You have to work for it, and you have no choice but to work for it. And that is a hard reality. Growing up in a pretty decent situation, and you are given everything, you become accustomed to your life which has been given [to you], that you haven't earned.

Now when you realize this is your lifestyle, you have to realize how hard you have to work to achieve that lifestyle. That is scary. You get demoted. I was up here and now I am down here, and that is scary. Medical and dental benefits, if I get a cavity, are my teeth going to fall out?

Richard ends the interview with an optimistic note, but is also somewhat damning of the boomer generation. His narrative describes the process of having to make it "on your own," without adequate supports:

It is possible to make it in this world. You could surpass your parents. You could do better than even them. These are times of opportunity. You have a chance to do what you really really want if you are committed to doing it.

... The amount of information you can get, you get information in a 100 different ways now. My generation is going to be running this country. The baby boomer generation is coming to an end. I think we are more intelligent, not as closed minded. Learning has gotten more sophisticated. We have been taught better. There will be a lot of improvements in the world. We have to see how it happens.

... For us, we're still living by your rules .... The people who are governing are worried about themselves, not us. They are taking away medical benefits that people will need. So many things that are messed up. People are worried about themselves. People are not worried about their children. I am going to make rules that will help 60 year olds. People are not worrying about you in your 20s. Once you get out of the nest, no longer under mama's wings, you are on your own. No one is worried about us. Laws are not being made to help you in any way. Nothing is being done to help people survive in their 20s. We are like rubber balls. We are young enough to bounce back from pretty much anything.

The voices of emerging and young adults spoke of hope and possibility, as exemplified by Richard's optimistic stance that his generation "will bounce back from pretty much anything." Most of emerging and young adult participants believe that their life will turn out well, a finding confirmed by Arnett (2004).

Intriguing questions have been raised regarding how we can best harness the possibility and hope suggested by the participants, as well as design evidence-based interventions that make a difference in their lives. Their voices as well as those of parents and employers are textured and nuanced. Attempts to characterize emerging and young adults as a monolithic group appear foolhardy. The narratives provided by the stakeholders interviewed offer a wide range of perspectives and reinforce the significance of context in the lives of emerging and young adults. Their combined voices bring increased appreciation for the complexity of the issues, and the challenges encountered. It is the hope of the author that their rich voices are heard.

References

Apter, T. (2001). *The myth of maturity: What teenagers need from parents to become adults.* New York: Norton.

Arnett, J. (2004). *Emerging adulthood: The winding road from the late teens through the twenties.* New York: Oxford University Press.

Arnett, J. J. (2006). The psychology of emerging adulthood: What is known, and what remains to be known. In J. Arnett & J. Tanner (Eds.). *Emerging adults in America: Coming of age in the 21st century* (pp. 303–330). Washington, DC: American Psychological Association.

Bahney, A. (2006, June 8). A life between jobs. *New York Times*, E1.

Coontz, S. (2005). *Marriage, a history: From obedience to intimacy or how love conquered marriage.* New York: Viking.

Cote, J. E. (2006). Emerging adulthood as an institutionalized moratorium: Risks and benefits to identity formation. In J. Arnett & J. Tanner (Eds.), *Emerging adults in America: Coming of age in the 21st century* (pp. 85–116). Washington, DC: American Psychological Association.

Csikszentmihalyi, M. (1997). *Finding flow: The psychology of engagement with everyday life.* New York: Basic.

Dickerson, V. (2004). *Who cares what you're supposed to do: Breaking the rules to get what you want in love, life, and work.* New York: Berkeley.

Dvorak, P. (2006, June 26). Why management trends quickly fade away. *Wall Street Journal*.

Hassler, C. (2005). *20 something, 20 everything: A quarter life woman's guide to balance and direction.* Novato, CA: New World Library.

Henry, A. (2006, June 5–11). Boomers' kids raise self-esteem to extremes. *The Washington Post National Weekly Edition*, 32.

Masten, A., Obradovic, J., & Burt, K. (2006) Resilience in emerging adulthood: Developmental perspectives on continuity and transformation. In J. Arnett & J. Tanner (Eds.). *Emerging adults in America: Coming of age in the 21st century* (pp. 173–190). Washington, DC: American Psychological Association.

Miller, J. (2006). Commentary: Forced choices, false choices. *Research and action report: Wellesley Centers for Women, 27*(2), 16–17.

Nash, L. & Stevenson, H. (2004). *Just enough: Tools for creating success in your work and life.* Hoboken, NJ: John Wiley & Sons.

Schwartz, B. (2004). *The paradox of choice: Why more is less.* New York: Harper Collins.

Tanner, J. L. (2006). Recentering during emerging adulthood: A critical turning point in life span human development. In J. Arnett & J. Tanner (Eds.), *Emerging adults in America:*

Coming of age in the 21ˢᵗ century (pp. 21–56). Washington, DC: American Psychological Association.

Twenge, J. (2006). *Generation me: Why today's young Americans are more confident, assertive, entitled—And more miserable than ever before.* New York: Free Press.

Warner, J. (2005). *Perfect madness: Motherhood in the age of anxiety.* New York: Riverhead.

Appendix A
Methods

The material provided below describes the participants of the study as well as methods used to elicit their diverse perspectives. Appendix A describes the participants and the methods, and Appendices B, C, and D include the questionnaires specifically designed for each of the major stakeholders: emerging and young adults, parents, and employers.

Participants

The major stakeholders—two cohorts of emerging and young adults representing diverse socioeconomic backgrounds, parents, and employers—were selected for the purpose of gaining a richer, more textured understanding of the range of experiences and perspectives regarding the developmental period of emerging and young adulthood. Tables describing the characteristics of the two cohorts of emerging and young adults are presented, followed by tables describing the baseline characteristics of parent and employer participants. Table A.1 describes the characteristics of the total sample of emerging and young adults, whereas Tables A.2 and A.3 describe the characteristics of the affluent and less affluent (public university graduates), respectively. Tables A.4 and A.5 describe parents of emerging and young adults and employers of emerging and young adults.

TABLE A.1. Characteristics of total sample of emerging and young adults ($N = 64$)

Variable	n (%)
Age*	28.9 (SD = 3.5)
Sex	
Male	32.8
Female	67.2
Ethnicity	
African American	6.2
Mixed race	6.2

(Continued)

Table A.1. (*Continued*)

Variable	n (%)
Other	12.5
White	75
Educational level	
College degree	100
Graduate degree	42.2
Professional degree	9.4
Religion	
Christian—practicing	34.4
Christian—not practicing	34.4
Jewish—practicing	15.6
Spiritual	1.6
Atheist	12.5
Agnostic	1.6
Marital status	
Married	37.5
Single	62.5
Married with children	15.6
Single with children	4.7
Living arrangement	
Home owner	39.1
Rent (alone)	17.2
Rent (with family)	7.8
Rent (with girlfriend/boyfriend)	6.2
Rent (with roommates)	14.1
With parents	14.1
Other	1.6
Employment	
Full time	79.7
Part time	7.8
Unemployed	6.2
Other	6.2
Income	
$0–5000	7.8
$5000–10,000	4.7
$15,001–20,000	3.1
$20,001–30,000	6.2
$30,001–40,000	20.4
$40,001–50,000	18.7
$50,001–60,000	7.8
$60,001–75,000	17.2
$75,001–100,000	4.7
Over $100,000	9.7

*Mean (standard deviation).

TABLE A.2. Characteristics of affluent sample of emerging and young adults ($N = 31$)

Variable	n (%)
Age*	27.58 (SD = 2.9)
Sex	
Male	35.5
Female	64.5
Ethnicity	
Mixed race	6.4
Other	6.4
White	87.1
Educational level	
College degree	100
Graduate degree	41.9
Professional degree	12.9
Religion	
Christian—practicing	22.6
Catholic—not practicing	29.0
Jewish	32.4
Spiritual	3.2
Atheist	9.7
Agnostic	3.2
Marital status	
Married	29.0
Single	71.0
Married with children	3.2
Living arrangement	
Home owner	29.0
Rent (alone)	22.6
Rent (with family)	6.4
Rent (with girlfriend/boyfriend)	6.4
Rent (with roommates)	19.3
With parents	12.9
Other	3.2
Employment	
Full time	77.4
Part time	9.7
Unemployed	9.7
Other	3.2
Income	
$0–5000	9.7
$5000–10,000	3.2
$15,001–20,000	3.2
$30,001–40,000	16.1

(Continued)

TABLE A.2. (*Continued*)

Variable	*n* (%)
$40,001–50,000	12.9
$50,001–60,000	9.7
$60,001–75,000	25.8
$75,001–100,000	6.4
Over $100,000	12.9

*Mean (standard deviation).

TABLE A.3. Characteristics of sample of emerging and young adult graduates of public university (*N* = 33)

Variable	*n* (%)
Age*	30.2 (SD = 3.6)
Sex	
Male	30.3
Female	69.7
Ethnicity	
African American	12.1
Mixed race	6.1
White	63.6
Other	18.2
Educational level	
College degree	100
Graduate degree	42.4
Professional degree	6.1
Religion	
Christian—practicing	48.5
Christian—not practicing	36.4
Atheist	15.1
Marital status	
Married	45.4
Single	54.5
Married with children	27.3
Single with children	9.1
Living arrangement	
Home owner	48.5
Rent (with girlfriend/boyfriend)	6.1
Rent (with roommates)	9.1
Rent (with family)	9.1
Rent (alone)	12.1
With parents	15.1
Employment	
Full time	81.8
Part time	6.1
Unemployed	3.0
Other	9.1

(*Continued*)

TABLE A.3. (*Continued*)

Variable	n (%)
Income	
$0–5000	6.1
$5000–10,000	6.1
$15,001–20,000	3.0
$20,001–30,000	12.1
$30,001–40,000	24.2
$40,001–50,000	24.2
$50,001–60,000	6.1
$60,001–75,000	9.1
$75,001–100,000	3.0
Over $100,000	6.1

*Mean (standard deviation).

TABLE A.4. Characteristics of parents ($N = 30$)

Variable	n (%)
Age*	57.6 (SD = 4.3)
Sex	
Male	20.0
Female	80.0
Ethnicity	
Mixed race	10.0
Other	3.3
White	86.7
Educational level	
Less than college	3.3
College degree	96.7
Graduate degree	46.7
Post secondary degree	13.3
Professional degree	13.3
Religion	
Christian—practicing	26.6
Christian—not practicing	23.3
Jewish—practicing	30.0
Jewish—not practicing	13.3
Atheist	6.7
Civil Status	
Divorced	10.0
Married	86.7
Single	3.3
Number of children*	2.3 (SD = 0.8)
Employment: job category	
Advertising	3.3
Admin/clerical	3.3
Consultant	3.3

(*Continued*)

TABLE A.4. (*Continued*)

Variable	n (%)
Education	20.0
Healthcare	
Mental health	20.0
Nonprofit—social services	13.3
Information technology	3.3
Media	3.3
Pharmaceutical	3.3
Science	6.7
Real estate	6.7
Retired	3.3
Unemployed	10.0
Income	
$0–5000	6.7
$10,001–15,000	3.3
$30,001–40,000	10.0
$40,001–50,000	3.3
$50,001–60,000	3.3
$75,001–100,000	23.3
Over $100,000	50.0

*Mean (standard deviation).

TABLE A.5. Characteristics of employers ($N = 30$)

Variable	n (%)
Age*	46.9 (SD = 9.3)
Sex	
Male	56.7
Female	43.3
Educational level	
Less than college	3.3
College degree	96.7
Graduate degree	40.0
Post secondary degree	10.0
Professional degree	16.7
Religion	
Christian—practicing	50.0
Christian—not practicing	3.3
Jewish	33.3
Agnostic	3.3
Atheist	6.7
Greek Orthodox	3.3
Marital status	
Divorced	6.7

(*Continued*)

TABLE A.5. (*Continued*)

Variable	*n* (%)
Married	76.7
Single	16.7
Number of children*	1.7 (SD = 1.0)
Employment: job category	
Advertising	6.7
Cosmetology	3.3
Education	13.3
Engineering	3.3
Government	3.3
Healthcare	
Medical/dental practitioners	10.0
RN/nurse management	3.3
Mental health	10.0
Nonprofit-social services	3.3
Biomedical	3.3
Information technology	6.7
Legal	6.7
Management	6.7
Marketing	10.0
Media	3.3
Retail	3.3
Sports	3.3
Number of supervisees*	18.9 (SD = 17.6)
Income	
$40,001–50,000	6.7
$50,001–60,000	6.7
$60,001–75,000	20.0
$75,001–100,000	16.7
Over $100,000	50.0

*Mean (standard deviation).

Procedures

Two cohorts of emerging and young adults were interviewed by phone: (1) 33 individuals attending a public university in the northeast whose mission, in part, is to serve first-generation college graduates; and (2) 31 individuals who spent a majority of their childhood in affluent suburban towns located in the northeast. In addition, 30 parents of individuals ranging in age from 25 to 35, and 30 employers were interviewed. Employers, also located in the northeast, supervised a minimum of five emerging and young adults within the past three years.

Emerging and young adult participants, 25 to 35 years of age, were randomly selected from a list of graduates provided by the alumni office of a public university. Participants were contacted by mail and/or e-mail, informed of the purpose of the research, and if interested were asked to contact the researcher. A phone interview was scheduled at a mutually convenient time. Participation in the interview process occurred only after the individual read the information sheet provided, and gave his or her consent. The average time needed to complete the phone interview for each of the stakeholders was 60 minutes. A convenience sample of 31 graduates, 25 to 35 years of age, served as a comparison group. Graduates were recruited from advertisements appearing in preselected affluent towns located in the northeast, or via recommendations of the participants. The towns were selected based on public information available regarding average single-family tax bills. Participants were asked to contact the researcher, and once contact was made, the same procedure as described above was followed.

The convenience sample of 30 parents was recruited from advertisements appearing in preselected affluent towns in the northeast, or via recommendations of the parent participants. The same procedure as described above was followed. The sample of employers was a convenience sample, recruited from the researcher's professional contacts. In order to qualify as an employer, the individual was required to be in a managerial position, supervising a minimum of five individuals ranging in age from 25 to 35 within the past three years. Effort was made by the author to interview employers representing a diversity of work contexts (e.g., size of company, area of expertise).

The responses of all the constituents—college graduates, parents, and employers—were confidential. All of the participants were informed that their participation was voluntary, and that they could withdraw from the study at any time. They were also informed that identifying information would be altered to ensure anonymity.

The narrative data were analyzed following the principles of phenomenological psychology (Camic, Rhodes, & Yardley, 2003; Giorgi, 1985) and grounded theory (Glasser & Strauss, 1967; Henwood & Pigeon, 1992, 1995; Strauss & Corbin, 1998). Specifically, both grounded theory and phenomenological psychology emphasize the meaning an individual gives to his or her experience and thus attempt to understand participants' experiences on their own terms. This approach emphasizes the importance of lived experience as a valuable and legitimate source of data (Giorgi, 1985). The strength of using this type of qualitative research approach is that the richness and complexity of an individual's lived experience is emphasized. In addition to examining the meaning and context of lived experience via qualitative analysis, limited quantitative analysis was used to complement and enhance the data obtained. For example, each of the participants was asked to rate levels of satisfaction in their professional lives on a Likert scale.

The author wanted to understand participants' experiences in their own terms. Thus, in attempting to explore and capture the experiences of individual participants, the author and her graduate assistant, a seasoned mental health professional, reviewed each protocol in order to identify themes that emerged from the narrative data. Unclear responses, as well as any disagreements over category inclusion were addressed in the following way. The data were reviewed, and responses were included in a given category if both of the reviewers felt confident that it was the most appropriate category match. Interview questions appear in Appendices B, C, and D, respectively.

References

Camic, P., Rhodes, J., & Yardley, L. (1995). *Qualitative research in psychology: Expanding perspectives in methodology and designs.* Washington, DC: American Psychological Association.

Giorgi, A. (1985). *Phenomenology and psychological research.* Pittsburgh: Duquesne University Press.

Glasser, B. & Strauss, A. (1967). *The discovery of grounded theory.* New York: Aldine.

Henwood, K. & Pidgeon, N. (1992). Qualitative research and psychological theorizing. *British Journal of Psychology, 83*, 97–111.

Henwood, K. L. & Pidgeon, N. (1995). Grounded theory and psychological research. *The Psychologist, 8*, 115–118.

Strauss, A. & Corbin, J. (1998). *Basics of qualitative research.* London: Sage.

Appendix B
Emerging and Young Adult Questionnaire

1. Age: _____
2. Gender ☐ Female ☐ Male
3. Ethnicity: _____
4 a. Education: _____
  b. Education of parents:
  c. Growing up, did you view yourself as working class, middle class, upper class, or a variation of the above?
5. Religion: _____
6. Employment

  ☐ Part-time ☐ Full-time ☐ Unemployed ☐ Self-employed
  ☐ Other _____

7. Current Job: _____
8. Duration: _____
9. Current Income

  ☐ 0–$5000   ☐ $5000–10,000   ☐ $10,001–15,000
  ☐ $15,001–20,000 ☐ $20,001–30,000 ☐ $30,001–40,000
  ☐ $40,001–50,000 ☐ $50,001–60,000 ☐ $60,001–75,000
  ☐ $75,001–100,000 ☐ over $100,000

10. Previous Employment: _____
_____

11. Duration: _____
_____

12. Past Income: _____
_____

13. Relationship Status
  ☐ Single   ☐ Married   ☐ Divorced ☐ Widowed ☐ Engaged
  ☐ Involved   ☐ Cohabitating ☐ Separated
  monogamously
14. If you have ever been married, how many times? _____

15. Do you have children? ☐ Yes   ☐ No   If yes, how many? _____
    How old? _____
16. Living arrangement

    ☐ Rent Alone   ☐ Rent with roommates   ☐ Home owner
    ☐ With parents   ☐ With other family   Other _____

---

1. Tell me a little about your work life.
   a) On a scale from one (least satisfied) to ten (most satisfied), how satisfied are you?
   b) What needs to happen to increase your level of satisfaction?
2. What did you expect your work life to be like and what is it actually like?
   a) To what degree is your work life meeting your expectations?
   b) How is it not meeting your expectations?
   c) How would you rewrite the story of your career to date if you could?
3. a) What did you expect your personal life to be like and what is it actually like?
   b) How is it not meeting your expectations?
   c) How would you rewrite the story of your personal life to date if you could?
4. a) Where do you expect to be 10 years from now in your work life and personal life?
   b) What are your short-term goals?
5. If you had to describe your work life in terms of a metaphor, what metaphor describes it best?
6. If you had to describe your personal life in terms of a metaphor, what metaphor describes it best?
7. a) The average person has 8.2, 8.6 jobs by the age of 32, how do you understand that?
   b) Perhaps this seemingly homogeneous group with an average of 8.2 or 8.6 jobs, can be broken down to several groups; can you lend any insights regarding how they came to have 8.2 jobs and what motivates them.
8. a) Are we living in a time like no other in terms of the world of work? Please explain.
   b) Are we living in a time like no other in terms of relationships and people in their 20s and early 30s? Please explain.
9. In terms of the world of work, who seems to be doing well under these conditions? Who seems to be suffering?
10. What coping strategies serve you best under these times?
11. In terms of your work history, what led you make the choices that you did? What did the decision-making process look like?
12. In terms of your work life, what are some of life lessons that you have learned?
13. If you had to give advice to someone about to embark on his or her career path, what would you tell him or her?

14. a) How do your parents understand and perceive your choices around work and your personal life?

   b) How are their views the same/different from yours in terms of how one conducts himself/herself around work and relationships?

   c) How do your employers view people in their 20s and their early 30s and their approach to the world of work? How are their views the same/different from yours?

15. Is there a quarter-life crisis and if so, how do you understand it?

16. a) Individuals in their 20s and early 30s have been described as self-absorbed and narcissistic. What are your thoughts about these labels?

   b) Individuals in their 20s and early 30s have been viewed by some as delayed in terms of developmental markers such as establishing a career or establishing key relationships. Can you respond to this observation?

17. Individuals in their teens have been described as very pressured with many expectations imposed on them. On the other hand, we have a cohort of individuals in their 20s delaying their adulthood in terms of markers we associate with adulthood. How do you reconcile this?

18. a) How do you think people in their 20s and their early 30s (and you specifically) negotiate their/your friendships differently from your parents? Similarities and differences you observe?

   b) Do you have adequate social supports? Please elaborate.

19. a) How do you think individuals in their 20s and early 30s (and you specifically) negotiate their/your most intimate relationships differently from your parents (their generation)?

   b) Can you tell me about your plans for your career and personal life. (Do you see long-term commitment, marriage, children in your future and how do you see yourself adapting to the diverse roles you will be assuming?)

20. Given all the choices available to you, how do you decide on what it is you want to do professionally and personally?

21. a) To date, what do you find most difficult about living and negotiating these times? What do you find most satisfying about living and negotiating these times?

   b) What provides you with a sense of hope about your generation? What nurtures that hope?

   c) What provides you with a sense of despair about your generation. Please explain.

22. a) These times have been described as uncertain. Can you comment on how one best navigates in uncertain times and observations you have made regarding individuals in their 20s and 30s and dealing with uncertainty.

   b) How do you deal with uncertainty in your life?

23. Given the choices available, how does one best navigate an abundance of choices available to individuals in their 20s and early 30s? Observations you

have made regarding individuals in their 20s and early 30s and how do they deal with choice? What seems to be helpful and not helpful?

24. Do you think class and race informs this discussion and if so can you respond?
25. Any additional information you would like to share that captures the experiences of individuals trying to navigate their 20s and early 30s?

Appendix C
Parent Questionnaire

1. Age: _____
2. Gender ☐ Female ☐ Male
3. Ethnicity: _____
4. Education: _____
5. Religion: _____
6. Employment

    ☐ Part-time ☐ Full-time ☐ Unemployed ☐ Self-employed
    ☐ Other _____

7. Current Job: _____
8. Duration: _____
9. Current Income

    ☐ 0–$5000   ☐ $5000–10,000   ☐ $10,001–15,000
    ☐ $15,001–20,000 ☐ $20,001–30,000 ☐ $30,001–40,000
    ☐ $40,001–50,000 ☐ $50,001–60,000 ☐ $60,001–75,000
    ☐ $75,001–100,000 ☐ over $100,000

10. Relationship Status

    ☐ Single   ☐ Married   ☐ Divorced ☐ Widowed ☐ Engaged
    ☐ Involved   ☐ Cohabitating ☐ Separated
      monogamously

11. How many children do you have? _____
    How old? _____
12. Child's current job: _____
13. Child's current relationship status: _____
14. Child's current living arrangement

    ☐ Rent alone   ☐ Rent with roommates ☐ Home owner
    ☐ With parents ☐ With other family   ☐ Other _____

---

1. Tell me a little bit about your work life if applicable. How satisfied are you?
   a) On a scale from one (least satisfied) to ten (most satisfied) how satisfied are you?

2. What did you expect your child's work life to look like and what is it actually like?

   a) How is your child's work life meeting his or her expectations? Your expectations?

   b) How is it not meeting his or her expectations? Your expectations?

   c) Is there anything about your child's career path that you would rewrite? What would you keep exactly as is?

   d) Is there anything about your child's personal path that you would rewrite if you could? What would you keep exactly as is?

3. Where do you expect him or her to be ten years from now in his or her work life? What did you expect for your child's personal life?

4. a) If you were to describe your child's work life in terms of a metaphor, what metaphor describes it best?

   b) If you were to describe your child's personal life in terms of a metaphor, what metaphor describes it best?

5. The average person has 8.2, 8.6 jobs by the age of 32, how do you understand that?

6. a) Are we living in a time like no other in terms of the world of work? Please explain.

   b) Are we living in a time like no other in terms of relationships and people in their 20s? Please explain.

7. Who seems to be doing well under these conditions in terms of the world of work and in terms of one's personal life? Which seems to be suffering?

8. What coping strategies serve one best under these times?

9. a) In terms of your parenting your child in his or her 20s and early 30s, what are some of life lessons that you have learned?

   b) If you had to give advice to a parent about to embark on parenting a young adult in his or her 20s or early 30s, what would you tell them?

10. If you had to describe major similarities and differences in the way you and your child view the world what would they be? Please explain.

11. Is there a quarter-life crisis and if so, how do they understand it?

12. How do you think employers are viewing individuals in their 20s and early 30s?

13. a) People in their 20s and early 30s have been described as self-absorbed and narcissistic. What are your thoughts about these labels?

   b) People in their 20s and early 30s have been viewed by some as delayed in terms of developmental markers such as establishing a career and establishing key relationships. Please respond.

   c) Individuals in their teens have been described as much pressured with many expectations imposed on them. On the other hand, we have a cohort of individuals in their 20s and early 30s delaying their adulthood in terms of markers we associate with adulthood. How do you reconcile this?

14. a) If you had the chance to do it all over again, how would you parent differently? How would you keep things exactly the same?

   b) In assessing your generation and how they have parented, what do you view as their overall strengths and overall weaknesses?

    c) In assessing your child's generation how do you think they will parent? What will be their strengths and weaknesses? What will they mirror? What will they change in terms of their parenting the next generation?

15. What pressing questions do you have as a parent of an adult in their 20s or 30s?

16. a) Describe a scenario that challenged you as a parent of someone in their 20s or 30s. What were the issues?

    b) How did you go about trying to figure things out.

17. The following are some questions that parents of individuals in their 20s have. What are your thoughts?

    a) How do I define my new role? What are my responsibilities? What should my child's responsibilities be with the goal of moving my child toward independent life?

    b) What does being a good parent look like for this developmental period?

    c) How much support—instrumental, emotional, financial—should I provide? How much of a safety net should I provide?

    d) How do I ensure and reinforce mature responsible behavior in my child? At what point do I say you're an adult, you need to be on your own?

18. To date,

    a) What provides you with a sense of hope about your child's generation? What nurtures that hope? Please explain.

    b) What provides you with a sense of despair about your child's generation? Please explain.

19. Any additional information you would like to share?

Appendix D
Employer Questionnaire

1. Age: _____
2. Gender ☐ Female ☐ Male
3. Religion: _____
4. Education: _____
5. Current Job: _____
6. Duration: _____
7. Current Income

   ☐ 0–$5000   ☐ $5000–10,000   ☐ $10,001–15,000
   ☐ $15,001–20,000   ☐ $20,001–30,000   ☐ $30,001–40,000
   ☐ $40,001–50,000   ☐ $50,001–60,000   ☐ $60,001–75,000
   ☐ $75,001–100,000 ☐ over $100,000

8. Number of people you supervise: _____
9. Relationship Status

   ☐ Single   ☐ Married   ☐ Divorced ☐ Widowed ☐ Engaged
   ☐ Involved   ☐ Cohabiting   ☐ Separated
     monogamously

10. Do you have children? ☐ Yes   ☐ No
    If yes, how many? _____
    How old? _____

---

1. Tell me a little about your work life.
   a) On a scale from one (least satisfied) to ten (most satisfied), how satisfied are you?
   b) How satisfied are you?
2. To what degree is your work life meeting your expectations?
   a) How is it not meeting your expectations?
3. If you had to describe your work life in terms of a metaphor, what metaphor describes it best?

4. a) The average person has 8.2, 8.6 jobs by the age of 32, how do you understand that?

    b) Perhaps this seemingly homogeneous group with an average of 8.2 or 8.6 jobs, can be broken down to several groups; can you lend any insights regarding how they came to have 8.2 jobs and what motivates them?

5. a) Are we living in a time like no other in terms of the world of work? Please explain.

    b) Are we living in a time like no other in terms of personal relationships? Please explain.

6. Who seems to be doing well under these conditions and who seems to be suffering?

7. What coping strategies serve someone in their 20s best in these times?

8. What are some of life lessons that many people in their 20s and early 30s need to learn?

9. If you had to give advice to someone about to embark on his or her career path, what would you tell him or her?

10. Is there a quarter-life crisis and if so, how do they understand it?

11. a) People in their 20s and early 30s have been described as self-absorbed and narcissistic. What are your thoughts about these labels?

    b) People in their 20s and early 30s have been viewed by some as delayed in terms of developmental markers such as establishing a career, establishing key relationships. Can you respond to this observation?

12. The current generation has been described as very pressured with many expectations imposed on them. We have, on the other hand, a cohort of individuals in their 20s and early 30s delaying their adulthood in terms of markers we associate with adulthood. How do you reconcile this?

13. Do you think people in their 20s and early 30s negotiate their friendships differently? If so, how?

14. a) These times have been described as uncertain. Can you comment on how one best navigates in uncertain times and observations you have made regarding individuals in their 20s and early 30s and dealing with uncertainty.

    b) How do you deal with uncertainty in your life?

15. Given the choices available, how does one best navigate an abundance of choices available to individuals in their 20s? Observations you have made regarding individuals in their 20s and dealing with choice?

16. It has been observed that mentoring is difficult for individuals in their 20s to procure. How do you understand it and what recommendation(s) can you offer to people in their 20s regarding mentoring?

17. To date,

    a) What provides you with a sense of hope about your employees' generation (25 to 35 years of age)? What nurtures that hope? Please explain.

    b) What provides you with a sense of despair about your employees' generation (25 to 35 years of age)? Please explain.

18. Any additional information you would like to share?

Index

Acculturation, defined, 30
Adulthood
    criteria for, 2, 30, 87
    developmental markers for, 1–2
    developmental time period for, 1,
        43, 99, 130
Adults
    emerging and young
        descriptors of, 1, 113–114,
            149–153
        interpersonal lives of, 59–78
        moving back home, 97, 99,
            143
        questionnaires for, 159–162
        social and cultural contexts of,
            2–3, 29–40, 99–100,
            130–134
    parents. *See* Baby Boomers; Parents
Adventure/exploration, personal
    lacking in China, 33
    need and desire for, 19–20, 93
Affluence
    expectations of. *See* Expectations
    more choices with, 85, 94, 135–136,
        142
    of participants/interviewees,
        151–152 *See also* Social
        class/es
African-Americans
    adulthood criteria of, 30
    family structure of, 73
    women, 22–23

Age
    of participants/interviewees,
        149–155
    significance of turning thirty years
        old, 112, 132
    work satisfaction by, 45
Agency, 17–18
"American Dream," the, 37–38, 141
Apter, T., 86–87, 102, 107–108, 130,
    137
Argentina, 30
Arnett, J., 17, 30, 130, 145–146
Asian Americans, 30
Authenticity, 23–24

Baby Boomers
    blaming of, 129
    as employers, 125–127
    impact of, 22, 145
    job loss of, 48, 133
    modern work models and, 48, 111
    trend of working longer, 112
    as working mothers, 120
Bahney, A., 140
Balance
    of one's life, 5–8, 94, 135
    in parent/child relationships,
        104–105
    of work vs. home, 118–121
Barry, L., 31
BlackBerrys, 46–47
Borderline personality disorder, 13

Boundaries
  between parents and children, 105
  in social norms, 18, 25
  between work and personal life,
    5–7, 118–121
"Brain drain," 75
Bulgaria, communist, 24–26
Business, changing philosophies of, 48

Cairns, Robert and Beverly, 107
Canada, 100
Capitalism, 39
Career pathways
  before commitment to life partner,
    59–61
  dissatisfaction with, 7–8, 22, 25
  versus having "a job," 22–23
  indecision in, 89–91
  multiple, sequential, 87–89,
    114–115
  postponements in, 3, 37–39
  pursuit of, 43–56
Casper, L., 99
Cell phones, 46–47
China
  adulthood criteria in, 30
  filial piety in, 32–33
Choice/choices, 81–94
  abundance vs. scarcity of, 85,
    135–136, 142
  analyses of responses to, 84–94
  available resources and, 87, 136
  freedom of, 19–20, 25–26, 138
  Internet-related, 117–118
  overwhelming nature of, 2, 44,
    81–83, 90, 136
  purposeful limitation of, 88–89, 137
Coburn, K., 104
College tuition costs, 37–38
Collegiality, 126
Communication
  with employers, 126–127
  skillsets in, 118
Confucian teachings, 32–33
Consumerism, 37

Control issues, 102–104
Coontz, S., 133
Corporate America
  characteristics of, 48–49
  modern culture in, 112
Costs
  of college education, 37–38
  of training personnel, 115
Cote, J., 13, 17, 67, 140
Creativity, personal, 34–36
Culture/cultures, 29–40
  adulthood criteria in, 30
  defined, 29
  modern shifts in, 43–44
  religious. See Religion/spirituality
    See also specific countries
Cynicism, 7

Dates/dating, 62, 66–68
Debt, personal, 37–38
Depression in emerging and young
    adults, 130
Dickerson, V., 141
Discrimination, 16–17, 22
Disillusionment
  about work, 7–8, 25, 50–54
  in romantic life, 5, 8, 9–10
Divorce
  avoidance of, 63
  fear of, 132–133
  future rates of, 141
Draut, T., 77–78
"Dream jobs," 54, 72–74, 135
Drifters identity group, 15
Drug abuse, 144
Durkin, D., 48–49
Dvorak, P., 132

Economics, personal
  globalization's effect on, 33
  modern constraints on, 39–40
  parental financial support and, 98,
    100–101, 143

Education
  careers after. *See* Career pathways
  choices in, 81
  cost of, 37–39
  delay of, 136
  disconnected to employment,
    45–47, 100–101, 113, 130
  of participants/interviewees,
    149–155
  religiously-affiliated vs. public,
    31–32
  time committment for, 100
  value of, 8
E-mails, 46–47, 134
Emotional support
  from friends, 68–69, 71–72,
    133–134
  from parents, 102, 107–108
Employees
  advice from, 44–45
  advice to, 126–127
  employer views of. *See* Employers
  frequent job changes of, 114–115,
    131
  termination of, 5, 48, 133
Employers, 111–128
  advice from, 123–124
  advice to, 125–126
  Baby Boomers as, 125–127
  characteristics of, 111, 154–155
  communication with, 126–127
  competence and support of, 44–45
  loyalty to employees, 6–7, 47–49,
    112, 131–133
  questionnaires for, 167–168
  selection of, 156
  tensions/concerns of, 124–127, 132
Employment
  altered expectations from, 44–46
  balanced with home life, 118–121,
    135
  changing landscape of, 2, 43,
    111–115
  disconnected to education, 45–47,
    100–101, 113, 130

  dissatisfaction with, 44–45, 89–90,
    100
  finding a "dream job," 54, 72–74,
    135
  firing and lay-offs in, 5–7
  fluidity of, 131–133
  jobs found on Internet, 117–118
  loyalty/security in, 6–7, 47–49, 112
  "opting out" of, 74–75, 140
  of participants/interviewees,
    149–155
  quality changes in, 44–45
  women's return to workforce, 75
  work environments in, 7, 126,
    131–133 *See also* Work
Entitlement, sense of, 116–117,
    124–127
Environment
  personal, 130, 133–134
  of "real world," 145
  at work, 7, 126, 131–133
Ethnicity/race
  as group identity, 16, 22–23
  modern tolerance of, 113
  of participants/interviewees,
    149–155
  perceived alienation because of,
    16–17, 22
  personal influence of, 86
Expectations
  alignment of, 54–56, 130
  of college graduates, 99–100, 138
  conflicting, of women, 72–76
  perfectionistic, inflated, 72–74, 83,
    134
  of wealth and affluence, 145

Faith/confidence in one's children,
    106–108
Families
  evolving structure of, 73–74
  financial burden of, 39
  varying importance of, 19–20
Fields, J., 99
Filial piety, 32–33

Freedom, personal, 19–20, 24–25, 138
Friendships
    emotional support from, 68–69,
        71–72, 133–134
    functions of, 68–69, 71–72
    time for, 70
    varying importance of, 19–20

Gender differences
    in friendships, 69
    of participants/interviewees,
        149–155
*Generation Me: Why Today's Young
    Americans Are More Confident,
    Assertive, Entitled—And More
    Miserable Than Ever Before*
    (Henry, A, 2006), 129
Generational differences, 22, 124–127,
    145
Germany, 100
Globalization
    effects on job security, 131–133
    effects on marketplace, 48
    effects on personal economics, 33
Grounded theory, 156
Growth, personal, 19–20
Guardians identity group, 14–15, 27

Harrison, J., 16
Hassler, C., 52–53, 83, 134–135
Hewlett, S. (et al), 74–75
Home buying, 37–39

Identity development, 13–27
    defined, 14, 18
    diverse pathways in, 19–27
    fluidity of, 18, 27
    group membership and. *See* Identity
        groups
    historical and cultural context of,
        13–15, 130–134
    parental role in, 103
    role of agency in, 17–18
    role of confusion in, 13–14
    work-related, 135

Identity groups
    ethnic, 16–17, 22–23
    generational, 22, 124–127, 145
    overlap of, 15
    perceived discrimination and, 16–17
    theory of, 14–15
Immigration process, 24–26
Income. *See* Money/financial
    reimbursement
Information overload, 117–118
Internet
    dating on, 66–68
    information overload from, 118
    job opportunities on, 117–118
    online communities of, 67
Interviews/interviewing procedures,
    155–156
Israel
    adulthood criteria in, 30
    mandated military service in, 32

Japan, 53–54
Jones, J., 66, 73
Josselson, R., 14

Koerner, B., 38

Latinos, 30
Letter writing, 67
Lifestyles
    affluent. *See* Affluence
    alternative, 113
    authenticity in, 23–24
    balance and imbalance in, 5–8, 94
    of parents, 114
Little Shop of Horrors (play), 39
Loans, student, 37–39
Loyalty/security in employment, 6–7,
    47–49, 112, 131–133

Macko, L., 63, 72
Marital status
    of participants/interviewees,
        149–155 *See also* Marriage

Marriage
  autonomy in, 10
  before career, 59–61
  delay of, 131–133, 141
  historical perspective on, 5
  as rite of passage, 2
Masten, A., 144
Maximizers, 82, 137
Medical profession, 120, 122
Mentoring, 121–123
  defined, 121
  key functions of, 122–123
Military service, 30, 32
Miller, Jean Baker, 141
Money/financial reimbursement
  meaning and significance of, 5
  parental financial support, 98,
    101–102, 143
  of participants/interviewees,
    149–155
  responsibility for, 21
  student loan debt, 37–38
Mormon religion, 31–32
Moses, B., 125–126
Myers, David, 130

Nash, L., 137
NEETS mnemonic, 54
Nelson, L., 31, 33
New York Times (newspaper), 140
Niedzviecki, N., 56

Parenthood
  careers and, 23–24
  delay of, 60–61, 65, 131–133, 141
  faith-based approach to, 106–108
  stay-at-home mothers, 75–76, 120,
    142
Parents
  adjustments to adult children,
    97–109
  advice to other parents, 108–109
  avoiding mistakes of, 63

  characteristics of, 153–154
  co-creating new relationship with
    children, 105–109
  financial support of adult children,
    98, 100–101, 143
  job loss of, 48, 133
  questionnaires for, 163–165
  selection of, 156
  struggle to "let go," 102–104
Participants/interviewees
  characteristics of
    affluent sample, 151–152
    diversity in, 3–10
    of emerging and young adult
      sample, 152–153
    of employer sample, 154–155
    of parent sample, 153–154
    total sample, 149–150
  descriptors of, 149–155
  overall demographics of, 3
  selection of, 155–156
Passion (fulfillment, meaning,
    excitement)
  defined, 135
  expectations related to, 54–56
  identification of personal, 52
  in one's work, 50–54, 123, 131
  in personal relationships, 64–65
  pursuit of, 134–135
Pathmakers identity group, 15, 27
Perfectionism, 72–74, 83, 134–135
Phenomenological psychology, 156
Philanthropy, 76–78
Piercings, body, 126

Quality of Life (QOL)
  employment changes for, 44–45
  facets of, 51
Questionnaires
  for emerging and young adults,
    159–162
  for employers, 167–168
  for parents, 163–165

Race. *See* Ethnicity/race
Relationships
  with employees, 5
  with employers, 6–7, 112, 126–127
  with family. *See* Families
  fluidity of, 61–62
  with friends. *See* Friendships
  interpersonal skills in, 118
  with parents. *See* Parents
  romantic. *See* Romantic
    relationships
Religion/spirituality
  mandated experience in, 30–32
  of participants/interviewees,
    149–155
  personal influence of, 9–10
Rich Dad, Poor Dad (Kiyosaki and
    Lechter, 1998), 26, 138–139
Risk management
  advantages of taking risks, 84–86
  of employers, 115
  in romantic relationships, 65
  when choices are scarce, 136
Rites of passage
  lack of, 99
  marriage as, 2
Romantic relationships
  different approaches to, 6, 21, 133
  disillusionment in, 5, 8, 9–10
  failure in, 36, 143
  fluidity of, 133
  negotiation in, 64–65, 133–134
  risk management in, 62–63, 65
  technology's influence on, 65–68
Rubin, K., 63, 72

Satisficers, 82, 137
Schulenberg et al, 43–44
Schwartz, B., 17, 81–83, 137
Scott, Walter Dill, 49
Searchers identity group, 15
Self-focus/self-concern, 116–117,
    124–127
Setterson, R., 43

Sexual revolution, 61–62
Sheehy, G., 61, 63
Shulman et al, 32
Social class/es
  "parallel ladders" approach to,
    34–36
  personal influence of, 33–34, 86 *See
    also* Affluence
Social norms/expectations
  as boundaries, 18, 25
  context of, 133–134
Stay-at-home mothers, 75–76, 142
Stevenson, H., 137
Substance abuse, 144
Sweden, 100

Tatoos, 126
Technology
  demands of modern, 46–47, 145
  inpact on employment
    opportunities, 117–118
  as tool of control, 65–66, 68
The American Paradox (Myers), 130
*The Hidden Brain Drain: Women and
    Minorities as Unrealized Assets*
    (Hewlett et al, 2005), 74–75
Therapy, family, 97
Thurow, Lester, 75
Time, personal
  for friendships, 70
  lack of, 92–93
  for shift from parents home to own,
    1, 43, 99, 130
  volunteerism during, 76–78
Treeger, M., 104
Tribal behavior, 69–70
Trunk, P., 126–127
Twenge, J., 125, 127, 130, 143

United States of America
  adulthood criteria in, 30
  "corporate America" in, 48–49
  women leaving home later in, 100
Utah, 31–32

Value systems, compromise of, 37–39
Video games, 37
Village Voice (Koerner, 2004), 37–39
Volunteerism, 76–78

Wakefield, M., 127
Warner, J., 61, 141
Waters, David, 97
Watters, E., 69–70
Women
    African-American, 22–23
    delayed home leaving by, 100

inflated expectations of, 72–74
mentoring of, 122–123
multiple roles of, 134
return to workforce of, 75
stay-at-home mothers, 75–76
Woods, G., 53–54
Work
    disillusionment in, 7–8, 25, 50–54
    meaning and significance in, 4,
      50–54
    satisfaction levels at, 44–45, 89–90,
      100 *See also* Employment

Printed in the United States
87301LV00003B/277-312/A